Since its creation in 1861, Italy has struggled to develop an effective political system and a secure sense of national identity. This concise history, which covers the period from the fall of the Roman Empire in the west to the present day, looks in particular at the difficulties Italy has faced during the last two centuries in forging a nation state.

The opening chapters consider the geographical and cultural obstacles to unity, and survey the long centuries of political fragmentation in the peninsula since the sixth century. It was this legacy of fragmentation which Italy's new rulers had to strive to overcome when the country became united, more by accident than design, in 1859–60. The book aims to weave together political, economic, social and cultural history, and stresses in particular the alternation between materialist and idealist programmes for forging a nation state.

Since its creation in 1861, Italy has struggled to develop an effective political system and a secure sense of national identity. This concise history, which covers the period from the fall of the Roman Empire in the west to the present day, looks in particular at the difficulties Italy has faced during the last two centuries in forging a nation state.

The opening chapters consider the geographical and cultural obstacles to unity, and survey the long centuries of political fragmentation in the peninsula since the sixth century. It was this legacy of fragmentation which Italy's new rulers had to strive to overcome when the country became united, more by accident than design, in 1859–60. The book aims to weave together political, economic, social and cultural history, and stresses in particular the alternation between materialist and idealist programmes for forging a nation state.

CAMBRIDGE CONCISE HISTORIES

A Concise History of Italy

CAMBRIDGE CONCISE HISTORIES

This is a series of illustrated 'concise histories' of selected individual countries, intended both as university and college textbooks and as general historical introductions for general readers, travellers and members of the business community.

Titles in the series:

A Concise History of Germany
MARY FULBROOK

A Concise History of Greece
RICHARD CLOGG

A Concise History of France
ROGER PRICE

A Concise History of Britain, 1707–1795
W. A. SPECK

A Concise History of Portugal
DAVID BIRMINGHAM

A Concise History of Italy
CHRISTOPHER DUGGAN

A Concise History of Bulgaria
RICHARD CRAMPTON

A Concise History of South Africa
ROBERT ROSS

A Concise History of Brazil
BORIS FAUSTO

A Concise History of Mexico
BRIAN HAMNETT

A Concise History of Australia
STUART MACINTYRE

A Concise History of Hungary
MIKLÓS MOLNÁR

A Concise History of Poland
JERZY LUKOWSKI and HUBERT ZAWADZKI

A Concise History of India
BARBARA D. METCALF and THOMAS R. METCALF

Other titles are in preparation

A Concise History
of Italy

CHRISTOPHER DUGGAN

CAMBRIDGE
UNIVERSITY PRESS

PUBLISHED BY THE PRESS SYNDICATE OF THE UNIVERSITY OF CAMBRIDGE
The Pitt Building, Trumpington Street, Cambridge, United Kingdom

CAMBRIDGE UNIVERSITY PRESS
The Edinburgh Building, Cambridge CB2 2RU, UK
40 West 20th Street, New York, NY 10011–4211, USA
477 Williamstown Road, Port Melbourne, VIC 3207, Australia
Ruiz de Alarcón 13, 28014 Madrid, Spain
Dock House, The Waterfront, Cape Town 8001, South Africa

http://www.cambridge.org

© Cambridge University Press 1994

First published 1994
Reprinted 1995, 1997, 1998, 2000, 2004

Printed in the United Kingdom at the University Press, Cambridge

A catalogue record for this book is available from the British Library

Library of Congress Cataloguing in Publication data
Duggan Christopher
A concise history of Italy / Christopher Duggan.
p.   cm. – (Cambridge concise histories)
Includes bibliographical references and index.
ISBN 0 521 40285 9 (hardback). – ISBN 0 521 40848 2 (paperback)
1. Italy – History.   I. Title.   II. Series.
DG467.D84 1994
945 – dc20   93-30627 CIP

ISBN 0 521 40285 9 hardback
ISBN 0 521 40848 2 paperback

CONTENTS

ILLUSTRATIONS

MAPS

TABLES

PREFACE

A history of Italy on this scale can make no claims to originality or to comprehensiveness. My intention has been to provide a succinct, and hopefully clear, survey of some of the principal developments in the peninsula since the time of the Romans. I lean heavily on the work of others, above all in the early chapters and towards the end: I hope the authors concerned will exercise forbearance, and accept, collectively, my warm thanks. Perhaps inevitably, given limitations on space, my focus is primarily on political issues (in the event, though, rather more than originally intended). However, I have tried to weave in, at certain points, discussion of economic, social, and cultural matters; and in the introduction I have looked briefly at how Italy's location in Europe, its soil, climate, mineral resources, and physical geography have influenced its history.

The main problem with a work such as this is to find a thematic thread. In the case of Italy this is particularly difficult: the country has only been in existence since 1861, and strictly speaking 'its' history starts then, not before. Prior to that date the peninsula was a patchwork of states, each with its own history and traditions. One solution occasionally adopted is to abandon political narrative and instead to consider 'Italy' as essentially a 'geographical expression', a unit of territory whose history can be given coherence by focusing on broad socio-economic and cultural themes. This is not altogether satisfactory, however, since the unit of territory is still the national-political one, and for the most part bears little obvious or natural relationship to any such themes.

In so far as a single thematic thread exists in this book, it is that of the problem of 'nation building'. Italy came into being in 1859–60 as much by accident as by design. Only a tiny minority of people before 1860 seriously believed that Italy was a nation, and that it should form a unitary state; and even they had to admit that there was little, on the face of it, to justify their belief: neither history nor language, for example, really supported their case. The result was that after unity was achieved, Italy's rulers faced the difficult task of creating a sense of collective identity, and binding the peninsula's population to the new national institutions. They alternated between 'materialist' and 'idealist' solutions, but on the whole failed to come up with a satisfactory formula.

The first two chapters of the book are intended mainly to give some idea of the obstacles – natural and historical – that made the task of building a nation in Italy after 1860 so difficult. They do little more than provide an introduction to the main part of the book, which is concerned with the last two hundred years. As a result, the sections on the Middle Ages and the Renaissance are extremely cursory. I start with the fall of the Roman Empire, as it was then that the political fragmentation of the peninsula began. The final chapter comes right down to the present: however, Italy is currently undergoing a profound moral and political crisis, and this makes any conclusion or verdict more than usually risky. I may have been too pessimistic.

A number of people have been kind enough to look at drafts of this book. I am particularly grateful to Professor Adrian Lyttelton for reading the entire text, and commenting very perceptively on it. Denis Mack Smith, Professor Donald Matthew, and Professor John A. Davis read individual chapters, and made many extremely valuable suggestions. Dr Shirley Vinall, Professor Percy Allum, Dr Jonathan Morris, and Dr Patricia Morison, also read specific chapters, and offered much useful advice. Professor Giulio Lepschy indicated a number of improvements to the first section, and also helped with the map of Italian dialects and the table of dialect examples. My thanks to all concerned. I naturally take full responsibility for any errors that remain.

Introduction

In the late spring of 1860 Giuseppe Garibaldi, a flamboyant irregular soldier, who had spent much of his life abroad fighting as a guerrilla leader, set sail for Sicily from a port near Genoa. On board his two small ships was a motley collection of students and adventurers, many of them barely out of their teens. Their mission was to unify Italy. The prospects for success seemed limited: the group was ill-armed, and few among them had any experience in warfare or administration. Moreover, they did not constitute a promising advertisement for the nation-to-be. Among the thousand or so volunteers were Hungarians and Poles, and the Italian contingent included a disproportionate number from the small northern city of Bergamo. However, in the space of a few months they succeeded in conquering Sicily and the mainland South from the Bourbons; and in March 1861 Victor Emmanuel II, King of Piedmont–Sardinia, became the first king of united Italy.

The success of Garibaldi and his 'Thousand' was both remarkable and unexpected; and when the euphoria had died down, many sober observers wondered whether the Italian state could survive. France and Austria, the two greatest continental powers of the day, both threatened to invade the new kingdom, break it up, and reconstitute the Papal States, which had been annexed by Victor Emmanuel in the course of unification. A much more insidious long-term threat, however, to the survival of the new state, was the absence of any real sense of commitment or loyalty to the kingdom among all except a tiny minority of the population. The country's new rulers justified their demands for heavy taxes and military service, the often harsh repressive measures, and the unfamiliar institutions, by appealing to the sanctity and inviolability of the Italian 'nation': but for the overwhelming mass of Italians, the 'Italian nation', indeed 'Italy' itself, meant nothing.

The lack of loyalty to the new state haunted the country's intellectuals for many years after 1860. Initially, there was some hope that the introduction of liberal institutions and free trade would unleash the pent up talents and energies of a people who had given the world the civilisation of ancient Rome and the Renaissance; and the new prosperity, it was imagined, would generate support for the liberal order and its leaders. This soon proved illusory. By the late 1870s socio-economic unrest had begun to erode the old certainties. Disillusionment grew; and other less liberal political ideas surfaced that claimed to solve the problem of how to generate in Italians feelings of commitment to the state. These ideas culminated in the fascist experiment of the 1920s and 1930s. Ironically, though, it was the failure rather than the success of fascism that gave Italy its most cohesive set of values since 1860, the values of anti-fascism.

If the task of forging a collective 'national identity' proved so difficult, one reason was the absence of any political substance to the idea of a unified Italy prior to the nineteenth century. Patriotic historians and propagandists claimed to discern a national conscious-ness in the struggles of the medieval cities (or 'communes') against the Holy Roman Emperors, or in Machiavelli's appeal for the expul-sion of the 'barbarian' invaders in the early sixteenth century; but such interpretations were strained. The history of the peninsula after the fall of the Roman Empire was one of confusion and division, a 'hurly-burly of peoples, states, and institutions', according to the philosopher Giuseppe Ferrari in 1858. The historian Arnold Toyn-bee observed that there were more independent states in central Italy in the fourteenth century than in the entire world in 1934. Given this tradition of political fragmentation, it is hardly surprising that so many Italians found it hard to identify with the unified kingdom after 1860.

This is not to say that the idea of Italy was wholly without political meaning before the nineteenth century. The papacy from the time of Gregory VII in the later eleventh century had urged 'all

Italians' to resist the claims of the German emperors to sovereignty in the peninsula; and in the thirteenth century the Hohenstaufen ruler of Sicily, Manfred, had used 'Italy' as a stick to beat his French opponents. However, the concept was not very widely employed, and its primary appeal was to writers and poets, not politicians. The Renaissance humanists were especially fond of it, though much of their enthusiasm for the term *Italia* derived from the fact that it had been widely used by the Latin authors they wanted to emulate. During the *Risorgimento* – the movement of national revival in the early to mid-nineteenth century – many famous patriots were, like Alessandro Manzoni, professional writers, or else had very strong literary leanings, like Massimo d'Azeglio or Giuseppe Mazzini. A remarkable number of Garibaldi's 'Thousand' produced accounts of their exploits in 1860. Garibaldi himself wrote poetry.

If the idea of Italy flourished strongly among men of letters, it owed much, too, in the Middle Ages and later, to the thoughts of expatriates and exiles. Probably no other region of Europe has produced so many emigrants over the centuries, partly because the population of the peninsula always tended to outstrip the available resources, and partly also because banishment was for a long time a standard punishment for political troublemakers. Under the influence of nostalgia, and thrown together perhaps for the first time, Neapolitans and Sicilians, Piedmontese and Venetians, could forget their differences and summon up an imaginary community to which they all belonged. It was while in exile that the thirteenth-century Florentine rhetorician Brunetto Latini came to the conclusion that 'Italy is a better country than France'; Petrarch discovered his great love for 'Italy' during his time in Avignon; and Mazzini's devotion to the cause of Italian unity was sustained during thirty years in the London suburbs.

If a sense of being 'Italian' often arose through contact with the outside world, it also rested on certain real cultural premises, at least from the Middle Ages. Dante complained that Italy had over a thousand different languages in his day; but the fact remains that merchants, mercenaries, artisans, friars, and beggars criss-crossed the peninsula and presumably made themselves understood without too much difficulty. The development of a common literary language from the fourteenth century, based on written Tuscan, helped draw together the educated; while the artistic and intellectual achievements of the Renaissance, and the huge wealth of the city states, gave many Italians feelings of distinctiveness and superiority. 'From morning to night', said the sixteenth-century writer Matteo Bandello, alluding to the achievements of explorers such as Cristoforo Colombo and Amerigo Vespucci, 'we hear that the New World was discovered by the Spanish and Portuguese, whereas it was we, the Italians, who showed them the way.'

These glimmerings of cultural nationalism, however, contrasted strongly with the political fragmentation of the peninsula from the sixth century. A succession of foreign invasions, the plethora of states, disputes over sovereignty, and endless domestic wars made the idea of Italy intellectually elusive. 'In what does [Italy] consist?', asked Giuseppe Ferrari: 'What is it that links the republics, the tyrants, the popes, the emperors? . . . Scholarship can shed no light: indeed, far from guiding us, it simply provides evidence of chaos.' The absence of any clear unifying themes in Italy's past made a coherent historical narrative of the peninsula, of a kind that would give substance to the idea of Italy, extremely hard to write, and none of the attempts made by humanist scholars in the fifteenth and sixteenth centuries came close to succeeding. The one possible exception was that by Francesco Guicciardini. The first 'History of Italy' in English, written by the Welshman William Thomas in 1549, had as its revealing subtitle: 'A Book Exceedingly Profitable to Be Read Because it Entreateth of the State of Many and Divers Commonwealths How they Have Been and Now Be Governed.'

The fashion for historical writing in Italy during the Renaissance declined in the seventeenth century, and nobody sought to follow Guicciardini and attempt a coherent history of the peninsula. In part this was because Italy's cultural pre-eminence, on which so much 'national' sentiment had rested in the later Middle Ages, disappeared; and scholars now had little grounds for viewing the peninsula as a distinctive whole. However, the coming of the intellectual movement known as the Enlightenment in the early eighteenth century, began to change this situation. A sense now developed among the educated that the various Italian states had fallen behind the rest of Europe; and this feeling, combined with a new interest in economic and social questions, encouraged writers once again to see the peninsula as a unit. The most remarkable historical work of the period, Ludovico Antonio Muratori's *Antiquitates Italicae Medii Aevi* (1738–42), achieved an integrated vision of Italy in the Middle Ages by abandoning the conventional framework of political narrative, and focusing instead on broad categories such as law, trade, and warfare.

However, the Italian scholars of the Enlightenment belonged to a cosmopolitan movement, and their concern was not so much with establishing the specific identity of Italy, but rather with bringing the peninsula into line with the rest of Europe through the elimination of feudal anachronisms and privileges. The French Revolution and the birth of romantic nationalism destroyed this cosmopolitanism. The idea of Italy now acquired a new radical complexion, as the view emerged that the peninsula was not only distinct, but also a 'nation', deserving independence as much as France or Britain. Propagandists scoured Italy's past for evidence to support this belief, well aware, as the Piedmontese aristocrat Cesare Balbo wrote in 1850, that, 'in the absence of virtuous conduct (and this is sadly the case with us), history is indeed of the greatest use, the best possible foundation for a national political programme'.

The problem, however, remained: what was the essence of Italy? Those, such as Giuseppe Ferrari, who favoured a federal solution to the national question, emphasised the struggles of the communes in the Middle Ages for independence from the Holy Roman Empire: Italy, according to this view, was the sum of its autonomous parts. By contrast, those like Cesare Balbo who hoped the papacy would take a leading role in shaping the new nation, preferred to underline the stand of the medieval popes against the German emperors, playing down the fact that often the papacy and the communes were also at odds. Sometimes, what was in reality a social revolt or a local conflict, was recast in a 'national' mould. Michele Amari, the great Sicilian historian (and future Minister of Education), wrote an account of the brutal rising in Palermo against the French of 1282, known as the Sicilian Vespers, depicting it as an episode of revolutionary nationalism rather than (more prosaically and properly) a *jacquerie*.

The distortions to which the historical record was subjected in the national cause indicate how far the idea of unity relied on a willing suspension of disbelief to carry it forward. Some patriots undoubtedly saw unification as a way of achieving rational economic goals, such as a larger internal market or a uniform currency; but they were not a majority, nor especially influential. In the main, the *Risorgimento* appealed most to those sections of the middle classes – professionals, students, the provincial bourgeoisie – for whom the idea of Italy aroused strong but vague emotions that left little room for reflection. It was these people who applauded wildly any patriotic allusions in the operas of Giuseppe Verdi: the opening chorus of his *La Battaglia di Legnano* (The Battle of Legnano) (1849), for instance, ('Long live Italy! A sacred pact binds all her sons') was greeted on the first night with ecstatic cries of 'Viva Italia!'. The subject of the opera – the defeat of the Emperor Barbarossa by the Lombard League in 1176 – was one of the key episodes of nationalist historiography.

The extent to which rhetoric served to hide the truth about Italy's condition worried some patriots. 'A little bit of idolatry of the past, mingled with golden dreams of a remote future: reality, the present – never', complained the Piedmontese liberal Giacomo Durando, who wanted a federal solution to the Italian question. However, even the most sober succumbed to myth-making. The great Catholic writer, Alessandro Manzoni, dismissed the Middle Ages as a time of violence and division rather than of glorious proto-nationalism, but he still felt the need to create an alternative historical myth based upon the imagined forbearance and humility of ordinary Italians down the centuries. For him, the essential Italy lay in the obscurer and quieter moments of the past, such as after the Lombard invasions of the sixth century, or during the Spanish occupation of the seventeenth century, the setting for his most famous work, the historical novel *I Promessi Sposi* (The Betrothed), first published in 1827.

As the national movement gathered momentum in the 1840s, so too did the desire to ignore the divisions of the past. 'Have you not heard ... that the cruellest word that you can throw [at Italy] is "diversity"', Manzoni asked Alphonse de Lamartine in April 1848, 'and that this ... sums up a long history of suffering and degradation?' However, Manzoni's own humble vision of unity enjoyed very little favour with the public. Much more appealing were the vague grandiose claims for Italian greatness found in Mazzini's democratic programme (with its notion of a glorious 'Third Rome' that would

liberate all of Europe), and in the writings of such moderate nationalists as the Piedmontese priest, Vincenzo Gioberti. Gioberti's *Del
Primato Morale e Civile degli Italiani* (On the Moral and Civil Pre-
eminence of the Italians) (1843) enjoyed astonishing success (despite
its pedestrianism and long-windedness), a result largely of its rather
crude message about Italy's cultural superiority, ancient and modern.

The literary and rhetorical accretions that had accumulated around
the idea of Italy played an important role in generating enthusiasm
for unification; but they were also a serious liability to the new
kingdom. The reality of united Italy fell far short of expectations;
inevitably so, as centuries of political division and socio-economic
backwardness could not easily be overcome. This painful truth,
however, was difficult to acknowledge and even more difficult to
accept. Many, at all levels of society, from landowners and intellectuals to factory workers and peasants, turned their anger against the
new regime and its leaders. Under threat, and with their own faith in
what they had achieved diminishing, Italy's rulers began to toy with
political measures and methods that only served to weaken further
the credibility of the liberal state. The result was a crisis of legitimacy
that led in 1922 to Mussolini becoming prime minister.

The fascist regime strove resolutely to instil in the Italian population a sense of national identity, and thereby to overcome the
discordant local, sectional, and class loyalties that had brought the
country to the brink of seeming ungovernability on many occasions
since 1860. Freed from the ideological restraints of liberalism, fascism
used the power of the state on an unprecedented scale to coerce and
mould: propaganda, education, and war were the main tools of
indoctrination; and Ancient Rome was elevated into the historical
repository of national moral and political values. However, Mussolini's ill-fated alliance with nazism, and his attempt to import such
palpably alien doctrines as anti-semitism, destroyed much of the
credibility of the regime; and the fiasco of the Second World War did
the rest.

The collapse of fascism discredited the rhetoric of national greatness
(and to some extent the very idea of 'nation') that had underpinned
Mussolini's regime; but at the same time it helped to resolve the
country's political identity. For the reality of defeat in 1945 was that
Italy had no choice but to insert itself into the framework of western

democratic capitalism. However, the more general problem of
'national identity' remained. The new Republic was born under the
banner of 'anti-fascism': but the ejection of the Communists, the
most clearly anti-fascist of all the parties, from the government
coalition in 1947 invalidated this as a unifying principle. The Church
under Pius XII tried for a time to turn Italy into the flagship of
'Christian civilisation': but the growth of consumerism rendered this
a lost cause.

From the mid-1950s Italy seemed increasingly bereft of moral
foundations. The Christian Democrats, who dominated government
(and to a large extent the state too), paid lip-service to Catholic
values and exploited fears of communism; but their *raison d'être*
appeared, more and more, to be the retention of power for its own
sake. What legitimacy they had stemmed in large measure from the
often astonishing growth of the economy after the Second World
War. However, in the absence of any clear moral leadership, material
prosperity generated expectations that proved increasingly hard to
control. By the early 1990s the Republic faced a crisis of authority,
triggered by the mismanagement of public finances, pressure for
European integration, corruption, and the ideological earthquake
that had followed the end of communism. The search for a national
identity was evidently far from over.

1

The geographical determinants of disunity

The history of Italy is tied up inseparably with its geographical position. For centuries the peninsula formed the crossroads of Europe. To the north, the Alps were always much less of a barrier than their height suggested: of the twenty-three main passes, seventeen were already in regular use under the Romans. The relatively low Julian and Carnic Alps to the north-east offered an easy crossing point for invading armies. It was over them that the Visigoths, the Huns, the Lombards, and other central European tribes marched in the centuries after the fall of Rome. During the Middle Ages the dense flow of commercial traffic over the Simplon, the St Gotthard, and Brenner passes was crucial to the prosperity of Genoa, Milan, Venice, and many smaller cities in the Po valley. The accessibility of the Brenner to heavy German carts was particularly important for the Venetian economy.

Of no less importance than this close link with the continental land mass of Europe was Italy's position in the centre of the Mediterranean. With its long coastline, gently sloping beaches, and many natural harbours, the peninsula was highly attractive to overseas settlers. Greeks from Corinth, Euboea, and elsewhere, travelling west on the prevailing currents, landed in Sicily and on the southern mainland from the eighth century BC. Their settlements flourished: during the fourth century Syracuse was the most powerful city-state in the Mediterranean. The short distance between Sicily and North

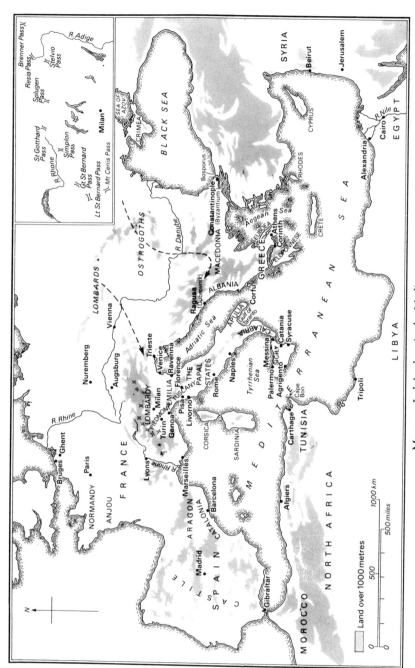

Map I   Italy's place in the Mediterranean.

Africa (about 160 km at the narrowest point) made it particularly prone to attacks from the south: the Carthaginians invaded on many occasions between the fifth and third centuries B C; and in the ninth century A D the Arabs conquered the island. In July 1943 Sicily was the first Axis territory to fall to the Allies following victory in the Desert Campaign.

If Italy's central location made it vulnerable to attack, it also provided excellent opportunities for trade. This was particularly true during the Middle Ages, when the Mediterranean formed the hub of Europe's commercial life. Naples, Pisa, Genoa, and Venice grew rich mainly because they were able to take advantage of their half-way position between the Asiatic and African caravan routes and the markets of northern Europe, and secure a near monopoly of traffic in spices, dyestuffs, and precious minerals. Italian merchants linked Spain to the Black Sea; and Italian trading posts appeared as far afield as the Sea of Azov. Plentiful supplies of timber (at least until the sixteenth century, when oak seems to have grown scarce) nurtured a vigorous shipbuilding industry. Genoese vessels in particular were renowned for their size and seaworthiness: it was Genoese galleys that pioneered the route to the northern Atlantic as early as the thirteenth century.

The fact that Italy cut the Mediterranean in two meant that the eastern and western sides of the peninsula tended to have different orientations. Until the fifteenth century Venice looked to the Levant, and its art and culture, with their concern for ornament and ritual, bore the imprint of Byzantium. The threat from Islam, and the challenge of Orthodoxy in the Balkan mountains, gave Catholicism in Friuli and the Veneto a distinctly militant flavour. Apulia, further south, faced Albania and Greece, and for long periods its history was more closely tied up with theirs than with that of the peninsula. The western seaboard moved in a different sphere. The papacy in Rome was shaped by forces emanating from France and Germany; Naples and Sicily were for centuries coveted by Spain; and the fact that the Renaissance emerged in the cities of the west of the peninsula was due in part to their economic ties with the great cultural centres of Flanders and Burgundy.

While Italy's position in the Mediterranean was an advantage in the Middle Ages, in the modern period it was more of a handicap.

The opening up of the Atlantic sea lanes in the sixteenth century, and the westward advance of Islam, pushed the axis of European trade northwards; and Great Britain, Holland, and France emerged as the new dominant powers. Italy's economic decline was accompanied by political marginalisation. In the seventeenth and eighteenth centuries events in the peninsula were contingent upon the affairs of the great states of northern and western Europe. The changes of dynasty and government that occurred were due to compensatory deals made at the diplomatic negotiating table; and the Italian states themselves had little say in the matter. Foreign interest in Italy was now more cultural than economic, and the northerners who descended on the peninsula did so to savour the ruins of ancient Rome or the art works of Bologna, Florence, and Naples.

In the first half of the nineteenth century the question of the European balance of power, and the ambitions of France in particular, gave Italy a new geo-political significance; and this was to contribute greatly to the process of national unification. Between 1806 and 1815, during the wars against Napoleon, Britain occupied Sicily to keep the Mediterranean open to shipping and to contain the French fleet; and the fact that Italy lay *en route* to Egypt, and thus to England's most prized colony, India, gave the peninsula added importance. During the 1850s, when France once again seemed a threat to European stability, the British government looked with cautious benevolence on the patriotic movement in Italy: the prospect of a major power in the Mediterranean that could serve as a counterweight to France, was attractive. Moreover, with Russia and Austria competing in the Balkans, and with Africa attracting colonialist interest, Italy was now in a key strategic position.

Italy's position in the Mediterranean determined many of the parameters of her foreign policy after 1860. A long shoreline, punctuated with cities that could be attacked from the sea (Genoa, Naples, Palermo, Bari, Venice, and even Rome), made harmonious relations with Britain, the greatest maritime power, seem vital. Furthermore, the main railway and telegraph lines ran along the coastal plains, and in the event of war communications between North and South might easily be severed by bombardment. However, geography did not permit Italy the luxury of focusing on naval defences alone, for the presence on its northern borders of two major and often hostile powers, France and Austria, necessitated the maintenance of a large army. The result was a huge burden of military expenditure; and Italy's wisest course (and the one it most generally pursued) was to avoid commitments that might lead to war. Better still was to try and pool responsibility for defence with other countries.

In the euphoria created by the industrial and agricultural boom of the mid-nineteenth century, many believed that Italy's geographical position could once again be turned to its economic advantage. Count Cavour wrote in 1846 of how the construction of a European railway network would make Italy 'the shortest and easiest route from East to West', and so allow it to 'regain the brilliant commercial position that it held throughout the Middle Ages'. The opening of the Suez Canal in 1869 and a little later of the Fréjus tunnel under the Alps, encouraged this idea. Brindisi, it was now imagined, would replace Marseilles as the main port for India, while Italy's merchant marine and its railways would be transformed by the new transcontinental traffic. Such hopes were not realised: the high tariffs for the Suez Canal restricted the volume of goods passing through it; and the Italian fleet had too few steam vessels to benefit from the new routes.

One consequence of this failure of the Mediterranean to re-emerge in the nineteenth century as a central axis of world trade was that the economic gap between the north and south of Italy widened. During the early Middle Ages the southern half of the peninsula had benefited from close links with Byzantium and the Arab world; it had also enjoyed good government and a healthy degree of political autonomy. As a result, towns such as Naples, Salerno, Amalfi, and Palermo grew into brilliant commercial and cultural centres. From the thirteenth century the situation began to alter. The South became detached from Africa and the Levant, and through conquest entered the orbit of France and Spain. Relegated to the periphery of the European market, it never recovered the prosperity that it had enjoyed in earlier centuries. Even the best endeavours of the Italian state after 1860 failed to make the South's economy competitive or self-sustaining.

Geography alone cannot explain the differences between North and South; but the North's proximity to the rich markets of France and Germany certainly influenced its economic and cultural life, and helped to make it distinct from southern Italy. For much of its history, in fact, the Po valley was more closely tied to northern Europe than to the Italian peninsula. Until 1860 the Piedmontese state straddled the Alps, and its rulers were often happier in Chambéry than in Turin. Its prime minister, Count Cavour, knew France and England well, but never travelled further south than Florence (which he disliked). Lombard culture had a strongly French flavour in the nineteenth century: for the writer Stendhal, Milan was like a second home. Venice had traditional links with Austria and southern Germany, and in the Middle Ages the Rialto was always thronged with German merchants. 'Germans and Venetians', wrote the patrician merchant and diarist Girolamo Priuli in 1509, 'we are all one, because of our ancient trading partnership.'

The south of Italy belonged to a different zone of Europe. Cut off from the rich land traffic of the north by the chain of the Apennines and its lack of roads, its culture often struck outsiders as deeply foreign. The Norman rulers of Sicily in the eleventh and twelfth centuries kept a harem, used Islamic and Greek officials, and developed a hierocratic view of kingship similar to that of the emperors in Constantinople. From the fifteenth century the influence of Spain prevailed: Naples grew into a picaresque city, full of beggars and vagrants, with a Spanish court and nobility, and a working population that catered largely to the needs of the rich and the clergy. Titles and privileges were avidly sought after; and vendetta was common at all levels of society. In Sicily, the Inquisition survived until 1782; and in the South as a whole, Catholicism acquired an exuberant character that was to nauseate many Piedmontese and Lombards when they arrived after 1860.

SOIL AND CLIMATE

If Italy's position in Europe and the Mediterranean determined the pattern of much of its history, the country's internal geography also dictated the main contours of its economic and social life. Mountains and rugged hills dominate the peninsula. The Alps in the north give way, after the broad and fertile Po valley, to the long chain of the Apennines, which spread in a great swathe south from Genoa, through central Italy, to Calabria and then across to Sicily. Sardinia,

Plate 1   The bleakness of Italy's southern mountains. A view
towards Monte Cammarata in western Sicily. In the foreground
are sulphur-mine workings.

too, is almost entirely mountainous. In much of the peninsula the
mountains reach down to the sea, leaving only a narrow coastal
plain. Apart from the Po valley, there are few extensive areas of
lowland; and those that do exist (the Tuscan Maremma, the Roman
Campagna, the Plain of Lentini in Sicily) suffered constantly, right
up until the present century, from an excess of water sweeping
down from the surrounding hills to form huge tracts of malarial
marshland.

The mountainous character of so much of the landscape made the
peninsula ecologically vulnerable. The forests, that in ancient times
covered the slopes up to a height of several thousand feet (as today
in the Abruzzi National Park), were a vital protection against soil
erosion; but once the trees began to be cut down to make way for
farming, the topsoil was exposed to the heavy autumn and winter
rains, and washed away. Nor was it quickly replenished: the woody
and resinous scrub that takes hold in the Mediterranean when the

forest is gone, does not produce a rich humus, unlike the deciduous
cover of northern Europe. Deforestation also caused springs to dry
up. Italy has thus always faced a serious problem with its land,
which, in the absence of careful controls, tended constantly towards
infertility.

Alongside the vulnerability of its soil, Italy has had to face problems of climate. The mountainous landscape has always ensured
abundant rain, even in the South, with annual averages of about
600–900 millimetres over most of the country, with rather higher
levels in the Alpine hills and in those areas, particularly in the west,
exposed to coastal winds. The principal variation is with distribution
throughout the year: the Po valley has a 'continental' style climate of
severe winters and warm summers, and receives most of its rain in
the autumn and spring; the central and southern areas, by contrast,
are more 'Mediterranean', and at least 80 per cent of their rain comes
in the winter months, leaving the land parched in the summer and
streams and rivers reduced to a mere trickle or nothing. The main
worry for Italian farmers has always been not so much the quantity
of rain but how to harness and store it.

This has required human intervention on a massive scale. In the
Po valley, the problem for centuries was an excess of water. The
great Alpine rivers – the Ticino, the Adda, the Oglio, the Adige, the
Brenta, and the Piave – were always liable to burst their banks when
they reached the plains. The Po itself, especially in its lower reaches,
flooded regularly in the Middle Ages, and in the twelfth century it
altered its course completely below Ferrara as a result of overflowing.
The result was extensive and barren marshland. Until quite recent
times, indeed, it was the South and not the North that had a
reputation for agricultural wealth, and it was only the construction
of great irrigation canals, such as the Naviglio Grande and the
Martesana, in the medieval period and later, that gradually allowed
the waters of the Po valley to be brought under control and the area
turned into one of the richest in Europe.

In the Centre and South, the countryside was also subject to a
great deal of human intervention over the centuries, but the results
were in general far less satisfactory than in the Po valley. Population
pressure caused the forests to be gradually cleared and the land to
be cultivated ever higher up the mountain and hill slopes. In some

areas this could produce well-built terracing, as in Tuscany, where in the sixteenth century the French writer Montaigne was astonished to find chestnut woods being replaced with vines, 'right up to the peaks'. In other regions, above all in the South, deforestation occurred with little thought for the longer-term consequences: without trees, the ancient topsoil was easily washed away; and the uncontrolled winter torrents produced flooding and then malaria in the plains, pushing more people up into the hills and setting in motion a vicious spiral.

If Italy's landscape has seen dramatic changes over time, so, too, have its crops and vegetation. Fruit trees of Asiatic origin, such as pistachio, peach, and almond made their appearance before the Romans; while cotton, rice, sumac, oranges, lemons, and mulberries were introduced some time between the fifth and tenth centuries, probably by the Arabs. Sugar cane was grown in the South in the Middle Ages; and by the fifteenth century, with the climate apparently becoming warmer, it was to be found as far up the west coast as Formia. The discovery of the Americas in the sixteenth century led to the introduction of tomatoes, prickly pears, and, most important of all, maize, which although far from ideally suited to the climate of northern Italy, soon became its main subsistence crop. Rice spread through the Po valley in the sixteenth and seventeenth centuries; so, too, did mulberry trees, the basis of the highly important silk industry.

While the types of crop grown in Italy have changed over the centuries (one important exception is wheat, which has been cultivated in the South from the earliest times), another, albeit negative, feature of agriculture has been more permanent. This is the absence of rich pastures and therefore of good quality livestock, especially cattle. The resulting shortage of meat in the Italian diet was a source of frequent irritation to northern Europeans, who were not accustomed to eating vegetable- or fruit-based meals without beef or pork. ('In Italy', observed Montaigne, 'a banquet is the equivalent of a light meal in France.') The lack of pasture also made it impossible to rear strong horses, which meant that farmers had to rely on mules and oxen for traction. This, as much as the thinness of the topsoil or the conditions of land tenure, helps explain why so many of the technological innovations of the 'agricultural revolution' failed to take hold in Italy.

Another important result of the shortage of livestock in Italy was a lack of manure. Without fertiliser, the soil easily became exhausted; and this explains why large areas of the peninsula often had to be abandoned or left uncultivated. The absence of technical instruction for most farmers until the late nineteenth century did not improve matters: crop rotation was only introduced in some places this century; and in the 1950s animal dung could still be found piled in the streets of Sicilian towns, since the peasants believed it would make the land 'dirty'. The poor quality of Italian soil was evident in its low yields. In the mid-nineteenth century parts of the South produced only four hectolitres of wheat a hectare, while the average for the country as a whole was perhaps nine hectolitres. This compared with other national averages of sixteen for Austria, nineteen for France, and twenty-five (and probably more) for Britain.

There were certainly areas of rich agriculture, above all in Lombardy and Piedmont, whose methods of farming were warmly praised by the economist Arthur Young when he visited Italy on the eve of the French Revolution. In general, though, the picture was a desolate one. The situation would have been less serious had the population kept pace with resources; but from the late seventeenth century Italy, in common with other European countries, began to experience a sharp fall in mortality rates, with the result that its population leapt from around 11 million in 1660, to 18 million in 1800, and almost 26 million in 1860. This produced a socio-economic crisis from which the *ancien régime* states failed to extricate themselves. Nor was the problem resolved with unification: agricultural yields improved only slightly in the decades after 1860, while per capita income actually seems to have fallen in many places, as the widespread incidence of the disease pellagra in the North or of lawlessness in the South might suggest (see Table 1).

One traditional answer to the problem of overpopulation was to emigrate. In the sixteenth century, when demographic pressures were already acute, enterprising Italians could be found throughout Europe: in general they were artisans with particular skills to impart (brocade weaving, glass manufacturing, majolica making). By the nineteenth century the desperate situation in the countryside was reflected in the ever larger numbers of peasants going abroad. Until the end of the century most of them came from the North. They

Table 1 *GDP in Italy 1861–1988 (today's borders and at constant prices)*

	(1) GDP (1861 = 100)	(2) Annual average increase of (1)	(3) Per capita GDP (1861 = 100)	(4) Annual average increase of (1)
1861	100	–	100	–
1896	131	0.8	104	0.1
1913	198	2.4	140	1.8
1922	231	1.7	157	1.3
1929	271	2.2	174	1.5
1938	315	1.6	187	0.7
1951	359	1.0	196	0.4
1963	719	5.8	365	5.3
1973	1249	5.5	589	4.8
1988	1965	3.1	893	2.8

Note the negligible growth of per capita GDP 1861–96. During the same period, France, Germany, and Britain had per capita GDP increases in the order of 40–50 per cent.
Source: V. Zamagni, *Dalla periferia al centro* (Bologna, 1990).

found seasonal jobs in central Europe, or even in Argentina where they helped with the harvests during what was winter time back home. Many also settled permanently in South America, as the string of opera houses from Rio de Janeiro (where Toscanini made his conducting debut) to deep inside the Amazon forests, testifies. From the 1880s southern Italians began to emigrate on a large scale, above all to North America, helped by the cheaper transatlantic fares that came with steam ships (see Table 2).

Emigration alleviated but did not solve the problems of the countryside. One possible alternative lay with revolution. The prospect of converting the sufferings of Calabrian or Sicilian labourers into a great political movement that would sweep away the existing order, inspired a succession of insurrectionaries, beginning with the *carbonari* in the early years of the nineteenth century and continuing from the 1830s with republicans such as the Bandiera brothers and Carlo Pisacane. After unification the Italian peasantry continued to attract revolutionaries and utopians. The great Russian anarchist, Michael Bakunin, spent a number of years in Italy trying to instigate risings in the countryside; and from the end of the century the

Table 2 *Emigration from Europe to non-European countries (in thousands)*

	1851–60	1861–70	1871–80	1881–90	1891–1900	1901–10	1911–20	1921–30	1931–40	1941–50	1951–60
Austria–Hungary[a]	31	40	46	248	440	1111	418	61	11[b]	—	53[c]
Denmark	—	8	39	82	51	73	52	64	100	38	68
France	27	36	66	119	51	53	32	4	5	—	155
Germany[d]	671	779	626	1342	527	274	91	564	121[e]	618	872
Italy	5	27	168	992	1580	3615	2194	1370	235	467	858
Spain	3	7	13	572	791	1091	1306	560	132	166	543
Sweden	17	122	103	327	205	324	86	107	8	23	43
United Kingdom and Ireland	1313[f,g]	1572[g]	1849[g]	3259	2149	3150	2587	2151	262	755	1454

Notes: [a] Republic of Austria from 1921 onwards. [b] 1931–7. [c] 1954–60. [d] West Germany in 1941–50 and 1951–60. [e] 1932–6. [f] 1853–60. [g] Excluding emigration direct from Irish ports.

Source: W. Woodruff, *Impact of Western Man* (London, 1966).

Italian Socialist Party, despite ideological reservations, found most of its support among the day labourers of the Po valley. After the Second World War the southern peasants were central to the strategy of the Italian Communist Party

One reason why so many subversives believed in the revolutionary potential of the Italian peasants was that they knew very little about them. Most of the leading republicans, anarchists, socialists, and communists came from urban middle-class families, and their knowledge of the countryside was rarely direct. The fact that in Italy a large cultural and to some extent economic divide existed between towns and countryside (many peasant families consumed what they grew and did not sell their produce at market) reinforced this ignorance. In such circumstances, it was easy for a romantic notion of 'the people' as an army of downtrodden soldiers waiting for generals to lead them to the promised land to flourish; and this idea survived many indications that a majority of peasants were in fact deeply conservative, if not reactionary. The extent to which Italian revolutionaries were influenced by the 'messianic' legacy of the Catholic Church is a matter for conjecture.

A serious obstacle in the way of the revolutionaries was that the peasants, despite their common sufferings, were far from being a homogeneous force. The labourers and leaseholders of the South were subject to a bewildering array of contracts that worked against the formation of class ties. Some were simultaneously owners of small plots of land, tenant farmers, and day labourers. Feudal privileges and obligations survived in many places at least until the late nineteenth century, and helped cement peasants to the existing order and often encouraged far from hostile attitudes to the local landowner. In the central regions of Italy, sharecropping prevailed. Here, as well, peasants frequently enjoyed close relations with their landlords. In the Po valley, a growing army of militant day labourers began to appear from the 1880s; but alongside them, particularly up in the hills, were a large number of smallholders, who were often fiercely independent, Catholic, and conservative.

The huge variations of wealth and tenure among the peasantry, and the fact that rural society was often riven with mistrust and competition, made the chances of a sustained revolutionary movement emerging in the countryside slight. However, spontaneous and

often violent risings were very common, and they terrified the
authorities. Fear of starving and mutinous peasants burning down
tax offices, killing policemen, and breaking open gaols, was one
reason why Italian governments embarked on major programmes of
social and economic reform during the eighteenth century. The
limited success of these created uncertainty as to what remedies to
try instead. For most of the nineteenth century repression was the
usual instrument of social control, above all in the years immediately
following unification in 1860 when the authorities felt (with good
reason) that the clergy, the republicans, and the anarchists were
attempting to incite the peasantry against the state.

The problem of how to ease tensions in the countryside without
destroying or even changing the basic social and political order,
preoccupied Italian governments during the nineteenth and early
twentieth centuries. Had Italy been better endowed with minerals,
one possible solution might have been to build up the country's
manufacturing base and thereby shift the surplus rural population
into the cities. However, the peninsula had no coal to speak of and
only some scattered deposits of lignite, a fact of crucial importance
to the country's modern economic development, for it meant that the
peninsula was largely excluded from the first industrial revolution of
the eighteenth and early nineteenth centuries. Only at the very end of
the nineteenth century was Italy able to overcome some of its relative
disadvantage in energy through the construction of hydro-electric
dams in the Alps.

The lack of coal was not compensated for by an abundance of
other minerals. Iron ore was mined on the eastern side of the island
of Elba from Etruscan times; and deposits around Brescia gave rise in
the Middle Ages to a major local arms industry (Milanese armour
was especially prized in the fifteenth century). In neither case, however, was the quantity very great. Tuscany produced a certain amount
of salt, borax, and gypsum in the Cecina valley, mercury and also
antimony near Monte Amiata, and ferro-manganese in Monte Argen-
tario. Sicily had very important sulphur fields, which, with more
efficient mining, could have provided a major source of revenue. The
richest mineral region was Sardinia, with deposits of lead, zinc,
silver, bauxite, copper, arsenic, barytes, manganese, and fluorite.

After the Second World War methane gas was discovered in the Po valley, and oil off the Sicilian coast; but these did not spare Italy from having to depend on imported oil for most of its energy needs.

With few minerals and a large underemployed rural population, it is not surprising that Italy's early industries were closely tied to agriculture. The spread of mulberry trees in the Po valley after the sixteenth century, for example, encouraged the development of silk production. The cocoons, grown mainly by small peasant farmers (or more precisely by their wives), were turned into semi-finished cloth in water-powered mills. An abundance of fast-flowing rivers in the north of Italy helped the industry to grow, and in the late seventeenth century Bologna was the most mechanised city in Europe, with over a hundred silk factories. In Piedmont and Lombardy, the two most productive regions, mills were linked to the agriculture of the less fertile hill zones and relied for their labour chiefly on seasonal work provided by the local peasantry, and in particular, by the women.

Until the second half of the nineteenth century silk was Italy's only major industry; and the fact that it was largely an offshoot of agriculture suggested that an autonomous and competitive industrial sector might be beyond the country's reach. Many mid-nineteenth-century liberals, Cavour among them, thought that Italy's future lay with agricultural exports; and Richard Cobden, the great Victorian apostle of free trade, agreed, saying with metaphorical concision that 'Italy's steam is her sun'. The weakness of agriculture outside the Po valley, however, largely precluded this option; and after the 1870s governments felt obliged to look instead to industrialisation. The absence of minerals and the fact of being a 'latecomer', meant that the state had to play a major part in the process, introducing tariffs, controlling the labour force, and salvaging bankrupt companies and credit institutions.

The creation (out of very little) of a broad industrial base was fraught with difficulties, and many within Italy's ruling classes were from the start sceptical about the wisdom of uprooting peasants from the countryside and throwing them into an urban environment. Despite a strong civic tradition dating back to Roman times, Italian society was still overwhelmingly rural in the late nineteenth century. For centuries the lives of the vast majority of the population had centred around small communities, many of which had distinctive customs, political traditions, and dialects. The mountainous nature of much of the peninsula had tended to reinforce this fragmentation. It is not surprising, therefore, that the migration of millions of peasants and their families away from the countryside and into the cities in the century after unification, should have produced tensions that the state was often hard-put to contain.

One important factor limiting the movement of the population before very recent times was the weakness of the internal market. The poverty of the soil and the harshness of the agricultural contracts imposed on most peasants by their landlords (who always tended, given their political power and the abundance of cheap labour, to have the whiphand), meant that few farmers were ever in a position to accumulate a surplus to sell. Perhaps two-thirds of all the grain produced in Italy before 1860 was consumed by those who grew it, and only in the wealthier areas of the North and Centre was there any real exchange between the towns and the countryside. Even here, though, commerce was almost exclusively local in character. Payment in kind was practised virtually everywhere, and very little money circulated. A good deal of the population thus lived outside the market.

Even had domestic demand been greater, producers would still have faced an enormous obstacle to trade in the absence of good internal communications. The peninsula lacked navigable rivers, which meant that Italy was deprived of the conditions that allowed London or Paris to develop into commercial centres. The only major waterway, the Po, suffered too much from seasonal fluctuations and silting to become very important. Land routes were similarly deficient. For centuries the great Roman roads remained the only significant arteries; and inland from these, many towns and villages, especially in the South, had to rely on mule tracks or sheep runs for links with the outside world. Even in 1890, according to one estimate, nearly 90 per cent of all southern communes were unconnected by road. Winter torrents and landslips took their toll, especially on bridges and the more precipitous tracks; and local initiative or capital was rarely forthcoming to make good the damage.

In these circumstances, the population of much of the peninsula remained beyond the reach of the modern world until after

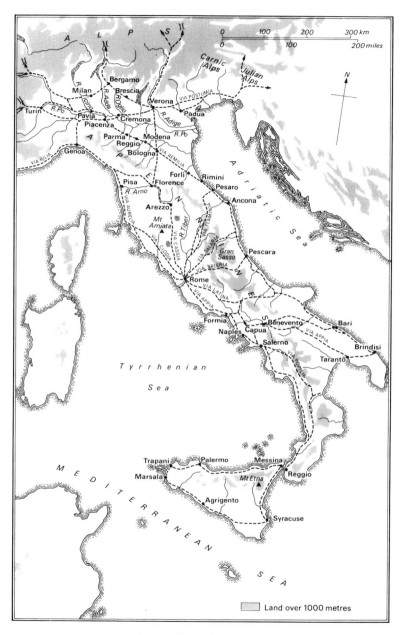

Map 2   Rivers, relief, and main Roman roads

unification. Even the Church failed to penetrate the remoter zones, despite its policy in the seventeenth and eighteenth centuries of trying to win new converts by proselytising the rural poor. The Jesuit missions to the South ('the Indies down below', as they called it) operated chiefly around the main urban centres; but even here they encountered extraordinary ignorance. Scipione Paolucci reported in 1651 on some five hundred shepherds he had come across near Eboli, who were 'hardly better informed than the animals they looked after'. When asked how many gods there were, 'some said a hundred, some a thousand, some even more, thinking that the higher the estimate they gave the cleverer they were, as if it were a question of increasing the number of their beasts'.

The Church, however, did manage to secure a greater hold over the Italian peasantry than any other force in the early modern period, which is one reason why the rupture with the Vatican after 1860 proved so damaging to the liberal state. Undoubtedly a good deal of rural Catholicism was far from being orthodox, and contained traces of superstition, folklore, and even ancient pagan practices. Mystical and millenarian elements surfaced in popular protest movements: in the 1870s, on Monte Amiata in southern Tuscany, Davide Lazzaretti and his humble followers proclaimed the third and last age of the world and the 'Republic of God' on earth, only to be shot by the *carabinieri* (military police). Despite such signs of waywardness, the Catholic Church managed to forge sufficiently close links with the peasantry (and the women especially) to withstand the assaults of the liberals and the socialists, and emerge triumphant after 1945 with Christian Democracy.

The Church's success at a popular level owed much to its welfare measures (caring for the sick, the elderly, and the destitute); but (and this was perhaps crucial to its influence) it could also cater to the needs of the powerful. Membership of a religious guild was often a status symbol for the local elite, especially if it involved organising the annual *festa* for the patron saint; and political faction fights could be given a veneer of respectability by being disguised as feuds between rival guilds. The cult of local saints and miracles (such as San Gennaro in Naples, Santa Rosalia in Palermo, the Madonna of Pompeii, or St Anthony of Padua) helped bolster civic pride; while in places the Church even managed to make an official accommodation with the lawlessness of the rich: in Sicily, prior to 1860, the ecclesiastical authorities published an annual list of (fairly light) penalties for a variety of crimes, including murder as an act of vendetta.

If the Church succeeded, through compromise and flexibility, in penetrating many of the communities of the rural interior, the state was often far less successful. Centuries of isolation bred habits of fierce independence that were hard to break, especially when it came to paying taxes or serving in the army. An inscription on an eighteenth-century map of Sardinia records, 'The Nurra: unconquered peoples who pay no taxes'. Law and order was a particular problem in the South. In many of the poorest and most remote areas, competition for resources led to strongmen or bandits acquiring power and influence, which they were not keen to share with the police. The fact that the local population colluded with them made the situation worse, and the authorities often faced a wall of silence when they tried to investigate crimes. In the Kingdom of Naples before 1860 the government took to enrolling brigands as policemen in a desperate attempt to overcome this problem.

The enforcement of law and order in the South was further complicated by the mountainous terrain, the lack of roads, and also by the patterns of settlement. In the Centre and North, the countryside was usually quite well inhabited, particularly in those areas, such as Tuscany and Umbria, where sharecropping was the usual form of agricultural tenure. Here the peasants lived with their families on the land they worked in sizeable farmhouses often supplied by their landlord. In the South, by contrast, the rural population was concentrated in large 'agro-towns' perched high up hillsides above the malarial lowlands. Every morning the peasants travelled to the interior to work their land, as much as ten or fifteen kilometres away, and returned at sunset. The vast stretches of desolate and uninhabited landscape, with their mountains, valleys, and caves, provided ideal territory for brigands, or indeed anyone who wished to hide from the law.

The remoteness and poverty of so many rural communities in Italy helps to explain why such a plethora of spoken dialects survived in the peninsula right down to the present; and the absence of linguistic uniformity was a further reason why the authorities often found it hard to establish their authority. It has been estimated that in 1860 only 2.5 per cent of the population understood Italian – in other words the fourteenth-century literary Tuscan that had come to be accepted since the Renaissance as the language of the educated (though in fact many in the ruling classes preferred not to use it: Victor Emmanuel II, the first king of united Italy, generally wrote in French, and spoke dialect at cabinet meetings; and his prime minister, Cavour, was visibly uncomfortable when using Italian in parliament). The majority of Italian speakers at the time of unification were concentrated in Rome and Tuscany.

Although a number of Italian dialects were recognisably 'Italian', many of them were in effect separate languages, with their own vocabulary, grammar, and cadence. In parts of the South, some even retained elements of archaic Latin and Doric dating back to pre-Christian times, a remarkable sign of how static their communities had been. More extraordinary still was the survival (down to the present) of Greek-speaking settlements in Calabria and Apulia, whose origins probably lay in the Byzantine period or possibly much earlier. Of more recent date, but equally indicative of isolation, were the Albanian towns of the South founded by Balkan refugees in the fifteenth century: their population numbered about 100,000 at the time of unification. At Alghero in Sardinia a Catalan-speaking community survives from the time of its original settlement by the Spanish in 1354.

During the late nineteenth century and throughout the twentieth century the quickening pace of industrialisation, increased attendance at primary schools, migration to the cities, and the spread of roads, railways, and the mass media all contributed to a steady decline in linguistic variety in the peninsula and to a growing familiarity with the national language. Nevertheless, for much of the population Italian continued to belong to an alien world, the world of literature not everyday speech, and the world, too, of officialdom and the state, towards which the poor in particular had at best ambivalent feelings. A survey of 1910 showed that at least half of school teachers were obliged to conduct lessons in dialect in order to be understood; and seventy years later, according to another survey, about 50 per cent of Italians still used dialect as their preferred first language.

In contrast to the situation in Germany (where from the sixteenth

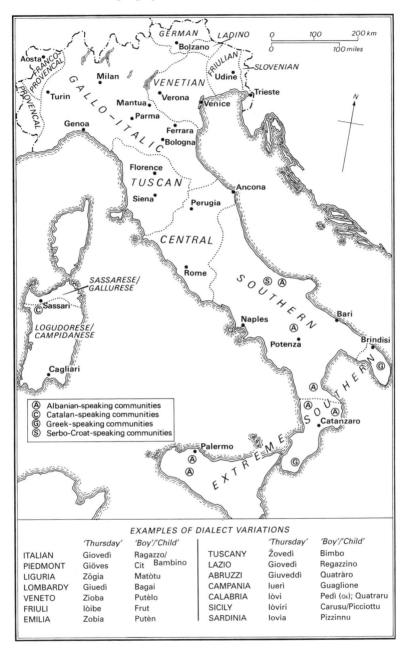

EXAMPLES OF DIALECT VARIATIONS

	'Thursday'	'Boy'/'Child'		'Thursday'	'Boy'/'Child'
ITALIAN	Giovedì	Ragazzo/	TUSCANY	Žovedì	Bimbo
PIEDMONT	Giöves	Cit Bambino	LAZIO	Giovedì	Regazzino
LIGURIA	Zögia	Matòtu	ABRUZZI	Giuveddì	Quatràro
LOMBARDY	Giuedì	Bagai	CAMPANIA	Iuerì	Guaglione
VENETO	Zioba	Putèlo	CALABRIA	lòvi	Pedì (Gk); Quatraru
FRIULI	lòibe	Frut	SICILY	lòviri	Carusu/Picciottu
EMILIA	Zobia	Putèn	SARDINIA	Iovia	Pizzinnu

Map 3 The principal dialect areas of Italy.

century all classes came to write, if not speak, the same idiom), language in Italy operated less as an instrument of integration and more as a wedge driven between the ruling elites and the great mass of the population. This was especially true in the early decades of unity when it proved yet another factor limiting the authority of the new state. In an attempt to remedy this anomaly, a number of heavy-handed efforts were made (especially in the fascist period) to impose linguistic uniformity by stigmatising dialect. However, the creation of a common language, like many other factors that ostensibly contributed to a sense of collective identity in Italy, was largely the product of socio-economic forces that were unleashed but not always controlled by the state; and as events in the twentieth century were to show, such forces had a strong capacity to bite the hand that fed them.

2

Disunity and conflict: from the Romans to the Renaissance, 400–1494

In the realm both of substance and ideals, long centuries of Roman domination bequeathed an enormous legacy to future generations of Italy. Clearance of the ancient forests began in earnest, and the South especially started to assume something of its modern appearance, with huge tracts of deforested rolling uplands covered with wheat-growing estates or *latifundia*. A network of roads was created, which, with the addition of the Via Francigena between Piacenza and Rome after 800, served as the basis for land communications down to the nineteenth century. Most important of all was the foundation of a string of semi-independent cities stretching across the Po valley, through central Italy, to the South. These *municipia* were the building blocks of the Roman administrative system, and their autonomy (albeit nominal at times) acted as a beacon that was to help inspire the civic tradition of the Middle Ages.

The achievement of the Romans in bringing first the peninsula and then the whole Mediterranean under their sway exerted a powerful influence on the minds of many of those who followed them. The idea of a strong emperor, who could eradicate warring and factionalism, was the dream of Dante in the early fourteenth century. Machiavelli's fascination with republican Rome two centuries later caused him to long for a revival of those civic virtues that had once made Italy great. The entire culture of the Renaissance, with its glorification of the classical world, led from the sixteenth century to a growing sense of failure, and a belief that Italians had a duty to make themselves worthy of their heroic past. This belief was to inspire many patriots of the *Risorgimento*. In a less savoury fashion it also fuelled the rhetoric of fascism, and much of its military aggression, too.

The collapse of the Roman Empire in the west was gradual rather than sudden. The event traditionally seen as marking it – the deposition of the Emperor Romulus Augustulus by the barbarian Odoacer in 476 – brought no special comment from western chroniclers. Since at least the second century Italy had steadily lost its central position within the empire, as the legions pushed through the Balkans and deep into Asia; and the urban population of the peninsula had begun to fall and its agriculture contract well before Constantine moved the imperial capital to the east in 326. After the first century relatively few Emperors were of Italian origin. Saint Ambrose, bishop of Milan, may have been exaggerating only a little when at the end of the fourth century he spoke of Bologna, Modena, Piacenza, and other towns along the Via Aemilia as 'corpses of half destroyed cities'.

The invasion of Italy by the Ostrogoths at the end of the fifth century did not result in any clear break with Roman traditions (the only mark of their presence that survives is the great tomb of King Theodoric (d. 526) in Ravenna); but it did usher in a century of ruinous warfare that was to shatter the political unity of the peninsula and lead to the destruction of much of the remaining machinery of the Roman state. In 535 the eastern Emperor Justinian set out to recover Italy from the barbarians, and for eighteen years his forces, under the command of Belisarius and later Narses, fought a succession of bitter campaigns against the Goths. The havoc wreaked by the 'Gothic wars' was enormous: famine became widespread; and Pope Pelagius I described his Italian estates in 556 as desolated. Amidst the chaos, the Church began to assume an increasingly important economic and administrative role.

In 568 a fresh wave of invaders descended on Italy from the north. The Lombards were a semi-nomadic people, adept at horse rearing and warfare but little skilled in the more peaceable arts. After driving back the Byzantines and confining them to the extreme south and the north-east around Ravenna, they established a new kingdom, centred on Pavia but with effective power in the hands of local 'dukes'. Politically, the Lombard invasion was a watershed: it marked the end of any vestige of political unity in the peninsula, for despite their military prowess the Lombards never managed to conquer all of Italy. The eastern Emperors continued to rule in Sicily and parts of the mainland South; while the popes, eager to assert their claims to sovereignty over the Church, struggled, with some success, to keep Rome and its surrounding territory independent.

Although from a political point of view the Lombard invasion was something of a turning point, in many other respects its impact was less dramatic. Rather than impose their own culture, the Lombards apparently respected that of the indigenous population and absorbed a good deal of it. The rulers, at least, became converted to Christianity; and by the eighth century most Lombards had abandoned their traditional forms of dress and appearance – clothes with multi-coloured stripes, and long hair parted down the middle – and adopted more sober Roman fashions, with short hair, instead. They even appear to have lost their own language. Lombard law, with its emphasis on kinship and private justice, became mingled with Roman law. Levels of literacy, at any rate among the top ranks of society, seem to have been very high by contemporary standards.

In the economy, too, the Lombard invasion did not produce any important innovations. Land clearance gathered momentum from the eighth century, often as the result of local initiatives by monastic houses; and the number of smallholdings may have increased. Arable farming prevailed, with wheat giving way in places to rye and other cereals, particularly in the Po valley where the drainage systems created by the Romans had grown badly decayed. The patterns of agricultural tenure seem to have varied greatly. At the base of the ladder were chattel slaves (though their numbers were declining); above them were tenant farmers owing a wide range of labour and other dues; and finally came the free owner-cultivators (a substantial class, it seems, by the eighth century) and the elite of big landholders.

The continuance of imperial rule in much of the South meant even less of a break with the past here than elsewhere. The wheat-growing *latifundia* (*latifondi*) survived the disruptions of war, and in Sicily, at least, land confiscation was limited, perhaps because of the Church's

Plate 2   The legend on which the papacy's claim to temporal power was based. The Emperor Constantine donating the western empire to Pope Sylvester. A twelfth-century fresco in the church of the Santi Quattro Coronati, Rome.

large holdings on the island. Rule from Byzantium produced a cosmopolitan if mainly Greek culture; and ports such as Naples and Bari (like Venice in the north-east) established lucrative trading links with the Levant. In contrast to the North, however, where the Lombards developed a well-integrated state using Roman administrative traditions, the South did not on the whole enjoy strong political structures. Benevento was an independent duchy, frequently at war with the Byzantines; while Capua, Naples, Salerno, and Amalfi all had varying degrees of autonomy and fought one another constantly.

A particular threat to stability in the South came from the Arabs, who, after a rapid expansion across northern Africa in the seventh century, launched a series of lightning raids on Sicily and the mainland coast. These culminated in the conquest of Sicily from the Byzantines after 827, and the occupation of sections of Campania, Calabria, and Apulia. Sicily under the Arabs was remarkably prosperous, even when allowance is made for the poetic exaggeration of contemporary accounts. A wide range of technical innovations appeared, including reservoirs, water towers, and mills for producing sugar. Silver, lead, and sulphur were manufactured; and many new crops were introduced. Palermo became a glittering capital, with more mosques, according to one tenth-century traveller, than any other city in the Islamic world except Cordoba.

The threatened elimination of the Byzantine presence in Italy had major consequences for one of the key forces in Italian history, the papacy. The popes had been in control of the city of Rome and its surrounding territory from an early date; but in the eighth century their position was menaced by a renewed expansion of Lombard power, which led to the ejection of the Byzantines from Ravenna, increased Lombard control in central and southern Italy, and demands that the papacy pay tribute. Faced with a loss of his independence, Pope Stephen II appealed to the Franks for help; and in 754 or 755 they responded by sending an army across the Alps. They returned again in 773 under Charlemagne, who entered Pavia in triumph and crowned himself king. From now on the northern half of Italy was in effect part of the Frankish Empire, with the papacy asserting its claim to a swathe of territory that ran from Rome north-eastwards, and included the former Byzantine provinces around Ravenna and Bologna.

The issue of papal independence, however, was unresolved, as Charlemagne had no intention of being a catspaw of the Church. In a bid to keep the initiative, perhaps, Pope Leo III placed a crown on the Frankish king's head in St Peter's, Rome, on Christmas Day 800; and Charlemagne assumed the title of 'Emperor of the Romans'. The legal authority for this move was a document known as the Donation of Constantine, according to which the Emperor Constantine had given all the western provinces of the Empire to the popes early in the fourth century, in atonement for his sins. Although a forgery, made probably in the papal chancery in the 750s, the Donation remained the basis for all subsequent claims by the papacy to temporal rule. However, Charlemagne enjoyed real powers in Italy that were not dependent on papal concessions; and he evidently believed he had rights over the Church itself. So too did many of his successors. The confusion was to be a source of bitter conflict in the centuries ahead.

For all their administrative sophistication, the Franks were unable to build up a durable state in Italy. Disputes over succession seriously undermined their authority from the late ninth century, and local counts profited from this to extend their own power by force of arms. Despite the weakness of foreign rule, however, no effective 'Italian' kingdom emerged to fill the mounting political vacuum. The absentee Emperors (who after 962 were German) tried to offset the influence of the counts by strengthening the hand of the bishops; but the counts simply moved to the countryside, where their fortified *castelli* were beginning to dot the landscape. The decline of central-ised authority also encouraged a growth of civic initiative and an increasing reluctance on the part of wealthy townsmen to defer to an imperial appointee, especially if he was a German-speaking bishop.

In the countryside, the ninth and tenth centuries saw some loosen-ing of feudal ties. Slavery declined and landlords took to renting out their demesnes, thereby freeing tenants from the bonds of labour service. By the late tenth century there is evidence that peasants were even able to sell leased land to other peasants. The general picture (and one which contrasts strongly with the situation elsewhere in Europe) is of a rise in labour mobility and a fall in the economic power of landowners. In some places, new agricultural tools, such as the heavy plough and the scythe, made an appearance; and there were fresh initiatives in drainage and land clearance, often carried out by monasteries and especially in the Po valley. These develop-ments helped to lay the foundations for the economic upswing that accompanied the emergence of the communes in the late eleventh century.

THE AGE OF THE COMMUNES, 1000–1300

The decline of urban civilisation at the end of the Roman Empire had never been more than partial. Of the one hundred or so *municipia* in northern and central Italy, over three-quarters were still functioning cities by the year 1000. The survival rate in the South was much lower. Structural decay undoubtedly increased, as temples and civic buildings were abandoned or used as quarries; but in most places, the town walls and even the forum were maintained, and the distinctive grid pattern of streets continued to be visible (and remains today in Turin, Milan, Piacenza, Cremona, Florence, and elsewhere). Churches became the new index of urban vigour: Lucca, the main Tuscan city, had at least fifty-seven before the year 900. In such places, numerous merchants and artisans, money-lenders and land-owners helped sustain an economic vitality that the confusion of war failed to crush.

By the eleventh century Italian trade was more extensive than that of any other part of Europe except Arab southern Spain. Salt from the lagoons of the Adriatic, the Tuscan coast, and the mouth of the Tiber was especially lucrative, and was one of the foundations of Venetian wealth. Venice was driven to trade from the start, as it lacked an agricultural hinterland; and it made use of its close political links with Byzantium, importing eastern artworks and cloth, and exchanging them for local grain and other commodities. A number of towns in the South also flourished on commerce with the Levant. Salerno by the eleventh century had grown into a great intellectual centre with a famous medical school. The case of Amalfi was particularly remarkable. Despite an almost inaccessible cliff-bound location, it became one of the richest ports in the Mediterranean in the tenth century: its wealth seems to have been the result of helping the Arabs in their raids on the Italian coast, and securing valuable trading concessions in return.

The prosperity of many Italian cities in the early Middle Ages was in part a consequence of the breakdown of centralised political control after the ninth century. This created the space in which local forces could surface, throw off the vestiges of imperial government, and set up autonomous cities or 'communes'. In most cases, the formal attainment of independence occurred only after 1080; but tensions had been mounting for some decades prior to this. Emperor Conrad II reported how the citizens of Cremona rebelled against their bishop in 1037, and 'threw him out of the city with great ignominy, and despoiled his goods, and destroyed to the foundations a tower of the castle ... They also razed to the ground the old city walls, and built another larger wall against our state.' The imposition by the bishop of tolls had been one source of friction.

The creation of independent communes, however, was also the result of a new and extraordinary growth in the economy, that was to continue until the fourteenth century and which generated the

Plate 3   The continuity of towns. An aerial view of Lucca
showing medieval houses built into the fabric of the Roman
amphitheatre. In the top right can be seen part of the intensively
cultivated hinterland or _contado_.

material conditions out of which the civilisation of the Renaissance,
with all its cultural and artistic achievements, developed. This growth
had already been started in many places during the ninth and tenth
centuries by commerce; but the dramatic upturn of the eleventh
century was apparent first in (and it seems was partly due to)
changes in the countryside, where land began to be cleared with a
new urgency, and the area under plough increased to levels probably
close to the earlier high point of the first century AD. These developments in turn stemmed from an increase in population.

The growing prosperity of the countryside allowed for an accumula-
tion of capital; and the fact that feudal ties had for some time been

breaking down encouraged mobility to the cities, where plenty of opportunities existed for investment in trade. The proclamation of the first Crusade in 1096 opened up new doors: in return for carrying knights to the Holy Land in their ships, the merchants of Genoa, Pisa, and Venice secured important commercial rights in the east that were to be a mainstay of their prosperity in the centuries to come. The trade in spices from the Levant (used both for cooking and medicine) was extremely profitable: a shipload of pepper, cinnamon, ginger, saffron, mace, cloves, or nutmeg commanded huge sums in the urban markets of western Europe. Venetian imports of pepper alone amounted in value in some years to more than a million pounds of silver.

The emergence of a new mercantile elite was an important factor in the establishment of civic autonomy at the end of the eleventh century. The struggles out of which the communes grew varied in character from place to place, but in general they were the product of an alliance between the old military families (*milites*) and the new social groups and their supporters (often referred to as the *popolo*), who found a common cause in limiting the jurisdiction of the local bishop or count. The communal leaders, known as 'consuls', ranged in number from two or three to over twenty. Their assumption of power was rarely due to a single revolutionary act: more often it arose from a gradual acceptance that they were better placed than anyone else to represent the interests of the city. In Milan, the consuls and the archbishop worked side by side until the early twelfth century; but tensions between them grew when the archbishop failed to support a war against Como for control of the Alpine passes.

The move towards communal autonomy took place in many areas of western Europe from the eleventh to the thirteenth centuries, but was greatest in northern and central Italy. This was partly because of the encouragement given it by the popes in their struggle against the Empire. From 1080 to 1130 Genoa, Milan, Mantua, Cremona, Piacenza, Padua, Florence, Pisa, and many other towns developed communal institutions. From the start lawyers played a prominent role in the new governments, defining their powers and vetting every decision and move of the consuls. This was to some extent a reflection of Italy's strong legal tradition that dated back to Roman

times; but it also suggested the insecurity of the consuls and their
wish to find legitimacy for their actions. In practical terms, their
power rested on their ability to express the interests of the leading
citizens, who met periodically in large assemblies; but in challenging
the Emperor, albeit with the support of the pope, the consuls
evidently felt the need for a higher sanction.

While the cities of the north and centre of Italy were pushing
towards autonomy, the situation from Rome southwards was very
different. For much of the tenth century the papacy had been a
pawn in the hands of local noble families struggling for control of
the duchy of Rome. In 1059, in a bid to strengthen his position, Pope
Nicholas II formed an alliance with the Normans (the most feared
contemporary fighters), who for thirty years had been marauding in
the South against the Byzantine government. He recognised their
power in Apulia, Calabria, and Capua, and encouraged them to
conquer Sicily (still in Arab hands) in return for an annual payment
and military support. His legal right to do this was unclear, but the
alliance suited both parties. In 1061 the Normans began the conquest
of Sicily; and by 1091, with the fall of Noto, they had control of the
whole island. The Norman state that emerged in the South was
strong and centralised; and local autonomy was not tolerated.

By the twelfth century the great southern ports were declining.
Amalfi was devastated by a Pisan attack in 1135 and never fully
recovered. The enmity between the Normans and the eastern Empire
closed off the trade routes with the Levant, to the advantage of the
northern cities, Venice in particular; and the taxes imposed by the
Norman kings on the merchant classes in the towns under their
control further weakened the South's commerce. The southern ports
might anyway have failed to compete with the North in the longer
term: their wealth rested heavily on their role as entrepôts, and they
lacked the dynamic agricultural hinterlands that were so crucial to
the prosperity of the towns in the North. Even in Apulia, one of the
richest areas of the South, production of wheat and oil for the
market seems to have been limited in the eleventh century.

The Normans were not unaware of the importance of trade; but
their main concern was with exercising political power and establishing their personal authority. Their state was one of the most remarkable of the medieval world. It had a huge revenue, a glittering court,

Plate 4   The brilliant eclecticism of Norman power in the South.
The twelfth-century Palatine Chapel, Palermo, looking west to
where the kings sat enthroned directly beneath an image of
Christ. The sumptuous roof is of Arab workmanship.

famous for science and poetry, and a sophisticated bureaucracy
staffed in Sicily by Arabs and Greeks. It was founded on a vision of
kingship that owed much to the eastern Emperors: subjects even had
to prostrate themselves before the ruler. Art and architecture were

used as propaganda: the great mosaics of Christ in the royal churches of Monreale and Cefalù stressed the idea of omnipotence; and another mosaic in Palermo showed the king being crowned directly by God. Such images, backed by the efficiency of the governmental machine, helped to legitimate the Norman state.

In rejecting rule by the German emperors, the communes of the north and centre of Italy made 'freedom' their proclaimed ideal. The executive officers were rotated regularly, and the consuls all swore elaborate oaths to one another and to the commune in an attempt to guard against any usurpation of power. However, this was not a recipe for strong government. The threat of a common enemy – a local feudal count, another town, or the Emperor – might generate a temporary sense of unity among citizens; but for most of the time (and increasingly in the late twelfth and thirteenth centuries) factional unrest was rife. Pitched battles, with crossbowmen shooting in the streets, buildings being set on fire, and dozens being killed and wounded, became regular occurrences; and at times, as in Florence between 1177 and 1179, near anarchy prevailed.

The vulnerability of the communes to factional unrest was due in part to the strength of family ties. Among the wealthy especially, kinship was crucial and served as a basis for both political and economic activity. Leading families often grouped together in the same neighbourhood or even, as with the Doria of Genoa and the Peruzzi of Florence, around a single piazza. Families had designated meeting places where they would assemble in times of emergency to deliberate and decide on a collective policy. Unity was reinforced by a certain degree of intermarriage, and was symbolised by the common patronage of a church or private chapel. However, the most power-ful source of cohesion, ironically, was feuding – whether between individual families or between groups of allied families called *consorterie*.

These *consorterie* could serve an innocuous economic purpose, such as cooperation in farming a tract of land; but among the powerful they were primarily sworn associations for self-defence, with the terms of agreement enshrined in contracts. According to one contract from Lucca in the thirteenth century, members were to meet in times of crisis and decide 'whether to serve the commune or to serve every one his friends'. Each *consorteria* had its fortified tower, a massive stone structure that could rise to a height of 250 feet. This served both for defence and attack in times of unrest: archers and catapults would be stationed on top and fire at neighbouring towers or down into the streets. The skyline of most cities was dominated by a forest of such towers: Florence had at least 150 in the early thirteenth century, each with a name such as 'the chestnut', 'kiss-cat', or 'lance'.

The struggle between families and *consorterie* for power both reflected and reinforced the political weaknesses of the communes. Without any strong executive power, the elite of landowning nobles and wealthy merchants, from whose ranks almost all civic officials were drawn, fought for supremacy. The feuding was often polarised between two dominant groups: in late-twelfth-century Florence between the Uberti and the Donati; in Brescia between the Rivola and Coglioni; in Cremona between the Barbarasi and the Cappelletti. The disputes were essentially about political control of the commune, but they were generally couched in the aristocratic language of 'honour'. Insults of one kind or another both started and sustained vendettas: the prolonged struggle between papal and imperial factions in Florence during the thirteenth century was said to have begun when Buondelmonte de' Buondelmonti was murdered after being lured into breaking off an engagement and marrying a member of the Donati family.

The internal instability of the communes had an economic as well as a political dimension. The cities expanded fast during the twelfth and thirteenth centuries, as the constant enlargement of town walls shows. The population of Florence increased from a few thousand in 1000 to perhaps 100,000 in the early fourteenth century, making it, along with Venice, Milan, Genoa, and Paris, one of the five greatest cities in Europe. The expansion seems to have been largely due to immigration from the countryside, as the unhealthy character of the towns is not consistent with a fall in mortality rates. The influx of peasants led to the growth of urban artisan industries, trade, and money changing, and provided new sources of support for the noble *consorterie*. The result was an intensification and broadening of the struggle for power.

One symptom of this was the appearance of a new political force within the communes known as the *popolo*. This was an organisation largely of non-nobles, with a complex military base, that started in the early thirteenth century to establish its own political institutions and to challenge the old *consorterie* for power. The *popolo* was founded on the guilds or *arti*, which represented the various economic interests in each city. In Florence, there were (eventually) twenty-one: seven 'major' and fourteen 'minor'. The guilds had their own armed companies and came together in sworn confederations with elected leaders known variously as *anziani* or *priori*. By the mid-thirteenth century the *popolo* (as the confederations were collectively called) were demanding a share of communal office, fairer taxation, and an end to the ruinous feuding of the nobles.

One reason why the *popolo* was so determined to bring the old *consorterie* under control was that from the second half of the twelfth century the communes faced a major external challenge to their independence from a resurgent Holy Roman Empire. Frederick Barbarossa was elected Emperor in 1152, and for the next thirty years he struggled to restore imperial authority in northern Italy. Despite five expeditions across the Alps, however, during one of which, in 1162, he captured and destroyed Milan, his efforts proved largely unsuccessful: in 1176 he was defeated at the Battle of Legnano by the combined forces of the northern cities grouped together in the 'Lombard League' (Lega Lombarda). Six years later, with the Peace of Constance, Frederick formally acknowledged the autonomy of the communes.

Barbarossa's grandson, the Emperor Frederick II, made a fresh attempt to subdue the communes between 1225 and his death in 1250. Frederick was brought up in Sicily, which at the end of the twelfth century had passed by inheritance from the Normans to the German Hohenstaufen dynasty. All his life Frederick bore the imprint of his childhood in the Palermo court. He loved science and literature (the first Italian vernacular poetry was due to his patronage), but combined it with a restless and authoritarian desire for the submission of his subjects and an exalted view of the role of kingship. His famous legal code of 1231, the *Constitutiones Augustales* (the Roman imperial title is revealing), embodied this desire, with their total prohibition of all private wars and the creation of a system of royal courts to coordinate the various legal traditions of his dominions (Roman-Byzantine, Lombard, Frankish, Norman).

Frederick's ambitions in Italy brought him into conflict not just with the communes but also with the papacy, which during the twelfth century had consolidated its position in and around Rome. The election in 1198 of the vigorous thirty-seven-year-old Innocent III saw the claims of the popes to temporal power carried to new and far-reaching heights. Building on the precepts of the Donation of Constantine, Innocent argued for special papal authority within the Empire and feudal lordship over certain kingdoms (Sicily, Aragon, Hungary). He also sought to secure the permanent independence of the papacy (now threatened by German power in both north and south) by establishing a strong state in central Italy. However, he faced the same problem as his predecessors: without his own military forces, he had to rely on others to do the fighting for him, which brought the issue of independence back to where it had started.

The conflict between Frederick and the papacy resulted in nearly thirty years of war, ending in the destruction of Hohenstaufen power in Italy. Both sides angled for support in the cities of the North: rival parties in the communes adopted the labels *Ghibelline* (empire) or *Guelf* (papacy) to signify their loyalty, although in practice the names meant little and served merely to give factions additional leverage (through alliances) in their struggle for local domination. Frederick enjoyed some success, particularly in the Romagna where he won the backing of an ambitious warlord called Ezzelino da Romano; but his cause was not attractive, for the communes were aware that his victory would mean a curtailment of their freedoms and the imposition of heavy taxes. The papacy, on the other hand, appeared a somewhat less awesome threat.

When he died in 1250 Frederick had few allies left in northern Italy, and the only clear result of years of fighting was widespread devastation. 'At that time', wrote a contemporary, '... men did not plough or sow or reap ... and wolves gathered in great packs around the moats of towns, howling for their raging hunger.' For a few years the cause of the Hohenstaufen was taken up by Frederick's illegitimate son, Manfred; but the pope turned to Charles of Anjou, brother of the French king, for help; and Charles marched into Italy, and defeated and killed Manfred at the Battle of Benevento in 1266. His reward was the kingdom of Sicily; and though Sicily itself was captured by the Aragonese in 1282, following the local uprising

known as the Sicilian Vespers, the Angevins continued to rule in
Naples for the next century and a half.

RENAISSANCE ITALY, 1300–1494

The campaigns of Frederick II and Manfred were the last serious
attempts to introduce a degree of political unity in Italy before the
nineteenth century. In the decades after the Battle of Benevento the
peninsula became steadily more fragmented, as the cities, freed from
the common threat of imperial ambitions turned their energies
against each other. The years of fighting had left a bitter legacy.
Guelf and *Ghibelline* factions competed for power, murdering or
expelling their enemies and generating a complex tangle of alliances.
'O servile Italy, breeding ground of misery, ship without a pilot in a
mighty tempest', lamented Dante, himself an exile, in the early
fourteenth century. Dante hoped an Emperor would come to restore
order; but no Emperor was again in a strong enough position to
make any lasting impact on Italy until the sixteenth century.

The end of imperial ambitions was matched by a decline in the
authority of the papacy. The attempt to create an independent state
in central Italy involved the popes in a morass of temporal politics.
The nadir came in 1303 when Pope Boniface VIII was arrested on the
orders of the French king after a quarrel over taxation of the clergy.
Thereafter the popes felt it wise to withdraw from Italy, and in
1316 the curia was established at Avignon, where it remained for the
next sixty years enjoying a fair degree of autonomy. In the meantime,
the Papal States, that comprised much of Lazio, Umbria, the Marche,
and the Romagna, were carved up among petty tyrants such as the
Malatesta in Rimini and the Montefeltro in Urbino. It was only in
the second half of the fifteenth century that the papacy emerged
again as a major political force in the peninsula.

The prolonged unrest of the thirteenth and fourteenth centuries
placed an enormous strain on the communal governments. The
popolo managed to broaden the political base of most cities (around
10,000 were eligible for office in Bologna in 1294 out of a total
population of 50,000 – a remarkable figure); but this did not induce
greater stability. Nobles, many of whom were active in trade, enrolled
in the guilds and pursued their vendettas from inside them; and

Plate 5   Siena in the fourteenth century. A detail from Ambrogio Lorenzetti's allegory of good government in the Palazzo Comunale, Siena, 1337–9. In the centre foreground a teacher delivers a lecture. Note the skyline dotted with towers.

where legislation by the *popolo* specifically debarred aristocrats from high office, the old families could simply change their names and repudiate noble status – as with the Cavalcanti of Florence, who renounced their past (symbolically at any rate) by becoming the Cavallereschi. The continuance of internal disorder led many to doubt whether communal government, with its faction-ridden councils and rapid turnover of officers, was any longer valid.

In the thirteenth century many cities had responded to times of crisis (such as imminent war with a neighbouring city, or financial insolvency) by appointing a temporary dictator, usually from outside. This officer, known as a *podestà*, received a precise mandate; and his term as governor was scrutinised by the communal authorities, who might dismiss him for breach of contract. The hope was that he would provide the impartiality and decisiveness called for by the situation; and once the crisis was over, he could be paid and sent home. In some cases, above all in the lower Po valley where the sheer number of towns made disputes between communes more common, the *podestà* became more permanent. This might be at the request of the city itself; often it was because a local warlord or faction leader had seized power by force and made himself governor for life.

The emergence of permanent lordships or *signorie* from the middle of the thirteenth century in Lombardy, the Veneto, Emilia, and the Marche, did not result in an immediate collapse of communal institutions. Some *signori*, such as Matteo Visconti in Milan, started as captains of the *popolo* and were simply re-elected to office for ever longer terms; and even those, like the brutal Ezzelino da Romano in the Veneto or Obizzo d'Este in Ferrara, who used force to gain power, often governed alongside the existing structure of councils and committees. Only gradually, in the course of the fourteenth and fifteenth centuries, did the formal institutions decay and the reins of government become concentrated in the hands of the *signori*, usually as a result of their proven ability in war or success in mediating between and appeasing the main merchant and noble families.

Many of the smaller lordships that sprang up in the Po valley and the Alpine foothills were short-lived. In the later fourteenth century they were conquered by Milan, which under the Visconti carved out a huge territorial empire in central northern Italy. Only in the Papal

States did minor lords manage to remain independent: the Malatesta of Rimini, the Este of Ferrara, the Montefeltro of Urbino. The insecurity of the new *signori* (some of whom, like the della Scala of Verona, were of humble origins) was evident from their often desperate search for recognition and prestige, whether through marital alliances, acts of patronage, or the purchase of titles and honours. The Visconti paid 100,000 florins to the Emperor in 1395 to become 'dukes', while the Gonzaga of Mantua, who became marquises in 1433, made great play of their right to wear the English royal livery, featuring it proudly in the Arthurian fresco cycle they commissioned from the artist Pisanello.

Signorial rule was restricted only to certain areas. In the north-east were two ecclesiastical principalities, Aquileia and Trent; while the north-west was dominated by the feudal counties of Savoy and Piedmont. The rulers of Savoy did well in the fifteenth century, and secured a ducal title in 1416; but their territories straddled the Alps, which made communications difficult, and they were forced to accept a good deal of local autonomy, with the court acting chiefly as a source of legitimation and patronage. Sandwiched between Savoy and Milan was a small feudal marquisate, Monferrat, which survived until 1533, despite its poverty, under the Palaeologi. In the south of Italy was a huge feudal kingdom ruled over by the Angevins until 1442; but here, too, communication was difficult, and many barons were laws unto themselves, obeying the crown only when it suited them: the Prince of Taranto was said in 1444 to possess 400 castles, had his own mint, and claimed to reign 'by the grace of God'. The Kingdom of Sicily was also difficult to control: for a century after its conquest by Aragon it was torn by baronial feuds, and only in the fifteenth century was a degree of order established.

The best known Italian states of the fourteenth and fifteenth centuries were neither feudal nor signorial. Venice was a republic, whose unique geographical setting among the lagoons had from an early date helped to foster a strong collective identity. The site was maintained only with great vigilance (for example, to prevent the waterways silting up), and this may have been one reason why its citizens had so much respect for public authority and why factionalism was so rare. The city was famed for its political stability. It was ruled by an hereditary aristocracy whose composition hardly

changed from the thirteenth century. However, social mobility
operated through an intermediate class of 'citizens', membership of
which was determined largely by wealth. Citizens enjoyed commercial privileges and had access to some public posts. They also
monopolised office in the prestigious *scuole grandi* (the city's five
largest confraternities); and they dominated the hundred or so lesser
confraternities.

Other factors made Venice into *la Serenissima*. The head of state,
the 'doge', was a largely symbolic figure; but the elaborate ceremonies
that surrounded him gave his office great mystique and made him a
powerful focus for public loyalty. Civic life was full of rituals and
processions: these encouraged corporate pride, and also had a specific
function to impress and entertain the poor. The relative absence of
social unrest, however, probably had more concrete causes, such as
the small number of unskilled workers in the city (the employees of
the arsenal were the main group: they enjoyed good pay and privileges, including the right to form the doge's bodyguard), and the
fragmentation of industry into a mass of small artisan workshops.
The fact, too, that nobles continued to live in popular districts and
did not withdraw to their own quarters (as tended to happen in
Florence), may well have encouraged loyalty to the ruling class.

Florence also survived as a republic – but not because it was
socially or politically very stable. The *popolo* defeated the old
nobility only after a fierce struggle, which at times in the late
thirteenth century reduced the city to anarchy, with whole quarters
burnt to the ground. Government was oligarchic and based on the
guilds, with the seven major guilds (*arti maggiori*) having the lion's
share of the offices. The executive (*signoria*) was filled rotationally
and by lot, while legislative power resided in large popular assemblies, which in periods of crisis could be replaced by smaller
committees known as *balie*. By contemporary standards this was a
remarkably open system, with perhaps two thousand citizens eligible
for office in the 1420s; but it did not prevent unrest flaring up
occasionally amongst the poor, especially the semi-skilled or unskilled
workers of the textile workshops who constituted the core of the
city's labour force.

Factionalism also persisted into the fourteenth and fifteenth centuries, though on a less disruptive scale than before. The richest

families of bankers, merchants, industrialists, and lawyers continued
to form large clienteles to further their political or financial careers.
The Medici owed their prominence in the fifteenth century to the
astute and subtle manner in which they constructed a huge network
of support, especially, it seems, among the upwardly mobile, whom
they could assist with loans. They also cultivated a large popular
following in their quarter of the city, San Giovanni. As their banking
empire grew (much helped by the acquisition of the papal account),
they increased their patronage; and in 1434, following a failed coup
by their rivals, they and their allies swept to power. From then on
they were in effective control of Florence, though they never overturned the city's constitution, relying instead on subtle manipulation
of the electoral process to maintain their supremacy.

The persistence of republican government in Florence was due in
very large measure to its economy, which was strong enough to
sustain a huge merchant and artisanal class with the will and
resources to crush the old nobility and whose interests were too
diverse to permit rule by a single lord. By the early fourteenth
century Florence was probably the wealthiest city in Europe. The
fast-flowing streams of its surrounding hills had fostered a huge
industry in finished cloth: the town had nearly 300 textile firms in
the mid-fourteenth century. Profits from manufacturing and commerce were transferred into banking, and Florentine financiers
became the paymasters of Europe. Loans from the Bardi and Peruzzi
allowed Edward III of England to launch the Hundred Years War in
the 1330s and 1340s (though his failure to repay destroyed them);
and the following century the Medici, the Pazzi, the Rucellai, and
the Strozzi were among the biggest names in international banking.

Florence, like many other cities of northern and central Italy,
continued to be highly prosperous throughout the fifteenth century;
but the rate of economic growth was much slower than in the boom
years of the twelfth and thirteenth centuries. The turning point seems
to have come (as elsewhere in Europe) in the first half of the
fourteenth century, although the well-documented case of the merchant Francesco Datini of Prato shows that it was still possible to
make a fortune in commerce in the later fourteenth century. The
exact reasons for the downturn are uncertain. Warfare and bad
harvests took their toll; so too did competition from English, Flemish,

and Catalonian merchants. The advance of the Ottomans in the east might also have played a part. The impact of the Black Death of 1348 upon the economy is hard to assess, though its demographic consequences are clear: Florence had a population of some 100,000 in the early fourteenth century; by 1427 it was just 37,000.

The slowing down of the economy was accompanied by a rise in social unrest. In the thirteenth century poverty had been linked with virtue by men such as Francis of Assisi and Dante; but in the fourteenth it became identified increasingly with subversion. The Apostolic Brothers, led by Fra Dolcino, preached community both of goods and women, until they were starved out by papal forces near Novara in 1306–7 and killed. The Spiritual Franciscans, the most austere of St Francis' followers, were similarly persecuted. The secular authorities faced difficulties as well. Revolts occurred in Siena in 1328 and 1349, in Florence in 1343 and 1345, and in Lucca and Perugia in the 1370s. The most famous rising was that of the so-called *Ciompi* in Florence in 1378, a large movement of unskilled workers seeking political representation. Rural unrest may have been growing, too. 'My Lord Jesus Christ', ran a fifteenth-century prayer, 'save me from the anger and hands of the peasants.'

The havoc wreaked by plague and the insecurities caused by social unrest might help to explain the extraordinary level of religious activity among the Italian laity during the fourteenth and fifteenth centuries. However, religiosity was also bound up with guilt: the Church officially condemned usury, and the anxiety of merchants and bankers (evident in their diaries) probably spurred them to charitable works or bequests to religious houses. So, too, did the goading of friars. Northern and central Italy may well, as a result, have had a greater concentration of hospitals, hospices, and orphanages than any other part of Europe in the later Middle Ages. Many were staffed by lay volunteers. Confraternities were especially popular with the wealthy. These associations had their own chaplains, encouraged regular church-going, and were responsible for particular acts of charity, such as comforting the condemned on their way to the scaffold or giving alms to the well-born poor.

Although many people felt some hostility to the worldliness of the Church and denounced the laxity of friars or the nepotism of prelates, they were nonetheless devout. A degree of anti-clericalism

Plate 6 Religious enthusiasm in the Renaissance. San Bernardino preaching in front of the Palazzo Comunale, Siena, and holding up the symbol of the Holy Name of Jesus. A midfifteenth-century painting by the Sienese artist, Sano di Pietro.

was perhaps unavoidable given the number of clergy in Italy: in the fourteenth century there may have been twice as many per head of the population as in England. The religious enthusiasm of the urban laity was apparent in a variety of ways: in the popularity of relics and indulgences, for example, or the growing cults of the rosary, the Stations of the Cross, and the Holy Name of Jesus. This latter cult, with its IHS symbol, was associated in particular with San Bernardino of Siena, the greatest itinerant preacher of his age, whose sermons generated extraordinary fervour in his audiences. So, too, did those of the Dominican prior Savonarola, who in the mid-1490s held Florence in thrall with his apocalyptic demands for repentance and the public burning of 'vanities'.

The tension that existed in the minds of some between wealth and religion could to a degree be sublimated through art. Great churches and chapels, altarpieces, frescoes, and sculptures served simultaneously as monuments to material success and glorifications of God. A sense of expiation was sometimes all too evident. The early fourteenth century Arena chapel in Padua, with its superb fresco cycle by Giotto, was built by the son of a local money-lender, Reginaldo Scrovegni, whose transactions earned him a place in Dante's *Inferno*. Even portraiture had religious roots: it owed less to a new sense of individualism than to an old-fashioned desire on the part of the deceased to be commemorated. Niccolò della Tuccia said he wanted to be included in a painting of the 'Madonna of Mercy' that he commissioned in 1458, 'not from pride or vainglory, but only in case any of my successors wishes to see me, he can remember me better thus, and my soul may be commended to him'.

However, not all commission were inspired by spiritual concerns. In the fourteenth and fifteenth centuries art was used increasingly as a means of enhancing worldly status. Among the greatest patrons were minor lords eager to atone for their somewhat unsavoury pasts, as in the case of the former mercenary, Bartolomeo Colleoni, in the Bergamasco, or Federigo da Montefeltro, another *condottiere*, at Urbino, whose palace was built to provide 'a beautiful abode, worthy of the rank and fame of our ancestors and our own standing'. Commissions were also employed to add lustre to confraternities (as with Carpaccio's cycle of paintings for the *scuola* of St Ursula in

Venice, 1490–8) or guilds: the statues on the exterior of Orsanmichele in Florence were paid for by the *arti*, with the wealthiest ordering works in bronze rather than marble; and it was the Calimala, the hugely rich cloth guild, that commissioned the 'Gates of Paradise' for the baptistry from Ghiberti.

Art had long had a civic role in Italy. Major buildings, sculptures, and paintings were commissioned by the government, and their size and quality were seen as enhancing the city's standing: Duccio's masterpiece, the *Maestà*, was carried in triumph from his studio through the streets of Siena on completion in 1311. Specific political messages could be conveyed through art. Donatello's bronze of Judith cutting off Holofernes' head was moved to a prominent position in Florence's central piazza in 1495 as a warning after the expulsion of the Medici. Ambrogio Lorenzetti's frescoes on the walls of the council hall of the Palazzo Comunale in Siena (1337–9) were intended to instruct the city's rulers. They showed allegorically the virtues and vices connected with good and bad government, and the material and moral benefits that accrued to both town and country-side when a state was well run.

The social and political value of art in Renaissance Italy made collecting and connoisseurship into fashionable pastimes; and huge fortunes, many of them amassed in banking or commerce, were deployed in acquiring paintings, sculptures, drawings, bronzes, medals, and tapestries. Ludovico Sforza of Milan, Isabella d'Este of Ferrara, and other patrons eagerly established close personal links with talented painters and sculptors, an indication perhaps of the rising status of the artist. The Gonzaga family stood as godparents to the children of Andrea Mantegna (who also received the title of count palatine), while Donatello's friendship with the Medici resulted in his being buried near the great Cosimo in the church of San Lorenzo. The idea of the creative genius, with a distinctive, difficult, and often tortured personality, was largely a product of this period and was one of the central themes of Giorgio Vasari's *Lives of the Artists* published in 1550.

The astonishing artistic achievements of the Renaissance were a product of the extraordinary economic and social environment of the city states; but Italian culture in this period was far from having indigenous roots only. Burgundian and Flemish painters were highly regarded in Italy, and their technical and stylistic influence on Italian artists was probably greater than contemporaries cared to admit. Cultural exchanges with the north of Europe were helped by the strong presence of Italian bankers and merchants in cities such as Bruges and Ghent: one, Tommaso Portinari, commissioned a great altarpiece in the 1470s from Hugo van der Goes (now in the Uffizi). In music, the north's supremacy was clear. French and Flemish musicians were in constant demand at the Italian courts, and during the fifteenth century the pope's choir consisted of singers recruited in Cambrai and elsewhere in northern Europe. It was only during the sixteenth century that Italian music began to establish a strong independent identity of its own.

The main source of inspiration for the culture of fourteenth- and fifteenth-century Italy, however, was the art and literature of the classical world. Interest in the writings of the ancients was far from unprecedented. In the twelfth and thirteenth centuries major developments had occurred in science and philosophy, mainly as a result of the influence of Aristotle. However, the Italian 'humanist' scholars were unusual in that they turned to Livy, Cicero, and Suetonius not so much for knowledge, but rather to extract a new moral system that would harmonise with the lifestyle of the merchants and bankers who had risen to prominence in the city states. The superiority of the active over the contemplative life, the ennobling power of wealth, the desirability of earthly glory, and the importance of civic patriotism could all be illustrated, if not proved, from ancient authors; and for men such as Francesco Sforza or Lorenzo de' Medici, they offered a convenient supplement to their traditional Christian religious beliefs.

However, the 'rediscovery' of the classical world from the mid-fourteenth century onwards, by Petrarch, Boccaccio, Salutati, and others, did not lead to a sudden transformation of Italian culture. Ancient models and motifs undoubtedly influenced painting and architecture, and sculpture was given fresh impetus by the unearthing of antique statues; but the new learning, with its desire to emulate the literary skills, the values, and even the lifestyle of the greatest Romans, was limited to a small if remarkable group of men, many of whom, like Petrarch, had first mastered Latin in the course of their legal studies. Most literate Italians in the fifteenth century probably remained largely untouched by humanism. Universities and grammar schools continued to teach traditional forms of scholarship, and differed from their counterparts in northern Europe only in the primacy of law rather than theology.

If humanist scholarship and its values were the preserve of an educated elite, whose influence was to be felt primarily in the centuries to come, Renaissance Italy was nonetheless an exceptionally cultivated world. The need for merchants and bankers to be numerate and literate had encouraged new forms of practical education. The arts of letter writing, accounting, and public speaking were taught, along with more traditional disciplines such as Latin composition and theology. The vernacular acquired a new prestige as the natural medium for business and government; and this in turn was a factor in the great flowering of Italian literature from the second half of the thirteenth century. Florence was particularly well known for its schools, and this, as much as the political dominance of the merchant classes, helps to explain why many of the most famous writers of Italian verse and prose (Dante, Petrarch, Boccaccio) came from Tuscany.

The growth of the peaceful arts, however, did little to curb the appetite of the cities for war and conquest. The need to supply food to the urban populations led, in the absence of a superior restraining power, to cut-throat competition. From the mid-fourteenth century the wealthiest Italian states consumed ever larger swathes of surrounding territory. Florence took Prato, Pistoia, Volterra, Arezzo, Pisa, and Livorno between 1350 and 1421; Venice seized Treviso, Vicenza, Verona, Padua, and Friuli in the same period; and Milan under the Visconti was similarly rampant. In the South, the accession of Alfonso of Aragon to the Sicilian throne in 1416 was followed by the conquest of Naples and wars against Florence, Genoa, Milan, and Venice. The turmoil and conflict in the peninsula was made worse by the papal schism: from 1378 there were two, and at one time three, rival popes encouraging their supporters and helping pit one power against another.

The election of Nicholas V as pope in 1447 marked the start of attempts to stabilise the situation. Fears of foreign intervention in the peninsula helped concentrate minds; so too did the capture of Constantinople by the Ottomans in 1453, with the threat this posed to the territorial and commercial interests of Venice, Genoa, and other

Plate 7   The Renaissance cult of ancient Rome. Part of Andrea Mantegna's series of nine canvases depicting the triumph of Julius Caesar. The series was commissioned by Mantegna's patrons, the Gonzaga of Mantua, *c.* 1480–95.

states. In 1454 Milan, Venice, Florence, the papacy, and Naples, agreed to bury their differences and set up the Italian League, an alliance that aimed to restore peace and uphold the status quo in Italy. Among their worries was France. The French monarchy had claims both to the Kingdom of Naples and, through the marriage of Louis of Orléans to Valentina Visconti in 1389, to the Duchy of Milan; and the fact that it had just emerged victorious from the Hundred Years War, and was now enjoying increased revenues and a greater degree of control over its nobility, made the prospect of invasion seem all the more likely.

The League, however, failed to secure peace. There was too much bad blood and ambition around, and too many pretexts for war. Alfonso of Aragon continued his struggle with Genoa; Sigismondo Malatesta of Rimini clashed with the pope, and ended by losing most of his lands; Pope Sixtus IV fell out with the Medici and brought Florence to the brink of war with Naples; and Venice fought unsuccessfully for control of Ferrara. Meanwhile the Turkish threat came closer. The Ottomans raided Friuli in the 1470s, and in August 1480 attacked Otranto in Apulia, desecrating its churches and taking nearly half its population into slavery. The danger from Islam did nothing, though, to curb the ambitions of the popes, who were determined at almost any cost to consolidate their claims in central Italy. It was against this background of uncertainty that in 1494 Charles VIII of France marched over the Alps.

3

Stagnation and reform, 1494–1789

Despite political and economic uncertainties, the leading families of the Italian city states in the later fifteenth century enjoyed a strong sense of superiority. They formed an elite, not entirely closed, but one whose values and aspirations were in general more aristocratic than those of their merchant forebears. The Medici and the Strozzi were still great banking families, but their wealth was invested increasingly in urban palaces, country villas, and works of art. Sensibility, learning, and a certain disdain for money *per se* became the touchstones of status: when Giuliano Zancaruol commissioned a painting from Giovanni Bellini, he stressed that the cost was unimportant, 'as long as it is beautiful'. The achievements of Alberti, Pisanello, Mantegna, Botticelli, Bramante, or Leonardo gave their patrons feelings of importance that spilled over all too frequently into complacency. There were many in Italy who felt that their civilisation not only rivalled but perhaps even surpassed that of the ancients.

The sense of self-assurance was undermined by the long sequence of wars that rocked the peninsula from 1494. Charles VIII's conquest of Naples and the subsequent invasions by Spanish, French, and Imperial troops were widely seen as acts of divine retribution, punishments for the excess of wealth and worldliness in Italy. The historian Francesco Guicciardini reported that the arrival of Charles VIII's army was preceded by awesome prodigies: in Apulia, three suns shone in the middle of the sky at night, while in Arezzo, 'an infinite number of armed men on great horses passed through the air, with a terrible noise of trumpets and drums'. By the time Guicciardini wrote this in the 1530s, the Italian states had been reduced to mere pawns in an international power struggle. Spain controlled Sicily, Naples, Sardinia, and Lombardy; the constitutions and boundaries of other territories had been radically redrawn; and Rome had been sacked. Disillusionment had begun to replace the earlier feelings of supremacy.

Contemporaries struggled hard to understand what had gone wrong. The Dominican monk Savonarola put the blame on blasphemy, gambling, low-cut dresses, paintings of pagan goddesses, and devotion to the classics. The Florentine diplomat and intellectual Niccolò Machiavelli, who saw the government of his native city overturned three times during his life, looked to ancient Rome for an answer, and argued that Italy's troubles stemmed from a basic lack of public morality or *virtù*. This, he hoped, might yet be restored. Guicciardini, his junior by fourteen years, was less sanguine. For him, 'the calamities of Italy' were the result of a seemingly incurable mixture of external aggression and internal divisions. Some humanists identified the problem as one of foreign 'barbarianism': but their argument was vitiated by the fact that many of the most brutal contingents in the invading armies were themselves Italian mercenaries.

To a large extent, as Guicciardini implied, the Italian states were victims of circumstances beyond their control. Their prosperity in the Middle Ages had depended in part on the inability of the Holy Roman Empire or any other power to subdue them: and this had allowed free rein to local political and economic energies. However, the strength of the communes had simultaneously worked against the emergence of extensive well-integrated territorial units; not least because the main cities had always been rich enough to put strong armies into the field, and defend themselves against the predations of neighbours. So long as other parts of Europe were weakened by rivalries between the crown and the feudal nobility, Italy was relatively safe; but once these disputes were resolved (as they began to be in France and Spain by the end of the fifteenth century), powerful monarchies suddenly appeared with an economic and military potential that outstripped anything in Italy.

The success of the French and Spanish kings in domesticating their nobility was accompanied by the acquisition of new lands and hence new revenues. The death of Charles the Bold at the Battle of Nancy in 1477 brought Louis XI a share of the Burgundian inheritance, while his successor secured the Duchy of Brittany, the last more or less independent area of France. In Spain, the marriage of Ferdinand and Isabella led in 1479 to the union of Castile and Aragon; and this was followed by the conquest of Granada from the Moors. The result was to give France and Spain the means to bear the immense costs of campaigning; and since neither side had any advantage in weaponry or soldiers, the wars were heavily protracted, and were decided in the end mainly by the exchequer. The importance of money was evident in the case of the Holy Roman Emperor, Maximilian. His problems with raising taxes made him the weakest of the foreign powers in Italy. In 1516 he had to abandon the occupation of Milan after one day when his paymasters ran out of cash.

If dynastic claims arising out of old marriage alliances, conquests, and papal grants furnished a tangle of pretexts for war, the ambitions and rivalries of the Italian states themselves confused the situation still further. It was Venice's hostility to Milan that led to Louis XII being invited to attack the Sforza duchy in 1499; and it was the ambitions of Pope Alexander VI, and after him of Julius II and Leo X, in central and north-eastern Italy that resulted in a bewildering diplomatic merry-go-round, directed first against one power then against another. In 1508 Julius II allied with Louis and Maximilian against Venice; three years later he did an about turn, and solicited Venetian and Spanish support in driving out the French. In 1515 Leo X joined France against Milan; in 1521 the French were driven from Milan by a combination of the pope and Spain. These twistings brought substantial gains for the papacy in the Romagna and the Marche; but in 1527 disaster struck: Rome was sacked by Imperial troops, an episode whose consequences were religious as well as political.

The fate of Italy was eventually sealed by a quirk of the dynastic lottery. Between 1516 and 1519 the Spanish, Austrian, and Burgundian inheritances all devolved on the Habsburg prince, Charles V; and in 1519 the Imperial title became his too. Charles' huge empire stretched from Silesia to the Straits of Gibraltar. In Italy, it included

Naples, Sicily, and Sardinia. However, it excluded Lombardy, which was controlled by France, an anomaly that made communications between the northern and southern halves of the empire difficult. In a bid to rectify this Charles went to war, and in 1525 he defeated and captured the French king at the Battle of Pavia. In 1530 Florence fell to Imperial forces: and Charles was now arbiter of the entire peninsula. He annexed Milan to Spain and restored Florence to the Medici (who became dukes, later 'grand dukes', of Tuscany); Savoy, Ferrara, Mantua, Urbino, Modena, and Parma were made into hereditary duchies, while Lucca, Genoa, and Venice stayed as republics. The popes were left to rule the Papal States. This arrangement was confirmed by the Treaty of Cateau-Cambrésis in 1559, and was to remain broadly unchanged until the upheavals of the eighteenth century.

It was ironic (though not entirely a coincidence) that the political and military humiliation of Italy in the first half of the sixteenth century was accompanied by the emergence of a form of national culture. Ever since Petrarch, humanist writers had made great play with the idea of *Italia*; and foreign invasion now gave it new poignancy and significance. In the last chapter of *Il Principe* (The Prince) (1513), Machiavelli appealed for a saviour of 'Italy' from 'the insolence of the barbarian'. However, the concept had far more substance at the level of literature than of politics. Through the advocacy largely of the Venetian humanist Pietro Bembo (1470–1547), Tuscan vernacular became widely accepted throughout the peninsula as the main literary language. Ariosto revised his great poem *Orlando Furioso* (1532) to fit in with the new linguistic canon, and Baldassare Castiglione did likewise in 1528 with his famous manual of etiquette, *Il Libro del Cortegiano* (The Courtier). Dialect continued to be used by some Italian writers and even flourished in some places during the seventeenth and eighteenth centuries; but Tuscan was henceforth supreme in educated circles.

As the sixteenth century progressed, Italian art and culture spread north and came to dominate much of Europe. Humanist education, with its rather romantic vision of the classical world and its stress on eloquence in Latin and Greek, became a hallmark of the rich from Scotland to Sicily. Italian dress, deportment, and even cooking set the standard at princely courts; and Naples became the European

Map 4   Italy, 1559–1796.

capital of taste and refinement. In England, Henry VII's tomb was commissioned from a pupil of Michelangelo; Wyatt, Surrey, Spenser, and other writers imitated Italian models; and Renaissance motifs began to adorn monuments and palaces, albeit somewhat haphazardly. Padua, Bologna, and other Italian universities led the way in anatomy and mathematics; while in astronomy, the Florentine Galileo Galilei provided incontrovertible evidence for the heliocentric universe and destroyed for good the Aristotelian cosmos that had been crucial to the medieval world view.

If Italian culture spread chiefly through being embraced spontaneously by outsiders, attracted by its connotations of wealth and sophistication, it was also disseminated as a result of a new attitude of the Church. The challenge of Luther and the humiliation produced by the sacking of Rome in 1527 gave rise to a militant era of Catholic reform, in which the power of the visual image was used to combat the austerity of Protestantism. Rome was transformed in the sixteenth century from a poor, rather decayed town, into a vibrant city, with great piazzas and churches, built and decorated by the best architects and painters of the day. It became the shop-window of the Counter Reformation, one of whose aims was to win over the rich and powerful not just through religious reforms but also by sanctioning the traditional passion of princes and aristocrats for worldly magnificence. Endorsed by the papacy, the extravagances of Mannerism and later the Baroque radiated out from Italy, across Europe, to South America and Asia.

SOCIAL AND ECONOMIC DEVELOPMENTS IN THE SIXTEENTH AND SEVENTEENTH CENTURIES

Italy's cultural achievements in the sixteenth century were underpinned by an economy that was still in many respects dynamic. One reason for this, or at any rate one factor behind the increased production evident in both industry and agriculture at this time, was a rise in population. From the mid-fifteenth century the damage caused by plague in the previous hundred years began to be made good; and the advent of peace after 1530 probably helped the process. The population of Sicily rose from 600,000 in 1501 to more than a million in 1607; and the town of Pavia more than doubled its number of inhabitants in the middle decades of the century alone. By 1600, according to one estimate, Italy was probably the most densely populated region of Europe, with an average of forty-four people per square kilometre rising in areas such as Lombardy and Campania to three or even four times this level. The figure for France was thirty-four, and for Spain and Portugal only seventeen.

The pressures of population resulted in fresh areas of land being brought under the plough. In sixteenth-century Tuscany, travellers were often struck by the degree to which the mountain-sides were newly planted with vines and other crops. In southern Italy, despite government strictures, the nobility tried to increase agricultural output by founding new towns: some four hundred were created during the middle decades of the century. In Lombardy, the response of landowners and governments to the population increase was characteristically energetic: new initiatives were undertaken in land drainage (Leonardo da Vinci was employed in bringing the waters of the Adda and Ticino under control); and by the late sixteenth century the region probably had much the same appearance as today, with regular fields lined with elms, mulberries, and fruit trees. The only notable difference would have been the absence of maize and large-scale rice growing, both of which appeared largely in the seventeenth and eighteenth centuries.

The textile industry flourished: wool production in Florence almost doubled between 1527 and 1572, while silk manufacture started to make its mark for the first time in areas of northern Italy. Banking enjoyed a particularly dramatic growth in both large cities and smaller towns: the proliferation of palaces and public buildings in the sixteenth century owed much to the easy availability of credit. Genoese bankers were especially powerful: the Doria, Grimaldi, Spinola, and Pallavicino family firms rivalled the great south German concerns of the Fugger or the Welser, financing Spain's huge trans-atlantic fleets and furnishing the gold with which Spanish troops in the Netherlands were paid. Florentine and Lucchese banks tended to work more with the French crown. All, however, were susceptible to government insolvency, and during the second half of the sixteenth century the growing inability of the Spanish crown in particular to repay its debts threatened many Italian (and German) bankers, and led in the seventeenth century to their ruin.

Plate 8   The Indian summer of Genoese prosperity. Marchesa Brigida Spinola Doria, by Peter Paul Rubens, one of a series of sumptuous portraits of members of leading Genoese families executed by the young Rubens on a visit to Italy in 1606.

Among the factors that helped sustain the Italian economy in the sixteenth century were improvements in land and sea communications, the invention of a new type of water-powered mill (that greatly benefited silk production), and an increase in tourism: more than half a million pilgrims visited Rome for the jubilee of 1600. In the South, the tendency of nobles to move away from the countryside and into Naples or Palermo in order to be closer to the viceroy and his court stimulated the manufacture of luxury goods: one report said that four-fifths of all Neapolitan workers were dependent on the silk industry in the late sixteenth century. However, the main spur to the Italian economy probably came from central government, whose powers and authority grew rapidly in most states from the mid-sixteenth century. The Venetian Senate undertook the drainage of huge tracts of marshland around Padua, while the Grand Duke of Tuscany turned the tiny fishing village of Livorno after 1592 into a great port with a population of over 10,000.

Economic prosperity was one important reason for the growing stability of the Italian states after 1530. As the century progressed, law replaced violence as the normal means of settling disputes between subjects, and revolts against the government were few. The Neapolitan revolt of 1585 was directed not so much at Spanish rule, as at local maladministration. Princes set out to legitimate their positions by drawing up new or revised constitutions (which were often well enough drafted to survive into the eighteenth century), and appeased their subjects through tax reforms and paternalism. As in other parts of Europe, the principle of monarchy was supreme, but councils, senates, or, in the case of Naples and Sicily, parliaments enabled the nobility to feel closely involved in government. The success of the new order was such that resentment at 'foreign' rule appears to have been minimal. Naples rose up against its viceroy to cries of *Impero* and *Spagna*.

However, beneath the orderly and prosperous facade some alarming features were appearing. One was the growing weakness of the bourgeoisie. In the course of the sixteenth century the merchant entrepreneurs, who had been the mainstay of the Italian economy since the Middle Ages, began almost everywhere to turn away from commerce and industry and adopt instead an aristocratic lifestyle. In Florence, according to the Venetian ambassador in 1530, anyone with 20,000 ducats invested half in a country house; and certainly by the end of the century the Torrigiani, the Corsini, and many other wealthy families were transferring their money from trade to land. The new Florentine elite lived on rent and patronage at the ducal court. In Venice, a similar process is detectable. In the South, the nobility grew in both size and political importance, assisted by the crown's sale of titles and its alienation of rights and dues. Between 1558 and 1597 the number of marquisates in the Kingdom of Naples seems to have trebled.

These tendencies were a symptom, and to some extent also a cause, of the growing vulnerability of the Italian economy. From 1580 the slide into recession gathered pace, and in the decades that followed Italian trade and industry experienced a catastrophic slump. Woollen cloth manufacture disappeared almost completely; shipbuilding collapsed; and the principal ports, with the exception of Livorno (which served as a staging post for vessels moving between northern Europe and the Mediterranean), contracted sharply. Merchant banking also declined dramatically. By the end of the seventeenth century Italy had become an importer of large quantities of finished products from France, England, and Holland, and an exporter of primary or semi-finished goods: wheat, olive oil, wine, and above all silk. It had moved from a dominant to a subordinate position within the European economy.

The reasons for this economic decline are by no means clear. Part of the explanation lies in the shift in the axis of world trade to the Atlantic, and the growing importance of commerce with non-Mediterranean countries. However, while this may account for some of the problems facing Italy's merchants, it cannot explain the failure of Italian industry to compete in Europe. One factor here was probably the historic power of the guilds and the controls they set on pay and work practices: the newer economies of England or Holland, free of such restrictions, could undercut Italian producers with cheaper goods. Another factor was perhaps the narrowness of Italy's home market. This stemmed from old rivalries between the Italian states (and hence their failure to build up commercial ties), and from the extreme concentration of wealth in the hands of an elite that preferred to invest in art and palaces rather than industry. The mass of the population was too poor to afford manufactured goods, and domestic demand was therefore weak.

Had Italian agriculture been more efficient, some of these problems might have been reduced. However, the population rise of the sixteenth century, while causing new areas to be brought into cultivation, did not engender real improvements in yields or in methods of production. The tendency of the urban middle classes to move their capital from trade to land led to a growing phenomenon of absentee ownership, which had especially harmful consequences in the South where large estates were often leased on short-term contracts to middlemen, who farmed with little concern for the well-being either of the soil or the peasantry; and output suffered accordingly. From the late sixteenth century Italian governments found it increasingly hard to produce enough food to feed all their subjects; and the situation was made worse by the fact that the Ottoman Empire was facing a similar crisis, which brought an end to the traditional reserve supplies of wheat from the Ukraine.

One symptom of the growing crisis in the countryside was banditry. In the last decades of the sixteenth century the number of reports of brigandage escalated, and governments became alarmed at the mounting threat to public order. 'In Rome this year', said a note of 1585, 'we have seen more heads [of bandits] on the Ponte Sant' Angelo than melons in the market.' Around Naples, watch-towers were built to warn of the approach of brigands; and in the Campagna, periodic brush fires were ordered to smoke out gangs of robbers. Calabria appears to have been particularly infested, largely because the terrain offered such good cover. On one occasion, according to a sixteenth-century account, bandits entered Reggio in broad daylight and opened fire with cannon, 'while the governor stood by helpless, as the townsmen refused to obey and come to his aid'. Banditry was caused mainly by rising unemployment and poverty; but the fact that Italy was a patchwork of states also encouraged it, as brigands could flee across a border when pursued.

The crisis in food production was accompanied by other difficulties and disasters, which made the first half of the seventeenth century one of the most dispiriting periods in Italian history. Plague returned with renewed virulence: Milan, Verona, Florence, and Venice suffered major epidemics in 1630-1, which killed between a third and a half of their inhabitants. The rise in mortality rates caused Italy's population to drop from about 13 million in 1600 to 11.25 million in

Table 3 *Population of Italy 1550–1800 (in thousands)*

	1550	1600	1650	1700	1750	1800	% increase 1700–1800
Northern Italy	4746	5412	4255	5660	6511	7206	+ 27.3
Central Italy	2542	2915	2737	2777	3100	3605	+ 29.8
Kingdom of Naples	3050	3320	2850	3300	3900	4847	+ 46.9
Islands[a]	1108	1424	1527	1456	1776	2136	+ 46.1
Total	11446	13111	11370	13193	15287	17795	+ 34.8

Note: [a] Including Malta and Corsica.
Note the particularly rapid rate of growth in the South 1700–1800.
Source: Ruggiero Romano (ed.), *Storia dell'economia italiana vol. II* (Turin, 1991).

1650 (see Table 3). A world recession beginning in the second decade of the century exposed the structural weaknesses of Italian industry and decimated production: in Milan, the number of silk looms fell from 3,000 in 1606 to just 600 in 1635. Unemployment and destitution increased rapidly. A study of the Piedmontese town of Saluzzo (where manufacturing was on only a modest scale) suggests that in 1624 two-thirds of its population was no longer able to support itself.

The effects of the recession were made worse by war. The dukes of Savoy, perennially ambitious, became embroiled from 1612 in a struggle with the Spanish for control of Monferrat and later of Mantua, a conflict into which the French were drawn in 1628. Venice took up arms against the Austrian Habsburgs in 1615; and from 1620 was involved with France, Spain, and Savoy in a dispute over the Alpine region of the Valtellina. In 1635 a new round of hostilities began, with France, Savoy, Parma, and Mantua allied against Spain. These and other conflicts in the north of Italy dragged on until 1659 and entailed huge government expenditures, paid for in large measure out of higher taxes. The result was to further depress consumer demand. Naples was forced to increase its subsidies to Madrid from 835,000 ducats in 1616 to over six million ten years later; and even the papacy (which also had territorial ambitions in this period) found its public debt tripling to 35 million *scudi* between 1620 and 1640.

One response of governments to their growing financial problems

Plate 9   A devotional image of Our Lady of Mercy, 1632, commemorating deliverance from the plague which, as the inscription relates, 'raged mightily in the city of Milan in 1630 and 1631'.

was to try and raise capital through the sale of crown lands, monopolies, titles, and privileges. This led, especially in the South, to a process that has been described as 'refeudalisation', whereby proprietors enjoyed a relationship to the land that was based more on archaic legal restrictions, rights, and immunities than on the criteria of the market. As a result, the power of landlords both lay and ecclesiatical tended to grow, to the detriment of the peasantry and in the longer term of central government too. However, this tendency was by no means general. In the North, farming continued to be largely modern and capitalist in character; and in some areas, such as Emilia, share-croppers began to be replaced during the seventeenth and eighteenth centuries by day labourers, a clear sign of increasing levels of commercialisation.

If the growth of feudal privilege in the seventeenth century was a result of government insolvency, it was also a response (albeit a short-sighted one) to agricultural recession. From 1620 a long-term decline in the price of wheat started, and landowners looked to shore up their positions by means of legal safeguards rather than through the more precarious channels of investment and enterprise. The results were evident in the widespread deterioration of the land and in the persistence of archaic methods of farming. Areas that had formerly been drained returned to being marshes – such as in the lower reaches of the Po, the Tuscan and Roman Maremma, and along the southern coasts. In the Centre and South, monoculture of wheat, alternating with fallow, was reinforced; so, too, was transhumance. The increased power of the nobility also led to large tracts of land being enclosed for hunting or for pasture; and one consequence of this was to accelerate the migration of unemployed and starving peasants to the cities.

However, the situation was not uniformly bleak. In parts of the North, and in the Po valley especially, landowners tried to minimise the impact of the recession by diversifying. Rice and maize were introduced and by the mid-seventeenth century had become well established in many areas. Continuous rotation was practised widely, often with industrial crops such as linen and hemp; and this helped to strengthen links between agriculture and manufacture, already evident so spectacularly in the case of mulberries and silk. Peasant holdings in the North frequently achieved a measure of stability in this period, as a result largely of equitable contracts with landlords. Piedmont seems to have reacted particularly well to the slump, splitting up large and unwieldy fiefs into more viable units. In Tuscany, there were still plenty of signs of economic initiative: the diarist John Evelyn was surprised in 1644 to find the Grand Duke himself active in the wine trade.

However, the general impression given by Italy in the seventeenth century is one of stagnation, both social and economic. A modern bourgeoisie, in any meaningful sense of the term, hardly existed, even in a quite advanced region such as Lombardy. Nobles everywhere constituted the ruling class; and despite their small numbers – in northern Italy, just over 1 per cent of the population – and the emergence from the sixteenth century of new groups of professional civil servants, they still dominated almost every branch of government and administration, especially in provincial cities. Their offices were frequently heritable. In many areas, above all of the South, aristocrats had settled in large numbers from Spain, bringing with them a cluster of traditional courtly values such as preoccupation with honour, privilege, and ritual, and a penchant for vendetta. They were also very often deeply pious; and during the years of Spanish dominance the Church in Italy received huge benefactions and grew enormously rich and powerful.

The hold of the nobility on society and the strengthening in many places of feudal practices polarised society dangerously. In 1647, following a series of bad harvests and a rise in taxes, a major revolt broke out in Naples. Its leaders proclaimed the equality of the poor and aristocracy, alleging (wrongly) that Charles V had once granted the city this privilege. The insurrection escalated into a full-scale war against Spain. The poor of Palermo also took to the streets and burned the town hall, opened the prisons, and forced the nobility into the countryside. Both risings were eventually put down by Spanish troops, but little was then done to tackle the economic and social causes of the unrest. In Palermo, the Archbishop of Monreale publicly exorcised the demons and witches that had driven the people to rebel; while the authorities, in order to save on food, ejected the unemployed on pain of death, together with anyone who had lived in the city for under ten years.

Such measures were simply cosmetic; and though, in a more

realistic vein, governments sought to deal with the serious imbalance between population and resources by trying to regulate the supply, distribution, and pricing of wheat, the issue of poverty remained unsolved. In Florence in April 1650 it was impossible to hear mass in peace, said one contemporary, so great was the importuning of wretched people, 'naked and covered in sores'. In 1674, as a result mainly of food shortages, an insurrection broke out in Messina. The response of the Spanish was to pull down the town hall, plough up the site, and sow it with salt. Nor did the new century bring much sign of relief. 'Just a few miles outside Naples', said a report of 1734, 'the men and women you meet are mostly naked . . . or else clad in the most disgusting rags . . . Their basic diet is a few ounces of unleavened bread . . . In winter, because there is no regular work . . . they are forced to eat plants without even oil or salt. If so much poverty is found in the province of the Terra di Lavoro, a region where mother nature is at her most bountiful . . . what can the situation be like in the other provinces of the kingdom?'

THE EIGHTEENTH CENTURY: THE ERA OF ENLIGHTENMENT REFORMS

In the last decades of the seventeenth century Italy enjoyed a period of relative peace. The Spanish remained the dominant force in the peninsula, ruling Milan, Sardinia, Naples, Sicily and an enclave in Tuscany called the Presidi, and indirectly controlling the activities of the other states. Their presence helped cocoon Italy from many of the social, economic, and cultural developments in northern Europe. The dukes of Savoy continued to hanker after new territory, exploiting their buffer position between the two greatest continental powers of the day. In 1690 Victor Amadeus II gave his support to Spain in an anti-French coalition, hoping to win Milan; when this failed, he made peace with Louis XIV and secured the fortress town of Pinerolo instead. However, Spain's days as a world power were numbered, for its economy could no longer sustain the burdens of empire. In 1700 Charles II, the last of the Spanish Habsburgs, died, and a major European war broke out to establish a new international order.

The War of the Spanish Succession was fought out for over a decade between France, Austria, Spain, and Britain. Italy was drawn in, less as a willing protagonist and more as a prize to be shared out amongst the contending parties. The political map of the peninsula changed frequently. In 1707 Austria acquired Lombardy; seven years later, with the Treaty of Rastatt, it added the Duchy of Mantua and the entire mainland South, and so replaced Spain as the dominant power in the peninsula. The Duke of Savoy, who had switched sides in the war with customary opportunism, profited from backing England, and acquired Alessandria, Valenza, the Lomellina and the crown of Sicily; in 1718 he swapped Sicily for Sardinia, but kept his royal title. Sicily then passed briefly to Spain and in 1720 to Austria. Modena, Parma, and the tiny coastal state of Massa continued as duchies, Tuscany as a grand duchy, and Venice, Genoa, and Lucca as republics.

In 1733 war broke out again, this time over the Polish succession; and the map of Italy was redrawn afresh. Charles of Bourbon, the son of Philip V of Spain, took Naples from the Austrians and assumed the ancient title of King of the Two Sicilies. However, Austria received compensation in 1737 when the Grand Duchy of Tuscany passed to the House of Lorraine, a branch of the Austrian imperial family, after the death of Gian Gastone, last of the Medici. During the 1740s a further round of fighting (the War of the Austrian Succession) led to another slight reshuffle of the pack. Modena was occupied by the Habsburgs, while Parma, Piacenza, and Guastalla went to the Bourbons. The House of Savoy added to its earlier gains with new provinces on its eastern flank. In 1748 the Treaty of Aix-la-Chapelle ushered in a long period of peace, the longest in Italy's modern history; and the political map of the peninsula was now to remain broadly unchanged (apart from the Napoleonic interlude) until national unification in 1860.

The wars of the first half of the eighteenth century placed a huge strain on the economies and administrations of the Italian states and laid bare their weaknesses in devastating fashion. After two centuries of creeping fossilisation under Spain, exposure to the more efficient and centralised regimes of northern Europe produced a crisis of identity for Italy that was simultaneously political and cultural in character; and this in turn caused governments everywhere to embark on major programmes of reform in a desperate bid to increase their revenues and allay the threat of social unrest. Although the Italian economy began to show signs of recovery from the 1740s, with prices rising once again after more than a century of stagnation, the demographic trend was also upwards. Between 1700 and 1800 Italy's population increased by around 4.5 million to nearly 18 million, a less rapid rate of growth than in other parts of Europe, but enough to ensure that the peninsula remained caught in its Malthusian trap (see Table 3).

The first Italian state to introduce a serious programme of reforms was Piedmont, whose dukes, and then kings, had expansionist aims that would have been hard to achieve without an efficient, centralised bureaucracy. The main problem was taxation. Around one-third of the most profitable land was owned by the clergy and nobility, whose feudal privileges were such that they enjoyed fiscal immunity on at least 80 per cent of it. Moreover, tax collecting was farmed out in a manner that was both wasteful and open to abuse. To remedy this situation, the government undertook from the end of the seventeenth century a huge census of Piedmontese territory. Resistance was firmly suppressed: forty-nine people were hanged in the Monregalese area for opposing the royal surveyors. When the assessment was finally completed in 1731, it not only allowed the king to increase his revenue from taxes, but more importantly it enabled him to seize estates that had been usurped from the royal demesne, or to which owners could not prove an ancient title.

The Piedmontese land register reduced the power of the feudal aristocracy and strengthened central government. The estates confiscated by the king were used to reward loyal servants and create a new class of nobles who were dependent on, and committed to, service of the crown. This process of reinforcing royal authority was advanced in the first decades of the eighteenth century by a variety of other reforms. The legal system was reorganised to create a more coherent corpus of law; poverty and begging were tackled by founding hospices to train the unemployed for productive work; secondary and higher education were given a more secular slant in the hope of equipping the state with modern administrators; and industry was subjected to protective tariffs and to measures that had the effect of weakening the contractual position of workers. The upshot of these changes was that the state in Piedmont acquired a strength and authority unparalleled elsewhere in Italy.

However, the reforms in Piedmont were carried out within the traditional framework of absolutism. Little attempt was made to win the support of those affected; and no moral or theoretical arguments were developed to justify them. They were a product of expediency, and bore no traces of the Enlightenment ideas that were just beginning to circulate in other parts of Europe. They succeeded largely because the population was too loyal, deferential, or passive to resist them. Their main purpose was to strengthen the state for war; and the authoritarian fashion in which they were pushed through reflected the military ethos of a kingdom that had a standing army of 24,000 men – equivalent to one soldier for every ninety-two inhabitants. Their success spared Piedmont the necessity of further major reforms after 1730; and the tight control that central government exercised over society ensured that criticism and dissent were stifled. As a result, the Enlightenment in large measure passed Piedmont by.

Elsewhere the need for reform was even more urgent than in Piedmont. In Lombardy, nearly half the agricultural land was owned by the nobility in the mid-eighteenth century, and a further 20 per cent by the Church. In central Italy, 61 per cent of the Agro Romano was in the hands of just 113 families; and in the Kingdom of Naples some 40 to 50 per cent of landed income was divided between the Church and nobles. Most of this property was feudal and (apart from in Venice) exempt from land tax. The fiscal burden thus fell heavily on the poor: in Lombardy, three-quarters of all state taxes in the 1720s came from those owning a quarter of the wealth. Privileges of every kind abounded. Feudal lords exacted tithes and tolls, enjoyed hunting and fishing rights, owned monopolies, and claimed civil and even criminal jurisdiction over the peasants. Often they also expected to be above the law: the Sicilian Prince of Villafranca, who had tortured boys with burning irons for having mocked his carriage, successfully defended himself by saying that the case was no concern of the royal courts.

One of the greatest problems facing Italian governments in the eighteenth century was the chaotic state of the legal system. Italy had an enormous number of rival courts and jurisdictions, a result partly of the richness of civil society – lay and religious – in the Middle Ages, and partly, too, of the peninsula's long history of political fragmentation. The strength of the legal profession in Italy ironically helped sustain this confusion, for most lawyers had a vested interest in preserving the status quo and resisting efforts by the crown to extend its powers. This was especially true in the South where lawyers were not only numerous (in Naples 26,000 reputedly earned their living from the law in the mid-eighteenth century), but also came from wealthy families, whose immunities and privileges they were paid to defend. In Sicily, a clever advocate called Carlo di Napoli earned himself the gratitude of the nobility – and a public monument – by arguing successfully in the 1740s that the old Norman feudatories had been the legal equals of the king, not his vassals; and consequently that the Sicilian fiefs were in effect private property over which the crown had no rights.

The chaotic state of the legal system had some far-reaching consequences. It deprived the government of two important sources of revenue – fines and sequestrations. It also bedevilled commercial dealings, for without a unified system of courts there could be little certainty that contracts or debts would be honoured. In Sicily, the Inquisition, the Protonotary, the Chancellor, the Apostolic Legateship, the Royal Mint, the Admiralty, the Auditor General of the army, the customs, and the wheat export council all had separate jurisdictions. In Tuscany, the situation was even worse: Florence had more than forty tribunals, fourteen of them belonging to the city's guilds. The plethora of jurisdictions had major repercussions on policing. The fact, for example, that criminals could take sanctuary in ecclesiastical property meant that in 1740, according to one estimate, 20,000 felons were avoiding arrest in this way. Nor is it surprising, perhaps, that churches often served as the operational headquarters for thieves and murderers.

Administrative confusion and economic crisis provided the backdrop against which the ideas of the Enlightenment began to spread in Italy. The first signs of an intellectual revival can be dated to the closing years of the seventeenth century, when a few individuals started to take seriously the scientific and philosophical innovations occurring in the north of Europe. Inspired by the great French scholar, Jean Mabillon (who visited Italy in 1685), the Benedictine monk Benedetto Bacchini and his pupils Ludovico Antonio Muratori and Scipione Maffei, set out to apply 'reason' to a wide range of subjects – historical, legal, literary, and philosophical – with a view to denouncing the ignorance and superstition of Italy's past, and so freeing the present from the dead hand of tradition. Their works were remarkable for their erudition; and by exploring with unimpeachable scholarship the manner in which institutions and laws had developed, they hoped to pave the way for a better understanding of contemporary society, and a reform of its anomalies.

Given the strength of the Church in Italy, it was not surprising that Enlightenment reformers should deploy much of their armoury in attacking its privileges and powers. In 1723 a Neapolitan lawyer, Pietro Giannone, published his famous *Istoria Civile del Regno di Napoli* (Civil History of the Kingdom of Naples), a powerful denunciation of the processes whereby the Church had secured a pernicious stranglehold over the centuries on the state: the book forced Giannone into exile; and he died in prison. Elsewhere – in Venice, Milan, Modena, and Parma – the early decades of the eighteenth century witnessed other attacks in a similar vein on the secular claims of the Church. In the 1740s the temperature of the debate rose: the large number of religious holidays in Italy was condemned for fostering idleness and drinking; the Church's hostility to usury was denounced for the advantage it allegedly gave the Protestant merchants of north Europe over their Catholic rivals; and the existence or not of demons and magic became the subject of a fierce polemic.

The problem facing the Enlightenment intellectuals was how to convert their ideas into practical reforms. The hold of the nobility and the Church on Italian society was so strong, and the middle classes in general so weak, that it was unlikely that pressure for change would come from below. The parliaments of Palermo, Naples, and Milan were all bastions of privilege; so, too, were many of the other institutions that represented civil society. One possibility lay in trying to persuade the ruling classes that reform might be in their interests; and from the 1750s a number of journals were set up whose aim was to spread the teachings of Newton and Locke, Voltaire, and Montesquieu, and to generate simultaneously a climate of debate out of which reform could emerge. The best known of these journals was *Il Caffé*, published in Brescia between 1764 and 1766. It provided a platform from which some of the most remarkable intellectuals of the period, including Cesare Beccaria, Pietro Verri, and Gian Rinaldo

Plate 10 The entrenched power of the Church. The Inquisition conducting an auto-da-fé in front of Palermo cathedral in 1724. The Inquisition was not finally abolished in Sicily until 1782.

Carli, argued the case for radical change in spheres such as trade, agriculture, law, and science.

The new ideas won only limited support, but they did attract the attention in many states of rulers and governments eager, after the financial havoc caused by war and recession, and with poverty a constant threat, to find a solution to their economic and social difficulties. The urgency of reform was underlined by a series of disastrous famines that struck in the 1760s. In Naples in 1764 thousands of peasants starved in the alleyways of the city after fleeing from the countryside; and memories of bodies lying in the streets scarred a whole generation of southern reformers. In Tuscany, the famine years of 1763 to 1766 were almost equally traumatic. Here (as in Naples) the calamity was blamed on the *annone*, the powerful and often corrupt public agencies that had regulated the supply and price of wheat in most Italian cities since the sixteenth century. In 1767, in a bid to stimulate production, the Tuscan government passed a law introducing free trade in grain, a decisive break with the immobile and restrictive world of the *ancien régime*.

Under Grand Duke Leopold (1765–90), Tuscany developed into one of the most progressive states in Europe. This was due largely to Leopold himself – a man of great energy and vision who had read widely, if eclectically, among Enlightenment authors. With his support, various measures were introduced designed to promote public welfare and happiness through a rationalisation of the economy and the administration. Tax privileges were ended and the fiscal system simplified; communal land was sold off – in keeping with the reformist conviction that private property improved yields; the Florentine guilds were abolished and the principle of freedom of work asserted; local autonomies were attacked; and landownership, rather than nobility, became the main criterion for office. In 1786 a new criminal code was introduced. It was drawn up with the help of the great Lombard jurist, Cesare Beccaria, and was based on the latest humanitarian and rationalist precepts. It did away with the death penalty and torture and confirmed Tuscany's position in the vanguard of reform.

Leopold was helped in his reforms by a talented group of state officials (nearly all of them trained at Pisa university; which, said a government minister, 'alone rescued Tuscany from that state of ignorance into which almost all the rest of Italy has sunk') and also

– and more importantly perhaps – by a nobility whose commercial leanings had long ago taught it that cooperation with a well-run state might be in its interests as much as the ruler's. In Lombardy, the idea of partnership was less developed. From the sixteenth century, when Spain took over the duchy, the Milanese elite had acquired a strong sense of autonomy, and guarded its political privileges jealously in the local Senate. The fact that the region was so prosperous (Arthur Young described the plain of Lombardy as 'the finest farmer's prospect in Europe') made Milan's nobility particularly reluctant to let the foreign governments of Madrid and then Vienna meddle too much in its affairs.

This helps explain some of the limits of the reform movement in Lombardy. From the 1750s the Austrian government pressed energetically for change, and achieved some striking successes. A new land register was passed in 1757; ecclesiastical privileges were reduced, and the hold of the Church on the universities and secondary education was weakened; customs duties were revised, the tax system restructured, and guilds abolished. Plans were even drawn up to create a coherent system of elementary schools in the enlightened belief that popular education was necessary to the moral and material well-being of the masses. However, the pace of the reforms, and the fact that they were imposed from above with little attempt to win the support of those most affected, caused growing resentment. This was particularly true between 1780 and 1790 when Joseph II was emperor: his authoritarian manner alienated not only the Lombard nobility, but also intellectuals; and many of his reforms ran aground at a local level.

In the Kingdom of Naples, the mistrust between the nobility and the crown, the sheer extent of feudal and ecclesiastical privilege, and the scale of administrative disorder made the reformers' task daunting. However, the size of the challenge was itself a spur to action, and in the second half of the eighteenth century Naples became a laboratory of Enlightenment ideas, especially on economics. The key figure here was Antonio Genovesi, a priest who in 1754 was appointed professor of political economy at the university of Naples (the first chair of its kind in Europe). For fifteen years he imparted to a generation of younger intellectuals the lessons to be learnt from Holland, England, and other commercial nations, and drummed home to them the urgency of reform if an economic and social disaster of major proportions were to be avoided in the South. Genovesi was deeply affected by the harrowing scenes that accompanied the great famine of 1764, and it was these that converted him to supporting a policy of free trade in grain.

However, despite Genovesi's influence and reputation, Naples failed in the 1750s and 1760s to establish a close collaboration between government and intellectuals of the kind that yielded such impressive results in Tuscany and Lombardy. The chief minister of the kingdom, Bernardo Tanucci, was a wily and pedantic figure who deeply mistrusted abstract economic theory: he preferred to tackle problems for which immediate concrete solutions could be found – as in the spheres of law, and above all the Church. The Jesuits were expelled from the kingdom in 1765; convents were suppressed; tithes and mortmain were abolished; and royal consent was made obligatory for ecclesiastical decrees. Though such measures were seen by Genovesi as a step in the right direction, they did not address what he regarded as the fundamental economic problem of the South, namely the stranglehold of the unproductive feudal nobility and their allies, the lawyers, on the land.

Only after Tanucci's fall from power in 1776 was the way open for a more direct assault on the economy. A series of remarkable studies appeared, written by pupils of Genovesi, analysing the shortcomings of agriculture in the South with great acuteness; and throughout the kingdom, groups of enlightened reformers met in academies and masonic lodges to discuss new proposals for change. A sense of urgency was in the air: grain prices rose in the 1770s and the condition of the peasantry worsened. However, the problem of the nobility remained. Between 1781 and 1786 the viceroy of Sicily, Domenico Caracciolo, conducted a vigorous campaign in the island against noble privileges: 'One must save the peasantry from the fangs of these [baronial] wolves', he wrote. He made little headway. In Naples, certain reforms were introduced: but they did no more than dent the power of the barons; and once the French Revolution broke out, all attempts at change were halted.

Elsewhere in Italy the pace of reform in the second half of the eighteenth century was less intense. The Duchy of Parma, the most ecclesiastical of the Italian states – the pope claimed to be its feudal overlord – passed measures in the 1760s to reduce the power of the

Church; but it was less successful in other areas, and from the 1770s it reverted to its normal provincialism. For Venice and Genoa the eighteenth century was a period of decline: their ruling oligarchies were hamstrung by the deadweight of tradition and were unable to convert Enlightenment ideas into practical reforms. The same was broadly true of the Papal States, where hostility to change was fuelled by the religious equation of truth with permanence. Pope Pius VI attempted to grapple with his chaotic finances from the late 1770s, but was hampered by local opposition. Of the smaller states, only the Duchy of Modena had made much progress with reform by the time of the French Revolution.

Italy's attempts to free itself of the burdens of the *ancien régime* during the eighteenth century had met with mixed results. The balance sheet was healthier in the North and Centre than the South; but even in the North the fact that Piedmont's kings refused to restrain their absolutism, and turned their backs firmly on the ideas and ideals of the Enlightenment in the second half of the century, alarmed supporters of progress. In the decades to come Piedmont would produce some of Europe's best known defenders of reaction – among them the diplomat and writer, Joseph de Maistre. In Naples, the failure of the Bourbons to break the power of the feudal nobility left the southern economy vulnerable and southern society perilously unstable. More importantly, it reinforced the sense (apparent for a number of centuries) that real power in this area lay with privileged individuals or groups and not with the state, which remained at best a shadowy force.

However, at an intellectual level the Italian states had participated in the debates of the European Enlightenment with commendable vigour. The cultural isolationism of the seventeenth century had given way to active engagement in the world of modern ideas; and this in turn had generated fresh optimism about the possibilities of change and progress. Yet the rapprochement with Europe was by no means unproblematic. While it gave rise to new economic, social, and soon also, political ideals, to which reformers aspired, it also bred a corresponding sense of inferiority, a feeling that what was peculiar to Italy was anachronistic or of little worth. A crisis of identity had begun that was to trouble the course of modern Italian history, and which would lead in the next two centuries to a fragile oscillation between a desire to emulate foreign models and a frustrated, often angry, assertion of an indigenous tradition and character.

4

The emergence of the national question, 1789–1849

THE IMPACT OF THE FRENCH REVOLUTION

The optimism that had underlain the European Enlightenment, the belief that a more humane and prosperous world could be built with reason, tolerance, and the systematic elimination of privilege, ignorance, and inhumanity, became tinged with uncertainty during the 1770s and 1780s. Most of the Italian states had succeeded in reducing the powers of the Church; but the afflictions of poverty, banditry, begging, and vagrancy remained and seemed if anything to be increasing. According to the reformers, such evils would only be cured when the stranglehold of the unproductive nobility had been broken: but doubts grew as to the will of princes to achieve this. Some felt that the only hope for real reform lay in a radical reshaping of the entire system. A new and in some ways desperate utopianism began to emerge, evident first in the rapid spread of freemasonry in the 1770s, and then during the 1780s in the appearance of sects such as the *Illuminati* preaching egalitarian and communistic messages.

As faith in princes and governments declined, those who longed for a better world began to cast about for alternative vessels in which to place their hopes. Many looked with growing interest and sympathy at the masses, whose virtues had been so eloquently described by Jean-Jacques Rousseau; and they drew inspiration from the American war of independence with its revolutionary assertion of a people's right to determine its own laws. Some intellectuals, among them the

Neapolitan legal reformer Gaetano Filangieri, grew passionate in the 1780s about the idea of equality: today, he wrote, 'everything is in the hands of few. We must act to ensure that everything is in the hands of many.' Others became absorbed in the largely philosophical search for the historical origins of contemporary society. This led to a revival of interest in Giambattista Vico (1668–1744), the maverick but deeply original Neapolitan scholar whose researches had included a wide-ranging enquiry into the customs and cultures of different peoples.

As intellectuals began to focus their attention on 'the people', so the notion of popular sovereignty gained ground among radicals, encouraged by fashionable doctrines of universal natural rights; and this in turn raised the issue of the 'nation': the unit of humanity whose collective right it was to determine the form of government under which it lived. The Enlightenment was cosmopolitan in spirit; but the close links that had grown up among the Italian reformers, and the fact that the states of the peninsula were widely held to be afflicted with a common set of problems and subject to a common process of decline, gave the idea of 'Italy' fresh poignancy. Certain reformers, among them Genovesi, even talked of the need for greater economic unity in the peninsula. The concept of 'Italy' was thus reacquiring some of the cachet that it had enjoyed in the Renaissance; but it was also gaining political overtones that had been almost entirely absent during the fifteenth and sixteenth centuries.

The outbreak of the French Revolution in 1789 served as a catalyst to these ideas. The storming of the Bastille and the first phase of the revolution were greeted by the majority of Italian intellectuals with enthusiasm. Some set off for Paris; others, including Pietro Verri in Milan, stayed at home and tried to use the threat of unrest as a stick with which to beat their governments into granting fresh reforms. However, the Jacobin ascendancy, the September massacres in 1792, and the Terror of 1793–4 caused the more moderate to grow disillusioned. One of these was the playwright Vittorio Alfieri, a Piedmontese aristocrat who had spent much of his life travelling in Europe and whose works, based largely on classical themes, had contained ringing denunciations of tyranny and patriotic references to Italy. His early support for the revolution ebbed quickly: in 1792 he left Paris for Florence where he spent the next few years satirising events in France in his book, *Il Misogallo* (The Anti-Gaul).

The French Revolution brought an abrupt halt to reforms in the Italian states. The ideas of the Enlightenment were widely seen as having led to the breakdown of order in France; and princes, frightened of losing their thrones, reverted to the old practices of absolutism. Censorship grew stricter and use of secret police more extensive. Even Tuscany, which tried hard to keep faith with its reformist traditions, restored capital punishment and introduced partial controls on the grain trade. Freemasons were openly persecuted from Turin to Palermo. A particular cause of worry to governments was the increase in violent unrest among the peasantry in the early 1790s. Although localised and directed in the main against oppressive landowners or heavy taxes, this was a sign, as the authorities knew, of a general social crisis that might easily lead to a full-scale revolution.

The threat of internal unrest was all the more worrying because of the prospect of war with France. In November 1792 the Parisian government annexed Savoy in order to complete what it regarded as the 'natural frontiers' of the French nation; and in the months that followed, the leading Italian states joined Britain, Austria, and Prussia in an anti-revolutionary alliance. For a time, however, nothing happened: it was only in 1795, with France facing growing financial chaos and domestic discontent, that an invasion of Italy was seriously contemplated as a means of raising revenue and taking pressure off the French armies on the Rhine where the main offensives were being conducted. The French government was aware that the Italian 'Jacobins' (as the radicals were known more or less indiscriminately) did not make up a strong force; but they also knew that the Italian states were militarily weak and could not count on widespread popular support.

In the spring of 1796 the 26-year-old Napoleon Bonaparte led a French army over the Alps. He drove the Austrians from Lombardy, pushed into the Veneto, and 'liberated' Bologna and the Romagna. In Emilia, local Jacobins rose up and forced out their duke. The decisiveness and speed of Napoleon's victories left him free to act almost without reference to Paris. He carved out two new states in northern Italy – the Cispadane and Cisalpine republics; and in October 1797 concluded his campaign by signing the Treaty of Campoformio, by which Venice was handed over to Austria, with a

Plate 11 The fall of Venice, 1797. Napoleon gave orders for many famous Venetian works of art to be seized. The four bronze horses from St Mark's were shipped to Paris to adorn the Arc du Carrousel in the Tuileries Gardens.

whose
nment
iple of
ror' –
uding
selves
cracy
 and
itical
ment
ited
out

not
avy
or,
ere
99
to
h
a
s

b
d

. contemporaries. Venice's history as an inde-
ime quietly to an end. Napoleon left Italy in
rief foray into the peninsula had changed the
ion for good. France was now no longer fighting
iers', but was engaged in a war of expansion and
h it would be unable to extricate itself.

famous episodes of Napoleon's short stay in Italy
n launched in September 1796 for a prize essay on
ich type of free government is best suited to the
'. Italy, it was assumed, was a 'nation'; and those
petition were urged to foster national sentiment by
cient glories of Italy'. Most writers deferred to the
cal ideas of the French Revolution in suggesting a
and indivisible'; but a few, such as the leading
nni Ranza, argued that federalism was necessary
ly's great variety of regional customs and dialects.
on was won by Melchiorre Gioia with a proposal for a
y republic, in which a single system of laws would
reak down local habits and practices, and create a
lture.

perience of revolutionary government lasted until the
799 when coalition forces drove the French back beyond
Though brief, the period of Jacobin rule was extra-
not so much for what it achieved – which in most places
ed to the sale of church lands and the abolition of certain
ivileges – but rather for what it showed about the character
alian nation'. Once freed by Napoleon, many northern cities
egations to Paris and tried to extend their territory at the
 of their neighbours. Milan looked to take over much of the
Veneto. Bologna coveted Ferrara, the Romagna, and Ancona: but
rara preferred to be governed by Milan. Ancona hoped to win
control of the Marche, while Reggio sought to gain independence
from Modena. Rome, which became a republic in 1798 after the
French had invaded the Papal States, wanted Neapolitan territory;
but some Neapolitan Jacobins felt Rome more properly belonged to
them.

If these territorial rivalries damaged the revolutionary cause, so
too did divisions among the Italian Jacobins. The extremism of the

French Revolution had given rise to a new breed of reformers
ideas were often very different to those of the older Enlight
intellectuals. The Tuscan Filippo Buonarroti – who was a disc
Robespierre, and had been active in Paris during the 'Te
wanted to win over 'the people' with egalitarian measures, inc
the abolition of private property; but many Jacobins them
came from propertied families, and preferred to limit their dem
to the sale of church lands and the provision of state welfar
education. Another major source of disagreement was over po
unity. The more extreme Jacobins felt the revolutionary move
could only be sustained in the peninsula if the Italian people u
in some way; but the moderates were usually more concerned a
the independence and power of their own cities.

Such divisions weakened the Jacobins greatly; and they were
helped by demands from Paris for contributions to the war. He
taxes drove a wedge between the new governments and the po
and led to riots and disorders. The consequences of this w
particularly grave in Naples, which became a republic early in 17
in the wake of a French invasion. The failure of its Jacobin leaders
agree on measures that might have won them popular support – su
as the confiscation of feudal property – and their inability to keep
rein on taxes, alienated the peasantry; and attempts to suppre
charitable Church institutions in the South only made matters wors
'We do not want republics', said a Calabrian peasant, 'if we have t
pay as before.' The clergy, helped by various nobles, bandits, an
royalist agents, staged a counter-revolution; and in the summer o
1799 the 'Parthenopean Republic' was overwhelmed by Cardinal
Fabrizio Ruffo's 'Christian Army' of peasants, which ransacked
Naples.

In 1800 Napoleon crossed the Alps again to reassert French power;
and this time his victories led to a more permanent conquest. During
the next fifteen years, however, Italy became an arena for constitutional experiments, with boundaries being rubbed out and redrawn
with such frequency that many people must have been unsure at any
given moment exactly whose subjects they were. Napoleonic Italy,
indeed, made hay of legitimacy; and the more politically sensitive
in this period were driven by events to reflect on the nature of
sovereignty. Among the arrangements, the Cisalpine Republic was

restored, and then made into the Italian Republic; Tuscany became the Kingdom of Etruria; Piedmont was annexed to France, together with Liguria, Parma, Umbria, and Lazio; and a Kingdom of Italy was set up in the North in 1805, with Milan as its capital. Naples was conquered by the French in 1806 and its crown given to Napoleon's brother Joseph, and two years later to his brother-in-law Joachim Murat.

These changes were made without any reference to the Italian people. As in the sixteenth and early eighteenth centuries, it seemed that Italy had no voice of its own and was just a pawn in the diplomatic and dynastic games of others. Even Sicily and Sardinia – the two regions Napoleon failed to conquer – lost a measure of their autonomy. Sicily, to which the Bourbon king fled in 1806, was occupied by a large British garrison, ostensibly for his protection but in fact to prevent this strategically important island, with its valuable sulphur deposits, from falling into French hands; and for many years after the Napoleonic period the English maintained a strong commercial hold on the island and behaved towards it with at times high-handed possessiveness. Sardinia was the home of the Savoy dynasty in exile, and although it was never occupied by British troops, it owed its independence largely to the vigilance of the English fleet.

A dominant feature of the Napoleonic regime in Italy as elsewhere, was centralisation. This was especially so from 1805, when France's control over its Empire (proclaimed in 1804) became increasingly uniform and rigid. Even the Italian Republic, which enjoyed some degree of autonomy under its vice-president, the reformer Francesco Melzi d'Eril, had to take its orders directly from Paris as soon as it became a kingdom: 'Italy ... must blend its interests with those of France', Napoleon's viceroy in Milan, Eugène de Beauharnais, was told. Everywhere, the existing administrative arrangements were swept away and replaced with more rational systems; and no concessions were made to variations in local practice. A single pattern of departments and districts was set up; internal customs barriers were abolished; weights and measures were standardised; education was reformed; the tax system was reorganised; and the Napoleonic civil, penal, and commercial codes were imposed.

On the face of it, the past had been wiped out with a few bold strokes of the pen. However, many of the reforms were never put into practice. Old habits died hard, not least because the administrative chaos and corruption of the *ancien régime* had often benefited sections of the middle and landowning classes. This was particularly true of the South, where local power had long depended on the weakness of central government. As one Napoleonic official noted despondently, referring to the difficulties the authorities faced in introducing an effective unified system of customs in the Kingdom of Naples: 'It is unbelievable how much employees steal and embezzle; the vice has passed into their blood.' The impact of Napoleonic rule on Italian society was thus a good deal less than the volume of reforms implied. It was greatest in those areas that had the longest experience of direct French rule, such as Piedmont.

The Napoleonic system suffered from an excessive faith in rationalism and a conviction that what had worked in France could work anywhere; but in one important respect – its attitude towards the nobility – it was more realistic than earlier Enlightenment governments. 'Property' was an ideological cornerstone of the Empire; and while the abolition of feudalism encouraged the rise of middle-class landowners, Napoleon never set out to undermine the old aristocracy directly. He aimed at an integrated strongly hierarchical society, in which the individual subordinated his interests to the general will of 'the people'; and since the landowners still had great power, an obvious short cut to such a society was to harness them to the new 'revolutionary' order. Also, on a practical level, they were the only viable class of administrators in most places. The Italian nobility was thus courted by the Imperial governments and received important posts in the bureaucracy, at court, and in the army.

The continued political and social prominence of the old nobility was one important reason why less redistribution of wealth took place in Italy in these years than in France. As elsewhere, 'national land' – property taken from the Church or the old ruling houses – was sold off; but while in France it was often bought up by prosperous peasants, in Italy the principal beneficiaries were existing noble or middle-class owners. In one commune of the Romagna, the area of church land fell from 42.5 per cent in 1783 to 11.5 per cent in 1812; but those who acquired it were members of the bourgeoisie and nobility, whose share of the territory rose from 59 per cent to 88 per cent. In Piedmont, typical purchasers were noble families such as the Cavours and the d'Azeglios, who were later to be prominent in the movement for national unification and whose fortunes were made – or at any rate consolidated – in these years of French rule.

One of the most important measures undertaken by the Napoleonic regime, at least from a symbolic point of view, was the abolition of feudalism. The Jacobin administrations of 1796–9 passed laws to end labour dues, tithes, and other feudal residues, particularly in the North; but here as in central Italy feudalism was largely a thing of the past, and its formal suppression probably did not involve very much in practice. In the South, by contrast, feudalism was still entrenched; and the laws of 1806–8 that ended baronial jurisdictions, removed legal restraints on the alienation of properties, and made for the division of common lands had serious consequences. The government had not intended this: Joseph Bonaparte compensated the feudatories for their lost privileges and confirmed them as the legal owners of their estates – his aim being to introduce mobility of land, not to effect a social revolution. However, the loss of feudal revenues exposed the nobles to the chill winds of market forces; and many were driven to sell out.

The main beneficiaries of these developments in the South (as also of the sale of church lands) were the provincial middle classes. Local lawyers, doctors, estate managers, leaseholders, merchants, and money lenders descended on the newly liberated property and purchased it, often at very low prices. Common lands, so crucial to the economy of the poor, were also seized: legally, they should have been divided up between the barons and the peasants after 1806, but in practice they were often enclosed wholesale by an unscrupulous landlord. This left the commune with the arduous, expensive, and even dangerous task of going to law to recover them. In Sicily – where the nobles abolished feudalism in 1812 under pressure from the British – the small town of Salaparuta spent seventy-four years pursuing the Prince of Villafranca through the courts, attempting to get back an area of communal woodland that he had expropriated and then, in a gesture of defiance, burned.

The unlocking of the landmarket and the sale of church property in the South did little to benefit either the peasantry or agriculture. The new middle-class owners were usually indistinguishable from the nobles in both their attitudes and practices. In time, some of

them acquired aristocratic titles; and many lived away from their
estates, in Naples or Palermo, where they could appear at fashionable
salons, the opera, or at court. Like the old barons, they saw land
more as a status symbol than as a vehicle for profitable investment.
In the North, a wealthy family such as the Cavours believed power
and status should be linked to an active often very sober pursuit of
commercial gain within the framework of the law; but in the South,
a less progressive and largely feudal social vision prevailed, according
to which a man's status was gauged by his capacity for leisure and
largesse, and by his ability to wield private force, coerce the peasantry, and if need be, flout the law with impunity.

The Napoleonic era was one of mixed gains for Italy. Many of the
old privileges and much of the administrative chaos that had so
plagued pre-revolutionary governments, formally disappeared; yet
the benefits were far less than they might have been. In part this was
because of Napoleon's attitude to Italy: he viewed the peninsula not
so much as a nation to be liberated, but rather as a territory to be
carved up and given as a reward to members of his family. More
important, perhaps, he assigned the peninsula a largely ancillary role
within the Empire. Italy's main function was to help finance France's
campaigns; and as a result, the spirit of the Revolution, with its
ideals of equality and freedom, was often sacrificed to fiscal and
political considerations. Land was sold off, and even feudalism
abolished, more to raise cash for the Parisian exchequer (without
stirring up too much opposition among the rich and powerful) than
to introduce any fundamental social changes.

However, the experience of French rule had some important
consequences for the development of Italian national sentiment. The
French Revolution had unleashed the idea of the nation; Napoleon,
with his drive for uniformity, seemed bent on stifling it. Among
those most angered by this were poets and writers (not least because
of Napoleon's attempts to make French the official language of the
Empire), and a number responded by resurrecting that 'cultural
nationalism' which had first appeared in Italy during the Renaissance.
The best known of these 'nationalist' writers was the Greco-Venetian
poet Ugo Foscolo, whose most famous work, *Dei Sepolcri* (Of
Sepulchres) (1807), was written in protest at a French ruling that
burials should no longer be allowed in churches. For Foscolo, tombs,

especially those of the great, as in Santa Croce, Florence, were a vital means of preserving the collective memory and inspiring a sense of reverence for the glories of the past, without which a nation could not hope to be morally strong.

In other ways, too, the Napoleonic era had important consequences for the future. The abolition of customs barriers, the new commercial code, and the greater degree of access to the profitable markets of northern Europe benefited Italy's merchants and traders hugely; and the major roads built in these years – particularly those over the Alps – were a further demonstration of what could be achieved with a progressive and determined government. The Cavours and the d'Azeglios took the lesson to heart. In addition, the incorporation of Italy into the body of Europe seemed to many of those who had been receptive to the ideas of the Enlightenment the fulfilment of a dream; and the fact that thousands of Italians had served with distinction in Napoleon's armies appeared to show the vitality of this new integration. It also heartened those who felt that the 'Italian nation' had for too long been saddled with an image – to a degree self-imposed – of decadence, cowardice, and moral corruption.

Italy's links with continental Europe were henceforth (with moments of hiatus) to grow increasingly strong; but the question of the character and identity of the 'Italian people', an inevitable corollary to the principle of nationality, was still far from settled. As a political problem, indeed, it had only just begun to be addressed. While some, especially in the north of the peninsula, believed that Italy should imitate contemporary French or British systems of government, others maintained that it should look rather more to its own past for guidance – to the world of the medieval communes, to the papacy of Innocent III, or to ancient Rome; still others preferred, in the course of time, to cast their gaze beyond Europe to arrangements that had been adopted in countries such as Russia or even China. The search for the 'Italian nation' proved far from simple, and gave rise to an awkward and often unstable dialectic of hope and disillusionment.

FROM RESTORATION TO REVOLUTION, 1815–1849

The collapse of Napoleonic rule in Italy in 1813–14 was not greeted with much visible dismay. For some years heavy taxes, rising prices,

Plate 12   Ugo Foscolo, 1778–1827. In Foscolo's writings, the
Romantic preoccupations with spiritual loss and personal identity crystallised around the idea of Italy. Exile in England after
1816 helped to fuel his patriotic nostalgia.

and the rapacity of landowners, old and new, had generated widespread popular discontent, particularly among the peasantry. Brigandage was one symptom of this rural unrest, fuelled by desertions from
the army. Opposition was also growing among sections of the
middle classes and was evident in the formation of secret societies
and sects. Catholic associations such as Christian Amity in Piedmont

and the Calderari in Calabria and Apulia, invoked the reactionary tradition of Cardinal Ruffo in Naples and sought to stir up peasant revolts in the name of the Church; while 'liberal' secret societies, often made up of former Jacobins disenchanted with the social conservatism of the Napoleonic regime, conspired to create a more egalitarian order. Among the best known of these was the *Carboneria*, whose chief stronghold was in the mainland South.

These opposition forces were too divided, however, to play a major role in the overthrow of the Napoleonic governments. Nor (unlike in Germany and Spain) did they operate under a 'nationalist' banner. Some members of the liberal sects certainly spoke of the 'Italian nation', but their main goal was more the downfall of Napoleon than the setting up of a unified state. The only really serious calls for a national revolt came from the British and Austrians – for reasons of self-interest – and from the King of Naples, Joachim Murat. In March 1815, after Napoleon's escape from Elba, Murat attempted to rally liberals throughout the peninsula, appealing to them to rise up in the name of Italy and expel the British and Austrians: 'Was it in vain that nature formed the Alps as your defence, and gave you the even greater barrier afforded by differences of language, customs, and character? No! Away with foreign domination!' His appeal went largely unheeded, and a few weeks later he was defeated at the Battle of Tolentino.

The success of the Austrian armies in Italy in 1814–15 led to the swift restoration of the deposed rulers. Victor Emmanuel I returned to Turin, Ferdinand III to Florence, and the pope to Rome. The peace settlement of Vienna (1815), drawn up by the victor powers, made 'legitimacy' its guiding principle, but in practice it ensured that Austria gained near total dominance of the peninsula. Lombardy and Venice came under direct rule from Vienna; the duchies of Modena and Parma were given to members of the imperial family; and Ferdinand IV was restored to his throne of Naples only after he had agreed to a permanent defensive alliance with Austria. The one more or less independent state in Italy was Piedmont, whose strategic importance as a buffer between France and Austria enabled it to recover Nice and Savoy and also to annex the Republic of Genoa.

A few Italian liberals, above all in Lombardy, tried to win recognition for Italy's national claims, and appealed to the victor powers to

stop the blanket restoration of Austrian dominance; but in general
the 1815 settlement met with little (visible) resistance in the peninsula.
One reason for this was that many of the socio-economic and
administrative changes that had occurred during the Napoleonic
period were accepted by the restored governments. New landowners
had their property rights confirmed; civil servants in the main kept
their posts – even in the South, where King Ferdinand issued a full
amnesty and abstained from a purge; and a good deal of the
Napoleonic bureaucratic and even judicial machinery was preserved.
In Lombardy–Venetia, the Austrians tried to prevent any local dissatisfaction at 'foreign' rule through efficient government; and theirs was
certainly the most effective and least corrupt administration in Italy.

Paradoxically, the most reactionary restoration government in
Italy was also the most independent. From the moment Victor
Emmanuel of Piedmont–Sardinia re-entered Turin, pointedly sport-
ing an *ancien régime* peruke and pig-tail, he made clear his determination to put the clock back to before 1789. He sacked French appoint-
ees, reinstated Roman law, and restored aristocratic privileges. There
was even talk of pulling down the newly built 'Jacobin' bridge over
the Po. The Jesuits returned and were given charge of education and
censorship, and the Jews were once again put into ghettos. Although
a good deal of the Napoleonic bureaucratic machinery was as
elsewhere retained, customs barriers were reintroduced, both at the
borders and internally, with damaging results for the economy. In so
far as the crown sought at all to win popular support, it did so by
trying to raise its profile with heavy military spending and by
talking about a possible 'Italian role' for the House of Savoy.

Ideologically, the Restoration was marked by a rejection of any
notion of progress through the application of reason, and a belief
instead in the superior merits of tradition, authority, and hierarchy,
sanctioned by religion. Politically, the Austrians looked to safeguard
the cause of absolutism through an agreement by the victor powers
(the Quadruple Alliance of Britain, Prussia, Russia, and Austria) to
preserve the status quo in Europe and by extension to suppress
constitutionalism wherever it appeared. Britain had serious reservations about such a reactionary policy, feeling that it might well do
more to encourage than prevent liberal opposition; but despite this,
the Austrian chancellor Prince Metternich won acceptance in 1820

for the principle of intervention to put down revolutionary movements; and since the whole of the peninsula was regarded as being of immediate concern to Austria, this meant that a rising anywhere in Italy might be suppressed by Habsburg troops.

Despite attempts by restoration governments to keep the more attractive features of the Napoleonic system, the prospects of political unrest in Italy after 1815 were considerable. In Lombardy–Venetia taxes remained high, military service was more onerous than before, and trade, to the annoyance of the commercial classes, was now restricted to the Austrian empire. The passion of the emperor for centralisation also meant that any *de facto* local autonomy soon disappeared. 'The Lombards', according to a report of 1820, '. . . loathe the system of uniformity by which they have been placed on a par with Germans, Bohemians, and Galicians.' In the Papal States, the fall of Napoleon meant a return to inefficient and corrupt rule, with the clergy resuming its monopoly of government. In the South, attempts to strengthen the hold of Naples on the state led to widespread resentment, especially in Sicily, which had received its own constitution in 1812 (now suspended) and where the nobility had grown accustomed under the British to having a relatively free hand.

Had the Restoration been accompanied by an economic upswing, it would have been easier for the new governments to secure political support. Unfortunately, for over thirty years after 1815 Europe went through a period of general slump; and the result for Italy was a near uniform stagnation in agriculture, which served to aggravate further the long-term crisis of the countryside that the Enlightenment reformers (and Napoleon) had failed to resolve. Small peasant farmers who had relied on quality crops such as vines for their income found it hard to make ends meet: many became day labourers, or else migrated to the cities where they swelled the ranks of marginal workers, beggars, and petty criminals; and some turned to banditry. Large landowners, confronted with falling profits, responded on the whole by intensifying labour. This was especially the case in the South where there was almost no tradition of capital investment; and the result was to further depress the living standards of the peasantry.

The poverty of the countryside was made worse by the relentless pressure of population. Some peasant farmers limited the size of their families in order to have fewer mouths to feed; but day labourers (of whom there were growing numbers) tended to have large families so as to have more units of labour to sell. This, together with declining mortality rates, helped push Italy's population up from some 18 million in 1800 to about 22 million forty years later; and the increase was restricted almost entirely to the countryside, for the population of most of Italy's cities in these years remained static or even fell, largely because of major epidemics – such as that of cholera in 1835–7 – which wiped out huge numbers of urban poor. (Average life expectancy at birth in the Naples slums at this time was not much more than twenty years.) With the countryside becoming ever more overcrowded, so competition for resources increased; and the threat of disorder and riots was constant.

One reason why the authorities were so alarmed by this state of affairs was that concern for the plight of 'the people' remained an issue with a small but energetic section of the educated classes. Not only did the ideals of the Enlightenment and the French Revolution persist among many older intellectuals, but also the new culture of Romanticism, with its passion for freedom and heroic action combined on occasions with a strong democratic strain, was starting to affect a younger generation. The threat to the government from 'liberal' doctrines appeared all the greater in that the number of university and secondary school students – the natural constituency for radical ideas – was growing fast. This was partly a result of the reforms in higher education carried out in the later eighteenth century; but it also reflected the new prominence of the rural and urban bourgeoisie, whose sons were being sent away to get degrees in law, medicine, or engineering.

The growing (if still tiny) number of middle-class intellectuals often seemed more threatening to the authorities than rural poverty. '[Today]', the King of Piedmont complained in the 1820s, 'the bad are all educated, the good all ignorant.' On their own, the peasants were generally too disorganised a force to pose a serious challenge to the state; and most were anyway deeply conservative. However, led by the middle classes or the clergy they could be turned into a frightening army. The great fear of governments after 1815 was that the educated might try and use popular unrest to start a revolution.

The alliance between throne and altar in the restoration states helped to appease the Church; but the urban intelligentsia proved harder to satisfy, for their expectations of what a modern state should be had been profoundly affected by the Napoleonic experience and also, increasingly, by their awareness of what was happening in progressive countries such as Britain and France.

The reactionary character of the restoration states, with their repudiation of progressive ideas and rigid censorship, forced opposition underground. As a result, the main vehicles for liberal dissent after 1815 were secret societies. Many of these had come into being in the Napoleonic period to oppose the social conservatism of the Empire; and they owed a great deal, in both form and spirit, to freemasonry: they had a panoply of rituals and symbols, and their structures and goals were obscure even to most members. The sect of the Sublime Perfect Masters, for instance, created by the best-known Italian conspirator, Filippo Buonarroti, around 1818, had three entirely separate grades: the lowest was aware only of its oath to deism, fraternity, and equality; the second swore to work for a unitary republic based on the people; and the third, that of the 'mobile deacons', was pledged to the abolition of private property, and answered directly to Buonarroti himself.

The main problem with the secret societies was that they lacked unity and a clear sense of what they hoped to achieve on a practical level. Most of Buonarroti's followers would have agreed that the first step should be to establish constitutional government; but whether this meant adopting the Spanish constitution of 1812, or something more conservative – the French *Charte*, for instance – was unclear. Equally undecided was the question of national unity. If Buonarroti and some of his closest supporters aimed secretly at a unitary republic (as a stepping stone to a universal social revolution), many liberals probably felt that the best they could hope for was some form of northern state. In the case of the *Carboneria*, the main secret society in the South, the confusion was even greater, for it did not have the coordinating structures that Buonarroti had tried to give the Sublime Perfect Masters. The *carbonari* were grouped very loosely into 'conventicles' and comprised a heterogeneous mix of army officers, professional men, artisans, and lower clergy, with political views that ranged from the fiercely democratic to the moderate.

The absence of clearly defined goals was a major weakness of the liberal opposition. So, too, was a largely uncritical faith in 'the people' and a vague assumption that both sectarians and masses had similar interests at heart. The consequences were disastrous. In the summer of 1820 a group of young officers staged a successful coup in Naples and forced the king to grant the Spanish constitution: but divisions soon emerged between those who felt that the Neapolitan 'nation' was best represented by landowners and others who took a more democratic line. As a result, the insurgents were unable to organise themselves in the face of the advancing Austrian troops. In Palermo, the political divisions were equally ruinous. Here, the revolution of 1820 began as a spontaneous workers' revolt. Sections of the nobility joined in hoping to turn it to their advantage and win independence for the island; but they lost their nerve when events began to slip out of control, and were relieved when the army arrived to put an end to the disorder.

Neither of these two revolutions had shown any concern with Italian unity. Indeed, the Sicilian rebels had been inspired mainly by their traditional hostility to Naples; and the Neapolitans had for their part been almost unanimous in opposing the island's demands for a separate government. In Piedmont, on the other hand, there was much more interest in the national question, partly because here 'independence' logically meant a war with Austria and the attractive prospect of making a strong northern state by annexing Lombardy. However, the liberals were probably even more divided in Piedmont than in the South. Moderates, such as the Catholic aristocrat Cesare Balbo, were eager for reform; but they balked at the idea of being disloyal to the throne. Accordingly, when in March 1821 a young cavalry officer, Santorre di Santarosa, staged a patriotic coup with the help of democratic sectarians, the moderates in Turin wavered. The king abdicated; but his successor refused to grant a constitution and the rising petered out amidst popular indifference.

Like many young well-born Italians of his generation eager for a cause, Santarosa went into exile; and like Lord Byron, whose search for passion and excitement had brought him to Venice, he later died fighting for Greek independence. The years that followed witnessed the high-water mark of reaction. In Lombardy, the Austrians rounded up members of the secret societies and sentenced many well-known

Plate 13   A Piedmontese aristocratic family, the La Marmoras, c.1825. Note the large number of army uniforms, an indication of the strong military traditions of the Piedmontese nobility.

liberals to long terms in prison. Among them was Silvio Pellico, whose memoirs, *Le Mie Prigioni* (My Prisons) (1832), became an international best-seller. Piedmont and the Papal States experienced similar repressions: in Piedmont, ninety-seven of Santarosa's fellow conspirators were condemned to death. In the South, where the government had adopted a rather conciliatory line after 1815, the 1820s saw sweeping purges of the bureaucracy, which not only caused hatred and bitterness but also deprived the kingdom of some of its ablest officials.

This was particularly damaging in the light of the Neapolitan government's attempts in the 1820s and 1830s to galvanise the southern economy. Apart from the threat to order posed by severe poverty, it now faced a further problem in a huge public debt after the Napoleonic wars. Luigi de' Medici, the chief minister in these years, embarked on a bold policy which sought through tariffs and state contracts to build up domestic industry while simultaneously helping the poor by holding down grain prices. Foreign capital was brought into the kingdom; and the region between Naples and Salerno became dotted with factories, many of them producing textiles and owned mainly by Swiss and English entrepreneurs. The government also set up an iron foundry and a plant for producing heavy machinery; and Naples became the first state in Italy to launch a steamship (1818) and build a railway (1839).

However, de' Medici's programme was heavily flawed. For political reasons, he was unable to stop the re-emergence of the Church's power; and clerical influence on government policy was damaging to the economy: Naples' failure to follow up its early success in railway building was the result in part of a ban on tunnels – regarded as a threat to public morality. A more fundamental difficulty, though, was the weakness of the domestic market. In the absence of serious improvements in agriculture, the great majority of the population was too poor to afford manufactured goods. As a result, the new industries remained dependent on state backing for survival and never succeeded in becoming self-sustaining. Another problem was foreign rapacity: Britain, France, and Spain all insisted on preferential rates for goods carried in their ships; and in the 1830s the British ruthlessly blocked attempts by the Bourbons to secure a monopoly of sulphur mining in Sicily.

De' Medici's programme was also politically contentious. By holding down the price of wheat and seeking to spread the burden of taxation in such a way as not to fall too heavily on the poor, the government risked antagonising the landowners; and attempts to encourage the division of large estates and set up a new class of smallholders loyal to the state, were similarly galling. Nor did the landowners benefit much from protectionism. Tariffs may have helped the Swiss manufacturers in Naples, but they did little for domestic producers – for example of olive oil – who had relied heavily on exports and now faced retaliatory duties. The result, in the longer term, was disastrous for the Bourbons. The great landowners became disenchanted, and turned increasingly to constitutionalism; and the peasantry remained desperately impoverished, the victims of an unreformed agricultural system and an administration whose writ scarcely ran in many of the remoter communities.

The volatility of the countryside, particularly in the South, helped keep alive liberal hopes after the failures of 1820–1. However, many of those who had participated in the revolutions of these years were now painfully aware that 'the people' were far from being a reliable force; and some of them began to think instead of persuading a monarch or a prince to lead a national liberal movement – the Duke of Modena, for example, was known to have territorial ambitions. However, there was no consensus on this; and Buonarroti for one found the idea of cooperating with princes abhorrent. When in 1831 a series of risings broke out in central Italy, inspired by the July Revolution in Paris of the previous year, divisions among the leadership again undermined any chances of forming a strong united front. Moreover, the short-lived revolutionary governments were dominated by conservative landowners, and failed to attract popular support; and the Austrian troops sent to put down the risings advanced in places to cheers from the peasantry.

One particularly disconcerting aspect of the 1831 revolutions, and another reason for their failure, was the inability of the different cities to lay aside their old rivalries and make a common cause. The first revolts broke out in the Duchy of Modena and then spread southwards to Bologna and the Marche: but the Bolognese liberals were deeply suspicious of the Modenese, whom they referred to as 'foreigners'; and indeed, when Modena sent troops to help Bologna against the Austrians, they were only allowed to enter the city on condition that they disarmed. In other places, too, old enmities came to the surface. Many of the smaller towns in Emilia took advantage of the unrest to establish their own administrations; and it was only after a great deal of acrimonious dispute that a 'provisional government of the states of Modena and Reggio' could be formed. Even then, Parma and Bologna insisted on retaining their separate governments.

The events of 1830–1 had a profound effect on the liberal movement both in Italy and in Europe generally. The July Revolution in Paris, which brought to the throne a new constitutional monarch, marked the return of France to the international stage and signalled the end of Metternich's hopes of freezing Europe around the settlement of 1815. France had also reasserted its claims to be the revolutionary nation par excellence; and older radicals – among them Buonarroti – took heart and set off for the French capital confident that a great European revolution was only just around the corner.

However, if many now felt that the march of progress had shown itself to be unstoppable, the situation in Italy was still far from reassuring. The 1831 risings exposed in the most painful manner the inadequacy of the secret societies and their leadership; and more alarmingly, they again demonstrated just how politically unreliable 'the people' in Italy were.

Among those who felt that a change of direction was called for was Giuseppe Mazzini, a young member of the *carbonari*, who was sent into exile in 1831 for attempting to organise a rising in Liguria. Mazzini was born in Genoa in 1805, the son of a university professor and a mother convinced her child was destined to be a new messiah. According to his own account, he became converted to the cause of Italian unity after seeing a group of Piedmontese liberals waiting on the quayside to embark for Spain following the abortive coup of 1821. From then on, he later wrote, 'I resolved to dress always in black, fancying myself in mourning for my country.' By temperament sensitive and philosophical, he had the single-mindedness of a zealot; and although he had never been further south than Tuscany in his life (and was to spend almost all his adult years abroad, mostly in north London), he never wavered from his conviction that Italy was destined for unity and for greatness.

Mazzini was a product of Romanticism rather than the Enlightenment. He accepted the principles of 1789, but believed that a new stage of history had arrived in which the collective struggle of 'the people' for freedom was replacing the struggle for individual rights. He was much influenced by contemporary German writers on nationalism, especially Herder; but his basic philosophy was the result of a religious intuition: a conviction that God had ordained nations to be the natural units of mankind. Italy was to be a republic, one and indivisible, made by 'the people'; and just as the eighteenth century had been the century of France, so the nineteenth would belong to Italy: 'I saw regenerate Italy', he wrote, 'becoming at one bound the missionary of a religion of progress and fraternity ... Why should not a new Rome, the Rome of the Italian people – portents of whose coming I felt I saw – arise ... to link together and harmonise earth and heaven, right and duty ... to make known to free men and equal their mission here below?'

The spiritual element was essential to Mazzini's vision of Italian unity, and indeed to the democratic movement as a whole; a movement which after 1831 began to distinguish itself sharply from that of the moderate liberals, who more and more looked to achieve reform within the existing framework of states. As heirs of the Enlightenment and the French Revolution, the democrats had a deep loathing of the Catholic Church; for not only was Catholicism a barrier to the dissemination of the 'gospel of humanity', but it was also a political obstacle in the path of revolution. The masses had to be persuaded that God no longer spoke through the pope but through 'the people' gathered together in nations, and that the cause of Italy was itself a divine mission requiring struggle, sacrifice, and if need be, martyrdom. 'As the standard-bearers of Italy's rebirth', said Mazzini of his followers, 'we will lay the foundation stone of her religion.'

Mazzini's emphasis on the 'nation' marked him out from the older generation of 'cosmopolitan' revolutionaries; so, too, did his stress on 'duties' rather than 'rights'. In 1831, in order to spread his beliefs and create a more effective instrument of revolution than the now discredited sects, he set up a secret society called Young Italy. This was like the *Carboneria* in its use of rituals and passwords; but it was more tightly organised, and aimed above all to make its goals explicit and thus avoid the confusion that had been so disastrous in the 1820s. Young Italy lasted only a few years, but attracted considerable support: among its members was a young sailor from Nice called Giuseppe Garibaldi. It brought attention to bear on the issue of unification; but perhaps more crucially, by asserting in unequivocal fashion that Italy should be a republic made by 'the people', it forced into the open the division between the moderate liberals and the democrats that till then had been partially obscured behind the banner of constitutionalism.

A fresh round of repression in the mid-1830s drove many of Mazzini's new followers (including Garibaldi) into exile; and for a time the cause of revolutionary nationalism appeared almost dead. Meanwhile, developments elsewhere in Europe helped to foster the idea of an alternative and far less radical version of nationalism, that was linked with political and economic liberalism. In the German regions of central Europe, the 1834 customs union or *Zollverein* showed how nationalism might be harnessed to middle-class commer-

Plate 14 The world of the secret societies. Mazzini (*right*) initiating Garibaldi into Young Italy (*Giovine Italia*) at the organisation's headquarters in Marseilles, 1833. The oath is taken before a bust representing liberty, a French Revolutionary symbol.

cial interests. The advent of railway building and a marked acceleration in the rate of industrial growth after 1830 suggested, too, that the future lay not with tariff barriers and government controls, but with larger more open markets, especially as the greatest commercial advances were being made in liberal states such as Britain, France, and Belgium.

In Italy, the 1830s saw only very limited industrial progress. Even Milan, which was by far the most economically advanced city in Italy, had by 1838 little more than one thousand manufacturers, merchants, and bankers, all told, out of a population of around 150,000. In these circumstances, and in contrast to Germany, the links between nationalism and the demands of a growing commercial bourgeoisie for political representation were slight; and even among the Lombard industrialists themselves, despite a certain resentment at Austria's commercial policies, the cause of Italian unity was never a burning issue. It was landowners, professionals, students, and intellectuals who made the running. Indeed, it was ironic that the most intelligent spokesman in this period for the Italian middle classes, Carlo Cattaneo, dismissed the nationalist movement as something of an absurdity given the economic, administrative, and moral disparities in so much of the peninsula.

Without a strong socio-economic base, the moderate form of nationalism that emerged in Italy during the 1830s and 1840s derived its momentum largely from political developments elsewhere in Europe. However, it owed a good deal also to the domestic tradition of 'cultural nationalism' which had been created by the Renaissance humanists and rekindled in the eighteenth century, and which was now built upon by a generation of journalists and writers who saw in literature a vehicle for manufacturing and spreading national sentiment. Inspired by the success of Walter Scott, they wrote historical novels with more or less thinly disguised patriotic themes: among the best known were Alessandro Manzoni's *I Promessi Sposi* (The Betrothed) (first edition, 1827) and Massimo d'Azeglio's *Ettore Fieramosca* (1833). They also published 'national' histories, and encouraged the setting up of associations – such as the Piedmontese 'Society for Patriotic History' – whose function was to increase historical awareness among the educated classes.

This nationalism was at heart rhetorical in character and was most intense in Piedmont and Lombardy where literary Romanticism had its stronghold in Italy. It became more political largely as a result of fear. In the early 1840s the economic situation throughout Europe was grave: in England, 1842 witnessed the Chartist general strike; and almost everywhere the spectre of revolution seemed to be stalking abroad. In Italy, the democrats enjoyed a resurgence: in 1840

Mazzini refounded Young Italy; in 1843 a revolt broke out in the Romagna; and in 1844 the Bandiera brothers of Venice attempted a rising in Calabria. Nowhere was the fear of unrest more acutely felt than in Piedmont, probably still the most reactionary state in the peninsula – the words 'nation', 'liberty', and even 'Italy' were banned – yet also the one in which the upper classes were most loyal to the ruling dynasty. Here the feeling fast developed that unless the king, Charles Albert, defused tensions with some gesture of reform, the Mazzinians would exploit popular discontent and mount a republican revolution.

It was against this backdrop of growing crisis that a number of Piedmontese liberals came forward with proposals for a conservative national programme. In 1844 the historian Cesare Balbo published his book *Delle Speranze d'Italia* (On the Hopes of Italy), in which he dismissed Mazzini's vision of Italian unification as 'a puerile idea, entertained at most by pettyfogging students of rhetoric', and suggested instead that the Austrians might be induced to leave the peninsula if they were offered compensation in eastern Europe out of the crumbling Ottoman Empire. Massimo d'Azeglio – Balbo's first cousin – was similarly determined to find a moderate solution to the national question. In October 1845 he had a famous interview with Charles Albert in which he told him that there was a widespread desire that the king should forestall further democratic initiatives by himself taking up the cause of Italian independence. To d'Azeglio's surprise, the king expressed sympathy with this idea.

However, the most famous moderate proposal of these years came from an exiled Piedmontese priest, Vincenzo Gioberti, who in 1843 published (in Brussels) *Del Primato Morale e Civile degli Italiani* (On the Moral and Civil Pre-eminence of the Italians), a long-winded hymn to Italian greatness, past and future. Despite (or maybe because of) its verbose erudition and somewhat chauvinistic message, it quickly went through numerous editions. Its key political idea was that Italy should become a confederation of states, supported by the Piedmontese army and presided over by the pope – a rather unrealistic proposition given that the papacy had turned its back on everything to do with the modern world after 1815 (including even street lighting); but Gioberti's 'neo-guelph' vision was sufficiently conservative to make 'Italy' for the first time into a legitimate topic of discussion for many people, and not least the clergy.

Despite the worsening economic situation, and signs that the pressure for reform was becoming overwhelming in many parts of Europe (in Britain, the Conservatives were driven to repeal the Corn Laws in 1846), Charles Albert of Piedmont refused to seize the initiative and act in the name of Italy. As a young man he had flirted with liberalism; but age had made him as reactionary and Catholic as his forebears. He was deaf to the extraordinary (and largely unjustified) clamourings of liberal optimism that greeted the election of Pope Pius IX in 1846; and even when a revolution broke out in Palermo in January 1848 and spread to the mainland, forcing King Ferdinand to grant a constitution, he still refused to make any concessions. It was only after the barricades had gone up in Paris that he was forced to bend: early in March he too conceded a constitution, though in deference to his horror of the term, it was called the *Statuto*.

A revolution in Vienna in mid-March triggered off a rising in Milan; and Charles Albert and his government, now headed by Cesare Balbo, was under enormous pressure to intervene and assist the Lombard rebels. The king wavered: he abhorred the idea of helping men who were probably tainted with Mazzinian beliefs. However, the demands for a patriotic war against Austria grew frenetic: 'The supreme hour for the Sardinian monarchy has sounded . . . Woe to us if . . . we do not arrive in time', wrote the young liberal Count Camillo Cavour. Fear of internal disorder forced Charles Albert to declare his support for the Milanese insurgents, and the Piedmontese army crossed tentatively into Lombardy. No preparations had been made for the campaign: there were not even any maps of Lombardy; and the slow advance allowed the Austrians to withdraw safely to the east, where they could wait for reinforcements.

When he reached Milan, where the rebels had forced the Austrian garrison to withdraw after five days of heroic street fighting, Charles Albert revealed his true colours. He disregarded the patriots and turned instead to the local aristocracy, whose liberal credentials were at best suspect. He also insisted on holding a plebiscite in order to ensure the fusion of Lombardy with Piedmont. This confirmed many Milanese liberals in their suspicion that the King of Piedmont was in fact conducting an old-fashioned dynastic war of conquest and not a war of liberation. It also served to deter those nationalists in Naples,

Tuscany, and Rome who were ready to fight against Austria for the sake of a new Italy. By the time Charles Albert was ready to advance again, at the end of May, all hope of defeating the Austrians had been lost: Marshal Radetzky had consolidated his forces, and in July he defeated the Piedmontese in a minor engagement at Custoza.

In the meantime, the constitutional governments that in the first months of 1848 had been formed in the South, the Papal States, and Tuscany, had run into trouble. So, too, had the Venetian republic, set up in March under the leadership of Daniele Manin. As in previous revolutions, the main problem was the split between the moderates and the democrats, to which was added a new division between a few mainly radical politicians who wanted a united Italy, and the bulk of the moderates who hankered after some form of Italian federation. In Sicily, the traditional demand for independence from Bourbon Naples further muddied the waters. The growing confusion had already, in May, permitted King Ferdinand to revoke the constitution that he had granted to Naples a few months before; and when Charles Albert was defeated at Custoza, and then signed an armistice and abandoned Lombardy (without even consulting his ministers), the future for constitutional government everywhere in Italy looked extremely bleak.

The failure of the war against Austria led to growing problems of law and order; and the democrats, bitter at the ineffectiveness of the moderates and the duplicity of the constitutional rulers, set out to profit. 'The royal war is over; the war of the people begins', Mazzini announced from his base in Lugano. In Tuscany, popular associations appeared preaching the cause of 'liberty' and 'independence'; and in October the democrats came to power following a wave of agitation. A month later the pope fled to Gaeta after a mob had assassinated his moderate minister, Pellegrino Rossi. Mazzini and his followers congregated in Rome, where an elected assembly had voted to set up a republic; but hopes that it might be the springboard for a national revolution were dashed by localist sentiment: Tuscany, Sicily, and Venice all rejected Mazzini's call for union with Rome.

In Piedmont, the defeat at Custoza had been followed by a series of short-lived administrations and demands by the democrats for a genuine war of national independence. It was largely fear of a republican revolution at home that drove Charles Albert in March

Plate 15 Secular icon: Giuseppe Garibaldi in 1849. In the background is the Castel Sant'Angelo, Rome. The cult of Garibaldi was fostered by idealised images such as this, which played up his supposed resemblance to Christ. (For a photograph, see page 138.)

1849 to resume the campaign against Austria. Once again, however, serious preparations were lacking; and the fact that the king had appointed a Polish general as his nominal commander caused major communication problems at the top, and depressed morale. On 23 March the Piedmontese forces were routed at Novara, and Charles Albert promptly abdicated. Genoa, a stronghold of the democrats, rose up in revolt, and there were demands for a continuation of the war alongside Rome, Florence, and Venice (where Daniele Manin's republic still survived); but General La Marmora brought the city to its senses, bombarding it into submission.

Piedmont's defeat left the way open for the restoration of the old order throughout Italy. In April Grand Duke Leopold was returned to Florence. Mazzini's Roman republic held out until July against a besieging French army, sent – in response to pressure from domestic Catholic opinion – to reinstate the pope: the heroic defence of the city was led by Giuseppe Garibaldi, whose astonishing military skills had been developed in exile fighting as a guerrilla leader for the emergent republics of South America. The last outpost of revolution was Venice, which resisted Austrian forces until the end of August. If 1848–9 had ended with a crushing defeat for the radical left in Italy as in other parts of Europe, the heroism of the Roman and Venetian republics won the democrats admiration and respect in many quarters, and provided the cause of Italian independence with some excellent publicity.

5

Italy united

The year of revolutions in Europe of 1848–9 was more an outcry at the shortcomings of the restoration states than a conscious struggle for a new social order. Many of the intellectual leaders or interpreters of this 'springtime of the peoples', from Karl Marx to Mazzini, hoped and indeed believed that a world free of oppressors and tyrants was about to be born; but the artisans, shopkeepers, and urban poor who made up the backbone of the insurrections, and took to the streets of Palermo, Berlin, and Vienna, threw up barricades and stormed town halls, acted more from a spontaneous anger at unemployment, prices, or taxes than a desire to create a wholly different society. Nevertheless, in at least one important respect 1848–9 did look to the future: it sounded the death-knell of absolutism. The idea that a government should prevent change and freeze society in the interests of a narrow elite, seemed untenable in a world that was already beginning to be transformed by industry and science.

The quickening pace of Europe's economic life from the 1830s was to quicken even more after the 1840s. Britain led the way: in the mid-1840s it had some 3,000 miles of railways; by 1850 this figure had more than doubled; and by 1860 the total stood at over 10,000 miles. Output of cotton and pig-iron, the cornerstones of industry in this period, soared; so too did production of an enormous variety of other often newly invented goods, as world demand, depressed for more than thirty years, picked up dramatically. Faith in the march of progress seemed boundless, and was enshrined in the Great

Exhibition, opened in 1851. In France, Belgium, and the German states the rhythm of economic life was similarly, if rather less dramatically, transformed. Small workshops became great factories; towns became sprawling cities; peasants became proletarians; and everywhere, the middle classes grew more numerous and assertive.

The contrast with the situation in much of Italy was marked. A number of regions, above all in the North, were certainly well advanced: 'We can show foreigners the plain of Lombardy entirely cultivated . . . More than 4,000 square kilometres are now irrigated; and through artificial canals there flows a volume of water estimated at over 30 million cubic metres a day', declared Carlo Cattaneo in 1844 in a passionate description of the agricultural wealth and technology of his native Lombardy. Outside the Po valley, however, the picture was much less encouraging. In the South, there were only sixty miles of railways all told by 1860; yields per hectare were on average a third of those in Lombardy; joint stock companies were non-existent, and the structure of banking, primitive. Even Tuscany, with its illustrious economic past, had little industry; and its agriculture was beginning to suffer from a doctrinaire adhesion by the great landowners to share-cropping, which they saw as promoting harmonious class relations, albeit at the expense of output.

The sense, as in the eighteenth century, of a growing gulf between Italy and the most advanced parts of Europe made the introduction of liberalism into the peninsula seem, to some at least, more pressing than ever. If constitutional government offered an antidote to social revolution, it also, as the examples of Belgium, France, and Great Britain suggested, appeared the best guarantee of prosperity. Political freedom, so the argument ran, allowed individuals to develop their talents to the full, unhampered by the controls, restrictions, and privileges that stifled enterprise in the *ancien régime* states; and the wealth of each would contribute to the prosperity of all. Tariff barriers were therefore anathema: 'Free trade', wrote the most ardent of the Italian liberals, Count Cavour, in the 1840s, 'is a goal towards which every civilised people is moving.'

Not surprisingly, perhaps, many of those who became leading advocates of political and economic liberalism in Italy during the 1850s had lived or travelled in northern Europe. Quintino Sella, the future Minister of Finance, was sent by the Piedmontese government to study at the Ecole des Mines in Paris. He also attended universities in Germany and England. The agronomist Stefano Jacini was a student in Berne and Vienna; and the great literary critic Francesco De Sanctis taught, while in exile, in Zurich. During his formative years, Count Cavour visited Britain and France on several occasions and met many statesmen and intellectuals. It was here, in the era of the Great Reform Act and the July Revolution, that his admiration for the politics and culture of both countries was born. His passion for England was to earn him the nickname of 'Milord Camillo'; and in later life he spoke of France as his second homeland.

Sella, Jacini, and Cavour, like the majority of the best-known Italian liberals of the period, came from the wealthiest regions of the North – Piedmont and Lombardy in particular. Their outlook was shaped by the vigour of the civil society into which they had been born; a society of entrepreneurial landowners – such as the Cavours – who read the latest scientific journals; and of silk, cotton, and wool manufacturers. For them it seemed natural that the state should act merely to facilitate and safeguard the activities of the industrious, as in Britain. In the South, by contrast, where most landowners were absentee, infrastructures lacking, and the rule of law weak, liberalism was conceived of in rather different terms: freedom had no meaning here, it was often felt, unless it was 'built' through strong state action: 'It is not enough', said the Neapolitan, Francesco De Sanctis, 'simply to decree liberty for it to exist.'

These two strands of liberalism were to compete for the soul of official ideology in Italy after 1860; and in practice they often fused. However, they were hardly representative of the views of the ruling classes as a whole in the 1850s. Cavour, indeed, was almost unique in the extent of his passion for progress and north European liberalism. In general, the bourgeoisie, both in the North and the South, saw modernisation as fraught with social dangers; and their fears were given moral sanction by the Church, which condemned the disruption to traditional economic relationships, and the spread of urbanisation, caused by capitalism. Intelligent social commentators, such as Count Petitti from Piedmont, repeatedly underlined their concern that industry would bring violent disorders; and Vincenzo Gioberti argued that Britain was inferior to Italy because it had failed to temper its economic energy with truly religious values.

Fear characterised the outlook of the majority of the rich and educated in Italy. The instability of the vastly overpopulated country-side had brought about a widespread belief that the social fabric could only be held together if the peasantry remained resigned. The pulpit for many was still the key to rural order. Popular education was regarded with suspicion, and materialistic ideas, whether social-ist, utilitarian, or even liberal, were seen as both inflammatory and immoral. Indeed, the low moral status attaching to materialist thought affected the left as well as the right, and made it hard in both the short and longer term for pragmatic socialism to make much headway in Italy. The democrats after 1849 were still domi-nated by the figure of Mazzini, who scorned materialism; and though socialist thought attracted some supporters in the 1850s (notably Carlo Pisacane), they were relatively few in number.

CAVOUR AND THE TRIUMPH OF THE MODERATES

The response of the Austrian government to the events of 1848–9 was to reinforce centralisation. The concessions made during the revolutions were almost all revoked, and administrative absolutism again prevailed. Strict censorship, political persecution, and an effi-cient if somewhat oppressive German-speaking bureaucracy were the main features of the Austrian empire in the 1850s. The central Italian duchies, dependent as before on Austrian troops, took their lead from Vienna and likewise revoked the reforms that had been granted in 1848. In the South, King Ferdinand, having weathered the storm without foreign help, grew isolationist and frightened of change and sank into a political torpor from which not even a severe agricultural crisis in the middle of the decade could wrest him. The pope, thanks to French arms, was restored to Rome.

The only Italian state to retain its constitution in 1849 was Piedmont. In part this was due to the Austrians: after the Battle of Novara they encouraged the new king, Victor Emmanuel II (whom they wanted as an ally), to keep the *Statuto*, believing he would be stronger with it than without it. Victor Emmanuel himself was willing to jettison it: like his father, he had been brought up in a strict military environment; was a staunch (if disobedient) Catholic married to a pious Austrian princess; and his sympathies were with absolutism. Fortunately for the future of Italian liberalism, however, he lacked the self-confidence to assert himself and almost invariably deferred to those with a stronger will. He kept up his self-respect by boasting of his physical courage (which was not inconsiderable) and of his sexual prowess – which was rather less than he liked others to imagine but sufficient for a joke to circulate that no sovereign had been a more successful 'father of his subjects'.

Despite Victor Emmanuel's opposition to it, the *Statuto* was in fact very conservative. It conceded remarkably little to the principles of 1789: only nine of its eighty-four articles dealt with the rights of subjects. It left the king with extensive powers: the executive was answerable to him, not parliament, and he could appoint and sack the prime minister in theory at will; he had sole responsibility for making treaties and declaring war; the upper house, the Senate, was nominated by him; the judiciary carried out justice in his name and was not an independent branch of government; and though parliament (comprising the Senate and an elected Chamber of Deputies) controlled legislation, the king had a right of veto and the power to issue 'decree laws' without parliament's consent.

The great achievement of the Piedmontese governments between 1849 and 1860 was to persuade the king to accept the principle that it was in practice parliament, and not the crown, that the executive answered to. However, the fact that the constitution failed to specify this (indeed failed to mention at all the role of the prime minister or President of the Council) left room for a good deal of ambiguity. One result in the longer term was that a rather uneasy relationship emerged between the executive and the Chamber of Deputies, with the latter seeing its task as to monitor, and if need be restrain, the government, and also ensure that sectional or even personal interests were not sacrificed to any claim by the administration to represent a higher 'national' interest. In this situation, a prime minister had to bargain hard and usually cajole if he wanted to remain in power for any length of time.

Another problem faced by the executive in its dealings with parliament was a widespread mistrust of 'parties'. Cesare Balbo and Cavour were unusual among the moderates in regarding parties and freedom as wholly compatible; for many, parties were little more than 'sects' that aimed to impose the will of a minority on the majority. Accordingly, party lines were never tightly drawn and party loyalty never something that acquired much moral force. This was an additional reason why ministers had to resort to bargaining with individual deputies for their support, often making unsavoury deals with them or their constituents; and the blatant character of such horsetrading damaged parliament's image badly after the 1860s. In general, however, the situation was made simpler for Piedmont's executive by the fact that many deputies had posts in the public sector and were unlikely to risk their careers by voting against the government.

The man who shaped Piedmontese politics after 1849 and gave them their liberal imprint, and who also, more than anyone else, was responsible for laying down the ground rules by which the parliamentary life of united Italy operated for over half a century, was Count Camillo Benso di Cavour. Born in 1810, the son of a landowner and one-time head of police, he was in many ways the product of a typical Piedmontese noble family. He did, however, have Swiss-Protestant relations, and it was largely from them that he absorbed some of his exceptional concern for freedom, religious tolerance, and the work ethic, a concern reinforced during his travels in northern Europe in the 1830s and 1840s. On social issues Cavour was always conservative; he believed strongly in private property, and was convinced that order and progress were inextricably linked.

Cavour's passionate faith in progress – economic, political, and moral – to a large extent determined his political philosophy. Revolutions, he maintained, were counter-productive: they caused disorder and invited reaction. True and lasting progress came about only through gradual change, and was best achieved by following what he called the *juste milieu* – the middle path between extremes. Britain in the 1830s and 1840s offered confirmation of the wisdom of this approach, he thought. Politics was the art of the practical (*le tact des choses possibles*); it was a question of responding with imagination to circumstances and not being constrained unduly by dogma or moral scruples. His hatred of Mazzini, indeed, stemmed as much from an aversion to the republican's uncompromising temperament as a dislike of his revolutionary ideas.

On the national question, Cavour's thinking was somewhat contradictory. He certainly believed that a sense of patriotism was important morally. As he wrote in an article of 1846: 'Every period of history shows that no people can attain a high degree of intelligence and morality unless it has a strongly developed sense of its national identity.' However, he was in general dismissive of the idea of Italian unity. This was no doubt partly because he considered it unrealistic ('He is still rather utopian', he said of Daniele Manin in 1856: 'He talks of unifying Italy and other such nonsense'); and partly, too, perhaps, because it savoured of Mazzini; but he might also have been unclear as to whether Italy really was a nation. After all, like many Piedmontese he was culturally more French than Italian; he spoke Italian only with difficulty; and, according to one close colleague, he knew little about Italian history.

Cavour said his goal was not so much unification as 'the independence of Italy and the aggrandisement of Piedmont', an ambiguous phrase and one which implied on a practical level resuming the fight against Austria. The lesson he had learnt from 1848–9 was that the European powers could not afford to let Piedmont lose territory, even if it suffered military defeat; for Piedmont was too important strategically, as a buffer state holding the ring between Austria and France. Accordingly, he believed, Piedmont had little to fear from a policy that involved the possibility of war. Cavour's programme contained two main strands, the one economic – to foster agriculture and industry, and create modern infrastructures, especially railways – and the other diplomatic; but to carry it out, he needed to create a political power base at home strong enough to allow him to act independently.

He first had to secure a solid majority in parliament. The Piedmontese elections of December 1849 had weakened the democrats and strengthened the moderates; and this fact, together with Napoleon III's conservative coup of 1851 in France, convinced Cavour that the threat of revolution in Europe had abated. Armed with this belief, he plotted to bring down the centre-right coalition of Massimo d'Azeglio (in whose government he was Minister of Agriculture) and replace it with a more centrist one that would leave the far right and far left isolated and allow him to pursue the *juste milieu*. This rather underhand move, which resulted in an alliance (later called the *connubio*, or 'marriage') with the centre-left, contributed to Cavour's appointment as prime minister in November 1852, and was seen by

Plate 16(a)   The pragmatist: Count Camillo Benso di Cavour in 1856.

him as his political masterpiece. It gave him a base in the Chamber strong enough to allow him to continue as head of government almost without interruption until his death in 1861.

Having mastered the Chamber (and his mastery was such that he once said that he 'never felt so weak as when parliament was shut'), Cavour now had to master the king. The turning point here came

Plate 16(b)   The dreamer: Giuseppe Mazzini, *c.* 1850.

with the so-called 'Calabiana affair'. In 1854 Cavour presented a bill
to parliament to suppress monasteries that had no educational or
charitable role. Victor Emmanuel's Catholic scruples (or those of his
family) led him to oppose this anti-clerical measure, and he conspired with the bishops in the Senate to block it. Cavour guessed
what was afoot and resigned in anger. The king was unable to find a

conservative alternative and had to face the ignominy of reappointing Cavour and seeing the bill passed. From then on, the relative independence of ministers from the crown was accepted – an arrangement that Victor Emmanuel soon came to acknowledge was beneficial, in that it spared him blame for unpopular decisions.

Under Cavour's energetic leadership, Piedmont forged ahead economically. Commercial treaties were signed with England, France, Austria and other countries; and a general free-trade tariff was introduced. Cavour was never a completely *laisser-faire* liberal, and believed that it was the government's role to provide the infrastructures necessary for private initiative to flourish. Hence the encouragement he gave to banking; hence, also, the enormous surge in railway building: by 1860 40 per cent of Italy's 2,400 km of railways were located in the regions of Piedmont and Liguria (see Table 4). The increase in public expenditure resulted in higher taxation and a huge public debt; but the overall success of Cavour's policies could be seen in almost every sphere, especially textiles, armaments, and shipping, and also (if less dramatically) in agriculture.

Against this background of economic resurgence, Cavour embarked upon an ambitious foreign policy. The breakdown of the relatively harmonious conservative order that had prevailed in Europe for over thirty years helped him. France under Napoleon III was now a revisionist power eager to undo the settlement of 1815; Britain was becoming alarmed by Russian ambitions in Asia; and Austria faced the challenge of Prussia for dominance in central Europe, and also rivalry with the Tsar in the Balkans. The air of insecurity was heightened by domestic pressures and by growing doubts about the capacity of absolutism to survive the challenges posed by liberalism and democracy; and it was out of this atmosphere of tension that the Crimean War emerged in 1854, with France and Britain joining forces to curb Russian expansionism in the East.

Despite opposition from the cabinet, Cavour was eager to join in the war against Russia. He wanted to raise Piedmont's standing with Britain and France, and secure a place at the conference table; but the king pledged his forces before any terms could be agreed and Piedmont found itself involved in the Crimea with no assurance that its interests would even be listened to once the fighting was over. However, at the Paris peace congress in 1856 Cavour succeeded in

Table 4 *Railways (open, in km) 1840–1900*

	1840	1850	1860	1870	1880	1890	1900
Austria–Hungary	144	1357	2927	6112	11429	15273	19229
France	410	2915	9167	15544	23089	33280	38109
Germany	469	5856	11089	18876	33838	42869	51678
United Kingdom	2390	9797	14603	21558[a]	25060	27827	30079
Italy	20	620	2404	6429	9290	13629	16429

Note: [a] 1871.
Source: B. R. Mitchell, *International Historical Statistics, Europe 1750–1988* (N.Y., 1992).

raising the issue of Italy; but he undercut this achievement by coming across as unduly bellicose towards Austria. This alarmed the British government, which thereafter never entirely trusted him. As a result, Cavour was forced to look to France for help against the Austrians, who were now (and this was an important consequence of the Crimean War) dangerously isolated after failing to commit themselves fully to either side during the hostilities.

From 1856 Cavour attempted to entice Napoleon III into a war against Austria. His task was made easier by the Emperor's desire to emulate his uncle, the great Napoleon, and also by the fact that in his youth Napoleon III had been a *carbonaro*. Already in 1852 the Emperor had spoken privately of his wish to do something for Italy, his 'second fatherland'. However, Napoleon's romantic leanings were tempered by practical political considerations: he could not countenance Italian unity, for that would have entailed destroying the Papal States and thus angering French Catholic opinion; and a united Italy was in any case not desirable strategically, for it would have meant creating a potential rival to France in the Mediterranean. What he aimed at was an enlarged kingdom in the North (to become a satellite of France), and for the peninsula as a whole a federal structure under the presidency of the pope.

In July 1858 Cavour and Napoleon met secretly in the Vosges to discuss terms for a war against Austria. Italy, it was agreed, was to become a confederation headed by the pope and split into four states: Piedmont would take over northern Italy, including the Romagna, and give Nice and Savoy to France; a new central Italian kingdom would be created around Tuscany; Rome and its environs would be left to the papacy; and Naples would remain unchanged. A pretext for war was to be found by using *agents provocateurs*, who would stir up a revolt in the territory of Modena and appeal to Victor Emmanuel for help. The Austrians would then be driven out of northern Italy. This deal, hatched between Cavour and Napoleon, almost folded when Victor Emmanuel balked at sealing it with a marriage between his pious fifteen-year-old daughter and the Emperor's dissolute cousin. Cavour forced him to see sense.

However, the war did not go according to plan. To start with, it almost failed to break out: the rising in central Italy was a damp squib; and it was only a miscalculation by the Austrians, who suddenly decided to teach Piedmont a lesson after thinking quite wrongly that Napoleon had lost his nerve, that led to the start of hostilities in April 1859. Then, despite a rapid push into Lombardy and major French victories at Magenta and Solferino, Napoleon, out of the blue, halted the campaign: he had discovered to his alarm that Cavour had been secretly working to annex part of the Papal States; and he had also learned that Prussia was about to intervene. He hastily concluded an armistice with Austria (Cavour was not even consulted), under the terms of which Lombardy was surrendered to Napoleon – who then passed it on to Piedmont – while Austria kept the Veneto. Cavour felt humiliated; and in a fit of anger, he resigned as prime minister.

Meanwhile, the war against Austria had sparked off a series of patriotic risings in central Italy. At the end of April Leopold of Tuscany was forced into exile; and he was followed after the victory of the French at Magenta by the dukes of Modena and Parma. Bologna, Perugia, and a number of other cities in the Romagna and Umbria also rose up against the pope. Cavour promptly tried to induce the provisional governments in these regions to accept fusion with Piedmont; but this annoyed many leading liberals, among them Baron Ricasoli in Florence, who suspected that Cavour's concern for Italian independence was far from altruistic. Moreover, traditional autonomist feelings and inter-communal rivalries were still strong. In the end, it was fear of social disorder as well as a possible restitution of the old rulers that led the provisional regimes to demand, and early in 1860 to secure, annexation to Piedmont.

1860

The war of 1859 may not have gone as Cavour anticipated, but it had brought into being an expanded Kingdom of Piedmont. Napoleon was far from content. The armistice with Austria had stipulated that the rulers in central Italy should be restored: failure to achieve this damaged his credibility. Furthermore, his high-handedness in the campaign had weakened his moral hold over Victor Emmanuel and left the Piedmontese government freer than it would otherwise have been to press ahead with the annexations. Napoleon did, however, gain a major concession: in return for recognising the annexations, he insisted that Nice and Savoy be handed over to France. Cavour (who returned to power in January 1860) accepted; and despite the scruples of the king and the protests of those who felt that western Piedmont would now be rendered militarily indefensible, he signed a secret treaty in March ceding these territories. He confessed in private that this was unconstitutional.

Among those who were particularly angered by Cavour's action was Giuseppe Garibaldi. He had been born in Nice and was mortified that this Italian city should be bartered away to the French in contravention of the national principle. His anger was all the greater in that after 1848–9 he had (like many other disillusioned followers of Mazzini) looked to Piedmont, in good faith, for leadership of the national cause. He was a member of the Italian National Society, a body set up in 1857 to promote Italian unity and backed, enthusiastically so it had seemed, by Cavour. In the war of 1859 he had been allowed to command a force of patriotic volunteers, many of them veterans of 1848. The cession of Nice in return for the central Italian duchies thus savoured of duplicity, and seemed to Garibaldi to confirm a long-held suspicion that Cavour was in fact more interested in the 'aggrandisement of Piedmont' than the cause of unity.

When in April news came through of a peasant rising in the west of Sicily directed, as was so often the case, against taxes, prices, and oppressive landowners, Garibaldi was approached and asked to lead an expedition to convert this *jacquerie* into a national revolution. For some time Mazzini and his followers had been plotting from London and Paris to launch such a movement: in 1859 Francesco Crispi had slipped into Sicily to teach local democrats the latest bomb-making arts. Now that so much of Italy had been liberated, it seemed imperative to try and finish the process and at the same time to wrest the initiative from Cavour and the moderates. However, as Crispi and Garibaldi both accepted, the only real chance of success lay in suppressing any hint of republicanism and appealing instead to Victor Emmanuel. Garibaldi was among those who believed, perhaps misguidedly, that the Piedmontese king was a more genuine patriot than his prime minister.

Garibaldi's expedition proved a brilliant success. With barely a thousand followers, many of them students or of student age and almost all without military training, he advanced inland from Marsala on the western coast of Sicily, proclaiming Victor Emmanuel king of Italy as he went. He dispersed a Bourbon force heroically with an inspired bayonet charge at Calatafimi, captured Palermo in June, crossed the Straits of Messina in August, and on 7 September entered Naples in triumph. This extraordinary feat owed much to the genius of Garibaldi; it owed a good deal, also, to the astute political handling of the revolution by Francesco Crispi, who courted the peasants with offers of land and lower taxes and the local middle classes with guarantees of property and law and order. On occasions, as notoriously at Bronte in eastern Sicily, peasants who rioted were summarily shot.

However, the main reason for Garibaldi's success lay in the convergence of a cluster of often negative feelings around the banner of revolution. For the peasants, Garibaldi offered the hope of relief from suffering; for the Sicilian landowners, the overthrow of the Bourbons meant an opportunity at last to secure independence from Naples; for the provincial middle classes, frequently caught up in bitter factional struggles, there was the chance to seize control of local government and worst their enemies. The majority of those who took part in the revolution probably did so with little clear sense of what they were fighting for. Most had never encountered the term *Italia* before: some even imagined that '*La Talia*' was the name of Victor Emmanuel's wife. Such vagueness may have been a source of strength in 1860, for it licensed even the wildest dreams; but it was to result in a great deal of resentment later, when the reality of Italian unification became apparent.

For Cavour, the events of the spring and summer of 1860 proved a

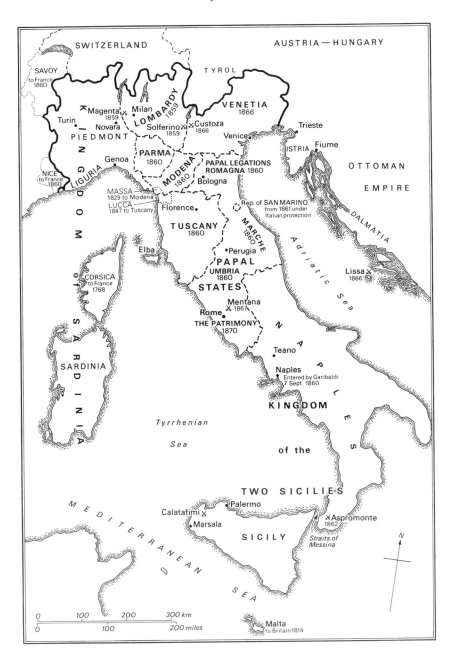

Map 5   The unification of Italy.

nightmare. He dared not oppose Garibaldi openly, since Piedmontese public opinion was enthusiastic about the expedition; so, too, was the king, who had a personal sympathy for Garibaldi. Cavour's great fear was that if Garibaldi and his army of young volunteers (most of whom were democrats) succeeded against all the odds in liberating the South, what was to stop them from dropping their support for King Victor Emmanuel and espousing instead the cause of republicanism, particularly if they conquered Rome, with its memories of 1849? Allied to this was Cavour's dread of foreign intervention. As it was, Napoleon was unhappy about the situation in Italy; if a rabble army of peasants and Mazzinians started bearing down on the Holy City, the pressure on him at home to send an expeditionary force would become overwhelming.

Cavour did his best to thwart Garibaldi and the Thousand covertly. He had their consignment of Enfield rifles sequestrated before they set sail. He ordered the senior Piedmontese admiral, Admiral Persano, to intercept the expedition as it headed south; but Persano failed even to locate it. When Palermo fell, Cavour dispatched one of his lieutenants, Giuseppe La Farina, to Sicily, to engineer the island's immediate annexation to Piedmont: but La Farina behaved with great tactlessness, and was sent packing. Cavour had better luck in Naples. Here he blocked attempts by the democrats to elect an assembly to decide on a new constitution, and persuaded Garibaldi to hold a plebiscite instead: voters were given a straight choice between accepting or rejecting a unitary state under Victor Emmanuel. They accepted overwhelmingly. However, the ballot was public and rigging clearly took place on a large scale. In Sicily, 432,053 votes in favour were recorded and only 667 against.

By the early autumn the Papal States were the only 'unliberated' region of Italy apart from the Veneto. Cavour was determined to occupy them before Garibaldi and wrest the political initiative from him. He let Napoleon know that he had to invade in order to stop Garibaldi marching on Rome. However, he probably failed to make clear what would happen to the Papal States later; and when the French saw what was going on, they protested strongly. Early in September Piedmontese troops crossed into the Marche. The pope's forces were beaten in a minor engagement at Castelfidardo, and by the end of the month Umbria and the Marche were conquered.

Peasants and priests offering resistance were summarily shot. Victor Emmanuel was elated by his success and pushed south. On 25 October he met Garibaldi near Teano, to the north of Naples. Garibaldi loyally handed over his powers in the South to the King. Against all the odds, and largely by accident, Italy had been made.

THE NEW STATE

The 'handshake at Teano' soon entered the pantheon of patriotic mythology. It became a symbol of the new state, forged, so the argument ran, through the harmonious convergence of 'the people', represented by Garibaldi, and the Piedmontese monarchy. The moderates and the democrats had complemented each other to perfection, it was said; and both had triumphed in 1860. The reality, however, was different. The unification of Italy had come about as the result more of a civil war than a war of liberation. It was a civil war that Cavour had been determined to win, and had won, using all his political skills. Having seized the initiative from Garibaldi with his daring invasion of the Papal States, he made sure that the new Italy owed nothing to the democrats. Garibaldi's services were dispensed with; his followers were sent home; and Mazzini remained in exile, bitter and disillusioned.

The character of the new state owed much to the partisan climate in which it was born. There was no discussion of constitutional alternatives; and the views of those, particularly in the South, who hoped for a measure of regional autonomy or who (like Carlo Cattaneo) believed passionately in federalism, were disregarded. In part, this absence of deliberation was pragmatic. Cavour felt a great sense of urgency in late 1860. He needed to present a *fait accompli* to Europe and feared that a discussion of the constitutional alternatives would expose the ideological rifts between the moderates and the democrats, and invite French or Austrian intervention. However, the lack of debate also had a more sinister dimension. To many, it seemed to imply that Victor Emmanuel and Cavour felt that Piedmont had conquered the rest of Italy, and therefore felt justified in imposing their own terms.

Very little was done to gainsay this impression. The king kept his royal title unchanged, and became Victor Emmanuel II of Italy.

Plate 17 The handshake at Teano. Garibaldi surrenders the South to Victor Emmanuel II (on the white horse). An idealised image by a Neapolitan artist, 1878. Whether the sheep are simply a bucolic touch, or a comment on the king's relationship to his subjects, is unclear.

Turin became the new capital, and when Italy's first parliament met there in January 1861, it was referred to as the 'eighth legislature of the Sardinian parliament'. The Piedmontese *Statuto*, administrative structure, tariffs, and commercial treaties were extended to the entire country. The legislation of the old states was kept in being pending the creation of unified legal codes, but certain key laws, such as those on education and the police, were applied to all of Italy from the start. The often insensitive manner in which the new structures were imposed caused a good deal of resentment; but Cavour remained confident about the outcome. 'If we show unbending will', he told the king, 'people will settle down and adapt themselves to our regime, for our institutions are in all respects preferable to those from which they were liberated.'

The sense that many Italians soon had of being 'conquered' by Piedmont was not tempered by economic benefits. The introduction of the new free trade tariffs led to considerable hardship, particularly in the South, where the fragile manufacturing sector had depended on protection for its survival. Almost overnight, Naples' textile and engineering factories closed. So, too, did many smaller artisan workshops. Rising taxation also produced much suffering. The government faced a huge public debt after 1860, more than half of it run up by Piedmont in the 1850s. Finance ministers wrestled with the task of balancing the budget, which became a national crusade in the 1860s and early 1870s (Quintino Sella called it 'a matter of "to be or not to be" '). The result was a great increase in the fiscal burden: between 1862 and 1865 direct taxes rose by 54 per cent, indirect by 40 per cent. In 1868 the notorious grist tax or *macinato* (on the milling of wheat) was introduced, which sparked off widespread rioting.

Another way for the government to raise revenue was by confiscating church and communal property. In 1866–7 2,000 religious congregations were deprived of legal status and 25,000 ecclesiastical bodies were suppressed. In the course of the next fifteen years, over a million hectares of church land were sold off. A similar amount of communal land also came under the hammer. Some people hoped that these sales would produce a new stratum of peasant smallholders, but the government's hunger for money was such that no adequate provisions were made for credit, and most of the land ended up in the hands of existing owners. Many peasants felt bitterly disappointed: they had often supported Garibaldi in 1860 believing they would receive a share of the commons. What is more, the closure of monastic houses left the poor without a major source of jobs and more importantly of welfare.

The government's economic problems after 1860 and its doctrinaire concern with balancing the budget weakened its already fragile support among the masses. Per capita income, it seems, remained static in the first decade and a half of unity: other European countries in this same period enjoyed marked levels of growth. The failure of the new state to reach out to the poor might, with hindsight, appear to have been impolitic; and certainly the moderates' fear of the democrats caused them to be less sensitive to social issues than even many conservatives thought prudent. However, the principal concern of Cavour and his followers was not with the poor but with the middle classes. In establishing the liberal regime, they sought to create an economic and political order that would guarantee leadership of society to the country's landowners, industrialists, and professionals; and this, they hoped, would unlock Italy's latent entrepreneurial energies, to the benefit of all.

Through the example of the propertied classes, it was believed, the masses would be morally raised up and the values of hard work, thrift, and self-help be disseminated. (Samuel Smiles, a former supporter of Mazzini, was hugely popular in Italy: his *Character* (1871) sold 7,000 copies in just one year; and he had numerous Italian imitators.) Private wealth was the main criterion of power in the new state, both in practice and legally. Under the country's electoral law, only men who paid at least forty lire a year in direct taxes (and were literate) had the vote. This limited the suffrage to less than 2 per cent of the total population, or about 8 per cent of males above the age of twenty-four. For local government, the electorate was somewhat larger, but a tax threshold was again applied. The sanctity of property was enshrined in the *Statuto*, and the 1865 civil code (which was based on the Napoleonic code) made the defence of property rights its central concern.

Italy's ruling class was not markedly different in composition from that of other European countries; but it was narrower (given the general weakness of the bourgeoisie in Italy) and included many fewer industrialists than in Britain, France, or Belgium. This narrowness gave rise to feelings of acute vulnerability, and was one reason why governments felt driven to use repression so often in defence of the status quo. Military barracks and police stations loomed large in the social geography of Italy's towns and cities; and in rural communities, the headquarters of the *carabinieri* was frequently the most conspicuous building. The army was regularly deployed to break up strikes and demonstrations; and when unrest was severe (as in Sicily in 1862, 1866, and 1894) military tribunals were instituted to mete out summary justice. The police had extensive powers: a man could be sent to a penal island for five years merely on suspicion of being a criminal.

The trouble with using coercion to defend the status quo was that it played havoc with the moral foundations of liberalism. 'We acted', wrote Massimo d'Azeglio ruefully in August 1861, 'on the assumption that any government unsupported by the people was illegitimate . . . But we need sixty battalions to control the South — and even that does not seem to be sufficient.' A vicious circle was set in motion: repression caused anger and hostility, and this made the country's rulers feel still more isolated and threatened. Desperation easily ensued. In late 1860 Luigi Farini, governor of Naples, and a future prime minister, wrote: 'In seven million inhabitants [of the South] there are not a hundred who want a united Italy. Nor are there any liberals to speak of . . . What can you possibly build out of stuff like this! . . . If only our *accursed* civilisation did not forbid floggings, cutting out peoples' tongues, and *noyades*. Then something would happen.'

The feeling of isolation was reinforced by political fears. The new state seemed to be assailed by enemies on all sides. Many democrats, among them Garibaldi (who turned up in parliament in April 1861 wearing a poncho and a redshirt and accused Cavour of having waged 'a fratricidal war'), still hankered after a national revolution made by the people. During the 1860s they aimed to use social unrest, especially in the South, as a springboard for a march on Rome: in 1862 Garibaldi crossed the Straits of Messina at the head of a volunteer force, only to be halted by the national army in Calabria. He tried again five years later, beginning in central Italy. This time he was stopped by papal and French troops. The intrigues of the

Plate 18   Garibaldi in 1862, showing the bullet wound in his
right ankle received during his encounter with Italian troops on
the slopes of Aspromonte in Calabria. The troops were sent by
the government to stop his revolutionary march on Rome.

democrats abated after 1867 and died out following the capture of
Rome in 1870; but in the early years of unity they terrified the
authorities and fuelled the climate of repression.

No less frightening was the hostility of the Church. After 1860 the
Papal States (for centuries seen by the popes as vital to their independence and security) were reduced to the city of Rome and a small area
of surrounding territory. Pius IX's anger was unbridled. He excommunicated the king and his ministers, appealed to France and Austria
for support, and encouraged Catholics to abstain from national
politics. The 1864 Syllabus of Errors widened the breach by pronouncing the incompatibility of Catholicism with liberalism. Lay organisations were founded (the first of the extra-parliamentary far right),
whose aim was to mobilise the faithful in defence of the Church and
so by implication undermine the new state from within. The government grew alarmed to the point of paranoia and began to blame the
mounting turmoil in the country, especially in the South, on clerical
conspiracies.

It was the South that caused the government the most severe problems after 1860. Cavour's last thoughts (he died after a short illness in June 1861) were of how to deal with the mounting chaos here. Repression was the main response: by the mid-1860s almost 100,000 troops were engaged in what the government rather speciously referred to as a 'war against brigands'. In reality, the unrest and lawlessness in the South were as much the result of political and social protest as of crime. In Sicily, one of the principal sources of opposition to the new state was military conscription (which was a novelty for the island). In the summer of 1862 General Govone undertook a particularly brutal operation to round up draft dodgers, besieging whole villages, cutting off their water supplies, and shooting on sight anybody 'with the face of a bandit'. When questioned about his methods, he added insult to injury by alluding in parliament to the 'barbarity' of Sicily.

In 1866 Sicily again became a focus of government worries. The war against Austria that summer led to a withdrawal of troops from the island. Local republicans and democrats, with the acquiescence of large sections of the middle classes and nobility, seized the opportunity to stage a rising in Palermo. They were aided by a groundswell of popular discontent. Squads of peasants (many of whom had fought with Garibaldi in 1860) marched down from the surrounding hills, and for a week the city was in the hands of perhaps 40,000 insurgents. General Cadorna regained control with the help of a naval bombardment, and imposed martial law. Summary executions took place, and attempts were made to pin blame for the revolt on bandits, 'the Mafia', and monks. Cadorna became so convinced of the idea of a clerical conspiracy that he even arrested as one of the ringleaders the Abbot of Monreale, a philosopher of international renown, then well over seventy.

Faced with so much opposition after 1860, and fearful that the state would fall apart, Italy's rulers held on to the reins of power with a desperate intensity. They were helped by an administrative structure that had been created initially in the age of absolutism, and then refined in the 1850s in an atmosphere of war. Centralisation was its essence. The state was split into provinces, each of which was governed by a government-appointed prefect: often he was a personal friend of the king or the prime minister and he usually came from

Plate 19 North meets South. An Italian soldier poses with the corpse of the bandit Nicola Napolitano. Between 1861 and 1865 almost two-thirds of the entire Italian army was deployed in trying to maintain order in southern Italy.

Piedmont. Each commune had its elected council: but the mayor was nominated by central government, while the main local official, the communal secretary, was a civil servant. The hold of the central authorities was further reinforced by the discretionary powers given to prefects to oversee, and if need be, veto, municipal decisions. Local councils could also be dissolved (and often were) on the grounds of some 'irregularity'.

In the first decades of unity in particular, a narrow elite of northerners dominated government and the bureaucracy. Not until 1887 did a southerner become prime minister. The king preferred if he could to have a premier from Piedmont (with whom he could speak in dialect), and if the occasion permitted – as during a war or in times of acute civil unrest – a general as well. Agostino Depretis and Giovanni Giolitti, the most successful of Italy's prime ministers between Cavour and Mussolini, both came from Piedmont. The army officer corps was predominantly northern: in the 1860s nearly three-quarters of all generals were Piedmontese. The upper echelons of the civil service were similarly northern-dominated. In the 1890s, according to one survey, 60 per cent of the top administrative posts were occupied by Lombards, Venetians, or Piedmontese. It was only in the early twentieth century that the civil service began to admit large numbers of southerners.

The sense of political insecurity, and the resulting mistrust towards civil society, that characterised much of Italy's ruling class after 1860, had a damaging effect on the bureaucracy. The absence of qualified and liberal personnel, especially in the South, meant that new appointments were often made on the basis of political loyalty rather than appropriate experience or skills. This fostered incompetence. It also blurred the dividing line between the executive and the administration, and so frustrated the hopes of those who had wanted to establish an impartial bureaucracy similar to the German *Rechtsstaat* that would guarantee citizens against the arbitrary actions of government. The tendency of politicians to use the civil service to build up personal clienteles by promoting friends and allies further encouraged this damaging process; while later attempts to 'neutralise' the bureaucracy by enveloping it in a web of administrative laws served in the long run only to induce paralysis.

From the start, therefore, the liberal state faced an overwhelming problem of legitimacy. Centuries of political and economic fragmentation were not easily transcended. The 'national' ruling elite was limited in both size and regional distribution; and without the backing of the Catholic Church, it had few sources of moral authority on which to draw. The nation lacked unifying symbols: attempts by propagandists after 1860 to rewrite Italian history in a patriotic key, or to endow the House of Savoy with an aura of greatness, were often too strained to be convincing. The haste with which unity had been imposed, and the cavalier, indeed brutal, fashion in which opponents of the new regime were swept aside, destroyed much of the goodwill that Garibaldi in particular had helped to generate. Disillusionment grew; poetry gave way to prose, as one writer put it; and the new state was left with its identity still unresolved and its future far from certain.

6

The liberal state and the social question, 1870–1900

Just as Austria's defeat by Prussia in 1866 had brought Italy the Veneto, so France's defeat by Prussia in 1870 led to the capture of Rome. Throughout much of the 1860s the Holy City had been defended by a garrison of French soldiers. When this was withdrawn in the summer of 1870 to fight Prussia, and Napoleon III was defeated and forced to abdicate, there was little to stop the Italian government seizing the historic capital. On 20 September, less than three weeks after the Battle of Sedan, Italian troops blew a hole in the Leonine walls at Porta Pia and marched into the city. Pius IX was left with the small enclave of the Vatican. A law was passed in May 1871 that guaranteed the safety of the pope, provided him with an annual grant, and gave him the full dignities and privileges of a sovereign; but Pius IX rejected it out of hand. The rift between the liberal state and the Church was now broader and deeper than ever.

The acquisition of Rome had long been the supreme ambition of most Italian patriots. For Mazzini's followers in particular, the city was always much more than just a piece of territory. It was a symbol of moral regeneration, pregnant with the idea of mission and responsibility; and just as the Rome of the Caesars and the Rome of the popes had each brought the world a new civilisation, so the 'Third Rome', that of 'the people', would arise and convey to the oppressed the gospel of liberation and peace. Even such a rational moderate as Quintino Sella could not escape the spell of Rome: he longed, he said, to underline the universal significance of destroying the pope's temporal power by making the city into a great centre for science. However, not everyone was smitten. Massimo d'Azeglio and Stefano Jacini objected to Rome becoming the capital of Italy precisely because of its historical associations, which, they felt, would weigh dangerously on the country's rulers.

Given all the messianic expectations, it was perhaps hardly surprising that the capture of Rome turned out to be an anti-climax. It seemed to many not so much the dawn of an era but the end of one; and a rather inglorious end at that. The city had owed its liberation, as with Lombardy and the Veneto, mainly to the victories of another nation's armies. Victor Emmanuel entered his new capital not in triumph but prosaically by train, and late. An ill-humoured remark, made in Piedmontese at the station, that they had 'finally arrived', was turned by propagandists into the grandiose 'here we are, and here we will stay'; but the lack-lustre reality was not so easily disguised and many, above all on the left, felt deeply disillusioned. Some withdrew from politics altogether; others, including Francesco Crispi, experienced a profound sense of disorientation now that unity was complete and began to cast around disconsolately for a new goal.

A sense of aimlessness seemed to have infected the entire political class. In the elections of November 1870, less than 46 per cent of the electorate bothered to vote. The turn-out was particularly bad in the northern cities, which ought to have been the most politically committed places: in Milan barely 35 per cent voted, and in Bologna just 28 per cent. The new Chamber of Deputies included more than 170 fresh members, but they, too, seemed hamstrung by uncertainty: the majority chose to sit on the central benches as if to underline that the old divisions between Right and Left (as the moderates and democrats were now known) lacked meaning any more. Many re-elected deputies appeared equally unsure of their political identity. Now that the issue of how and when to take Rome – the main bone of contention between Left and Right in the 1860s – had been resolved, it was hard to see where the party battle lines ran.

For many intellectuals and politicians, the completion of territorial unity in 1870 brought the nation face to face with itself for the first time; and the experience was daunting. '[Italy] must now look into its heart', wrote Francesco De Sanctis: '. . . It must search for itself, with unclouded eyes, free of illusion and prejudice . . . in the spirit of Galileo and Machiavelli.' But what did Italy stand for? What principles might guide the country's rulers and bind together the disparate population of the peninsula? The horrors of the Paris Commune in 1871 and the spread of the International Working Men's Association led many liberals to question their faith in economic progress: might not prosperity bring licentiousness and class war rather than increased social harmony? And did not Prussia's triumph in 1870 portend, perhaps, an era of force and authoritarianism: what place would there be in this new order for the democratic ideals of Mazzini?

Italy's rulers after 1870 found their options crowded out. With the Church more vehement than ever in its opposition to the state, hopes (entertained by some moderates) of anchoring the country's institutions to the rock of Catholicism appeared slim. The onset of an economic recession after 1873 made free trade seem increasingly untenable; and mounting social disorder, especially in the South, led to growing fears of revolution and prompted demands for a renewal of repressive action of a kind that had so troubled the more sensitive liberal consciences in the 1860s. Various enlightened conservatives drew attention to the desperate poverty of southerners and suggested that urgent social and economic reforms were needed to resolve what was now referred to as the 'southern question'; but when in 1874–5 the government proposed measures to help the poor, the landowners in the South threw up their hands in horror and defected to the opposition.

Politicians of both Right and Left were wary of economic and social change. Many feared that material progress untempered by moral restraints might plunge the country into chaos; and their fears were increased by the rise of socialism. The liberal programme of Cavour and the moderates, founded on the notion of an upward spiral of prosperity, rapidly lost credibility after the early 1870s; and some, particularly on the Left, looked instead to generate a national identity based upon ideals rather than materialism. They put their trust in education and sought to draw on the legacy of the democrats and build a secular patriotic ideology, in which anti-clericalism and a devotion to the institutions of the state featured prominently. From the 1880s a growing number of writers and politicians, conscious of the moral abyss that separated 'real' from 'political' Italy, came to feel that the best hope of 'making Italians' and destroying the moral allure of socialism, lay in a great national war.

The acquisition of the Veneto and Rome gave Italy an overall population of nearly 27 million. The United Kingdom at this time had 32 million, France 36 million. The country bore the hallmarks of demographic backwardness. A third of the population was under the age of fifteen, which reflected the unusually high birth rate. The death rate was also high: in 1871 nearly a quarter of children born alive died in their first year. Average life expectancy was probably little more than thirty. The situation improved gradually in the next few decades and by 1913 the mortality rate was over 30 per cent lower than in 1861. However, the birth rate remained doggedly high by European standards, and by the time the First World War broke out the population had reached some 40 million, despite massive emigration (see Table 5).

About 60 per cent of the population in the 1870s was directly dependent on agriculture. In 1911 the figure was still around 55 per cent, and only in the 1930s did it drop below 50 per cent. In the period between 1860 and 1918 Italy's agricultural sector was of greater relative importance to its economy than the United Kingdom's in the second half of the eighteenth century. Despite this, Italy was in many respects an urban society, as it had been for much of its history. According to the 1881 census, 34 per cent of the population lived in towns with over 10,000 inhabitants, and by 1911 the figure had risen to 42 per cent. The most populous city in 1871 was Naples. With 449,000 inhabitants, it was nearly twice as large as Rome and Milan. Rome and Milan grew fast in the last decades of the century and had populations of more than half a million by 1911; but they were still smaller than Naples (see Table 6).

A number of enquiries in the 1870s and 1880s revealed the appalling state in which the majority of the rural population lived. This was especially worrying given the conviction of many northern liberals in the 1860s that Italy's economic destiny lay with agriculture and the export of food and primary goods. Sidney Sonnino, one of the best

Table 5 *Demographic indicators 1860–1988*

	Italy			France			Germany			Russia			England and Wales		
	A	B	C	A	B	C	A	B	C	A	B	C	A	B	C
1860	38.0/30.9[a]	232[b]	30.5[a]	26.2/21.4	150		36.4/23.2	260	42[c]	49.7/35.4			34.3/21.2	148	42
1900	33.0/23.8	174		21.3/21.9	160		35.6/22.1	229	46	49.3/31.1	252	32[d]	28.7/18.2	154	
1920	32.2/19.0	127	46.6[c]	21.4/17.2	123		25.9/15.1	131		30.9			25.5/12.4	80	53[e]
1930	26.7/14.1	106													
1940	23.5/13.6	103		13.6/18.0	91		20.1/12.7	64		31.2/18.3			14.1/14.4	57	
1960	18.1/9.6	44		17.9/11.3	27		17.4/11.6	34		24.9/7.1	35	67[f]	17.1/11.5	22	
1988	9.9/9.3	9	77.3[g]	13.8/9.4	8	75[g]	11.0/11.2	8	75[g]	18.8/10.1	25	70[g]	13.8/11.3	9	75[g]

A = Births/deaths per 1000 of population
B = Infant deaths under one year per 1000 live births
C = Life expectancy at birth

Note the continuing fall in Italy's birth rate in the 1930s, despite the demographic campaign of fascism.

Notes: [a] 1861. [b] 1863. [c] 1875. [d] 1894. [e] 1913. [f] 1955. [g] 1985.

Sources: B. R. Mitchell, *International Historical Statistics, Europe 1750–1988* (N.Y., 1992); V. Zamagni, *Dalla periferia al centro* (Bologna, 1990).

Table 6 *Population of the main Italian cities (in thousands) 1800–1980*

	1800/1	1850/1	1860/1	1870/1	1880/1	1900/1	1910/1	1920/1	1930/1	1940/1	1950/1	1960/1	1970/1	1980/1
Genoa	91	120	129	130	180	235	272	316	608	635	648	784	812	760
Turin	78	135	178	208	254	336	427	502	597	629	711	1026	1178	1104
Milan	135	242	242	262	322	493	579	836	992	1116	1260	1583	1724	1635
Rome	163	175	184	244	300	463	542	692	1008	1156	1652	2188	2800	2831
Naples	427	449	417	449	494	564	723	722	839	866	1011	1183	1233	1211
Palermo	139	180	186	219	245	310	342	394	390	412	491	588	651	700

Note the continued growth of cities in the inter-war years (despite fascist attempts to encourage 'rurality') and the surge in the period 1950–70. Naples was Italy's largest city until the First World War.

Source: B. R. Mitchell, *International Historical Statistics, Europe 1750–1988* (N.Y., 1992).

informed observers of the period, claimed (not without justification) that the condition of Italian agriculture was worse than in 'every other region of Europe'. Most of the peasants, he said, were crushed by poverty and their burden of work: 'Any advice to save is an irony; every declaration by the law that they are free, and equal to all other citizens, is a cruel sarcasm'. The majority, he felt, knew nothing of what went on beyond their commune; and Italy signified to them simply 'military service, taxes, and the arrogance of the leisured classes'.

Hopes that unification and the advent of liberalism would provide a major spur to production, by opening up the national market, were belied by the extraordinary weakness of domestic demand. More than half of all the grain grown in Italy was consumed by those who produced it. Seventy-five per cent (often much more) of peasant expenditure went simply on food, the rest on clothing and shelter. This ruled out purchases of manufactures or quality agricultural goods, and so afforded little incentive to investment and expansion. Payment in kind was almost universal, and money was scarce outside the main urban centres: salt and pepper often served the peasants instead. Some trade operated between the towns and their rural hinterland, above all in the North, but the poor quality of the road system tended to preclude any long-distance internal commerce.

Certain categories of peasant could sustain a moderate standard of living. The sharecroppers of central Italy, for example, enjoyed some security of tenure, and their farms were often large enough to permit diversification and the spreading of risks. The smallholders in the Alpine valleys were also in general independent. The great majority of peasants, however, whether tenant farmers, proprietors, or day labourers (and many combined these roles) lived precariously. This was particularly true of the day labourers, whose numbers rose in the last decades of the century as the agricultural depression forced small farmers to the wall and drove big landowners, especially in the Po valley, to rationalise production. Day labourers were often lucky to find work for more than half the year, and theft or migration were for many the only means of staving off disaster.

The staple diet of most peasants consisted of *polenta* (made from maize) in the North, and bread of various kinds elsewhere. Acorns, chestnuts, rye, oats, or vegetables were commonly used to make the flour. Meat was eaten rarely, usually only at festivals or during convalescence. The basic diet might be supplemented with olives, nuts, greens, potatoes, water mixed with salt and a little oil (the *acqua e sale* of Apulia), or more rarely wine and cheese. Wheat was beyond the reach of much of the population: a study of 1903 suggested it was unknown in over one-fifth of all Italian communes. The indications are that the living standards of the peasantry as a whole were declining in the last three decades of the century (a remarkable fact given the general rise in prosperity elsewhere), and certainly per capita consumption of wheat dropped from an average of 1.79 hectolitres in 1870–4 to 1.23 in 1889–93 (cf. Table 1).

Poor diet weakened resistance to disease, and in the case of pellagra, the great scourge of the northern plains, effectively caused it. Over half the peninsula was affected by malaria: this was initially debilitating but in the long run fatal. It was only brought under control in the 1940s with the introduction of the insecticide DDT from America. Tuberculosis and other respiratory diseases were widespread, especially in the South. Pellagra was the result of a vitamin deficiency and produced dementia and then death. It was due primarily to a diet based too exclusively on maize, the staple food of the peasants of the Po valley. The incidence of pellagra certainly increased after the 1860s, and a survey of 1879 suggested that over 3 per cent of the population of Lombardy was affected by it, twice the figure for twenty years earlier. This again probably reflected a fall in living standards.

Poor conditions of housing also contributed to ill health. In the lower Po valley, according to Sonnino, most peasant families lived in a single room with a beaten earth floor that turned to mud during the wet winter months. This was true of many other areas as well; and all too often the room had to be shared with a mule or an ox. The immigrant workers of the northern rice fields were particularly ill served: only 20 per cent slept under cover in dormitories, the rest outside. In the South especially, and also in the Roman Campagna, caves, grottoes, and ancient necropolises were inhabited: the 1881 census recorded more than 100,000 people living in 'subterranean dwellings'. Sonnino described to the Chamber of Deputies how on a foray beyond the walls of Rome he had come across as many as forty men, women, and children packed together in airless huts or in chambers carved in the tufa.

Plate 20   The poverty of 'real Italy'. Rural labourers and straw
huts in the Roman Campagna. A photograph probably from the
end of the nineteenth century.

Italian manufacturing in the 1860s and 1870s was still in its
infancy, and almost no modern factory labour force existed yet. The
home market was too weak, and the agricultural sector in particular
too poor, to stimulate domestic production. What few large concerns
there were (such as Ansaldo) depended almost wholly on state orders
for railway equipment or ships. At the time of unification Italy had
500,000 cotton spindles: Britain had 30 million, France 5.5 million.
The annual output of pig iron was a mere 30,000 tons, compared to
four million tons in Britain and a million tons in France. The one
industry of international stature was silk, which claimed about a
third of the world market and employed 274,000 of Italy's 382,000
factory labourers in 1876. However, most of these worked only
seasonally, and half were women and children.

Despite a boom in the early 1880s, Italian industry continued to be
modest in scale until the end of the century and was confined to the
regions of Piedmont, Liguria, and Lombardy (see Table 7). Factory

Table 7 Italy in 1861: regional variations

	Population 1861 (millions)	Value of agricultural production (lire/ hectare) (c.1857)	Cotton spindles (c.1857)	Kms of railway in use (1859)	Kms of roads (1863)	Letters received per inhabitant (1862)	% Illiteracy (1861)	% Primary school attendance
Piedmont/Liguria	3.6	169	197,000	850	16,500	6.1	54.2	93
Sardinia	0.6	23	–	–	986	–	89.7	29
Lombardy	3.3	238	123,046 }	522	20,901	5.3	53.7	90
Veneto	2.3	128	30,000[b]	–	–	–	75.0	–
Parma/Modena	0.9	174	–	101 }	25,766[a] }	2.7[a] }	78.0	36
Papal States	3.2	68	30,000[b]				80.0[b]	25–35[b]
Tuscany	1.9	117	3,000[b]	257	12,381	3.1	74.0	32
Kingdom of Two Sicilies	9.2	81	70,000[b]	99	13,787	1.6	87.0	18
Italy	25.0	104	453,000	1829	–	–	75.0	43

Notes: [a] Excluding Lazio. [b] Estimates.
Source: V. Zamagni, Dalla periferia al centro (Bologna, 1990).

workers were subject to callous treatment and received almost no protection from the state. In 1876 half of them were women, and nearly a quarter were under fourteen years of age. It was not uncommon for children as young as four and five to be employed, particularly in the textile sector. Many mill owners (and politicians too) argued that since Italy had to catch up with other industrial nations, it needed cheap labour and could not afford the luxury of social legislation. A law was passed in 1886 making it illegal for anyone under nine (ten and fifteen in some industries) to be employed in a factory, but it was widely ignored.

Since many factory workers were, according to the season, also agricultural labourers, often working their own plot of land, their outlook tended to be more characteristic of peasants than an urban proletariat. Their sense of time in particular might well be leisurely. This was another reason why employers frequently ill treated them, seeing it as their task to instil in them, forcibly if need be, the disciplines of a modern industrial life. A few employers did take a more humane line. Alessandro Rossi, for instance, a Catholic wool manufacturer, believed that contentment among the workers was one of the best ways of maximising productivity: his factory at Schio was an experiment in harmonious class relations, with housing, leisure, and welfare all catered for and minutely monitored. However, Rossi's Catholic paternalism was intrinsically authoritarian and did not brook the idea of workers' rights.

Rossi was one of the most passionate spokesmen for Italian industry during the first decades of unity. However, his appeals for state assistance for manufacturing fell largely on deaf ears before the 1880s, as it was still widely believed by Italy's ruling class that the country's future lay with agriculture. The one sector of industry that attracted serious government attention in the 1860s and 1870s was iron and steel, for this was seen as vital to defence. It was mainly the deepening agricultural depression of the 1880s that pushed the government into taking up the industrial option, and relatively few were prepared to regard the move as intrinsically desirable. The idea that industrialisation would bring immorality and social disorder in its train continued to be widespread, and this helps to explain why the growth in manufacturing was little more than one per cent per annum before the 1880s.

The hope that economic progress could be achieved in Italy without changing the traditional social order led many (including Rossi) to regard schools as crucial to the moral fabric of the nation. Education was widely viewed as a way of binding the masses to the state and forestalling any perilous slippage towards socialism or clericalism. A growing awareness during the 1860s and 1870s of how intellectually destitute most Italians were added to the sense of urgency: at least two-thirds of the entire population was illiterate, and in many parts of the South the figure was closer to 100 per cent (see Table 7). Under the (for its time, quite enlightened) Casati law of 1859, which was extended to all Italy in 1861, it was incumbent upon local authorities to provide elementary schools and teachers, but a number of enquiries showed that between 40 and 50 per cent of children never set foot inside a classroom at all.

The problem was partly the lack of resources. The number of state primary schools nearly doubled in the first two decades of unity, but in practice most communes, especially in the South, were too poor to provide anything more than the most basic service. The school was often a single room and not large enough to accommodate all the pupils if they turned up. Teachers were badly paid, particularly in remote rural centres. In 1886 the writer Matilde Serao drew attention to instances of schoolmistresses who had died of hunger and neglect. Not surprisingly in these circumstances, qualified applicants were in short supply, and the local authorities frequently laid aside any ideological objections and turned instead to the parish priest: in 1867–8 28 per cent of elementary school teachers were clerics, but in Calabria the figure was 49 per cent.

However, there was also a deep ambivalence towards popular schooling among the Italian middle classes, both on the Left and the Right, and this was a further reason why provision was so frequently inadequate at a local level. A distinction was commonly drawn between instruction – which might simply equip the poor to read socialist newspapers – and education, which should aim to mould good citizens; and the function of elementary schools was in the main to educate, not to instruct. According to the education minister in 1886, Italians should be 'as far as is possible instructed, but above all, they should be honest and hard-working, an asset to their families, and devoted to their king and their country'. However, even such a controlled educational diet was regarded by some as dangerous. A meeting of Sicilian landowners in 1894 demanded an end to compulsory primary schooling on the grounds that this was turning the island's peasants into revolutionaries.

National loyalty and the ethic of work were the two main themes of popular education. One school song spoke of how the children would, when adults, 'rise up, as warrior cohorts', to fight for the king, and 'die, fair Italy, for thee'. The themes of patriotism and industriousness were often linked in school textbooks. Carlo Collodi, the author of *Pinocchio* (published in 1883, itself a fable about the results of sloth and dishonesty), explained in *Giannettino* (1876) the importance of increasing national production, 'so that Italians should not be forced to ask France, England, and Germany for so many, many goods, to pay for which, millions of lire are escaping beyond the Alps'. The most successful children's story of this period was Edmondo De Amicis' *Cuore* (Heart) (1886). Beneath its sentimental veneer lay a stern message about the need for loyalty to the crown, respect for the family, and inter-class harmony.

The largely ethical aims of primary education reflected the concerns of the Italian ruling classes more than the needs of the poor, and it was hardly surprising that many peasants looked upon it as an irrelevance. The fact that lessons were supposed to be conducted in Italian, when most children understood dialect only, was a further barrier to attendance (although in practice most teachers were forced to teach in dialect). If peasants did learn to read and write, it was often as a result of military service. In the mid-1870s about 65,000 young men were called up annually, and in many cases their three years in the barracks were more instructive than any time spent at school. This was to some extent as intended: the army was widely seen as the supreme instrument for 'making Italians', and a safer one than the village school.

If 'education' was for the poor, 'instruction' was for the middle classes. The aim of the moderates after 1860 was to open society to the leadership of the propertied, and the function of secondary and higher education was to define a national ruling elite. The *ginnasio-liceo* and the somewhat less prestigious *istituto tecnico* and *scuola normale* were subject to strict centralised control, and all gave access to university. They had uniform curricula built around classics, philosophy, linguistics, history, and literature. Science and economics were accorded little space, even in the *istituti tecnici*. Attendance at secondary schools underwent a huge expansion in the 1870s and 1880s, as an increasing number of middle-class families sought to take advantage of the liberalisation of the professions and the growth of the bureaucracy to gain access to the sphere of secure, respectable jobs.

The rush towards higher education still did not make the Italian middle classes, however defined, particularly large. Figures for 1881 suggest that proprietors, industrialists, professionals, teachers, private and public employees, and shopkeepers together numbered a little over one million or 6.7 per cent of the total population. In France at this time the figure was 14 per cent. Italy's main shortfall came in the private service sector: France had three private employees for every public one, whereas in Italy the situation was the reverse. The lack of a sizeable industrial base and the relative weakness of sectors such as insurance, banking, and accounting meant that the petty bourgeoisie tended to push their sons towards jobs in administration or the professions. This was especially true in the South.

By the turn of the century Italy had 24,000 lawyers, six times as many as in Prussia, which had a larger population. In the South, there were about twice as many lawyers per head of the population as in the North. Doctors were similarly abundant; so much so that it is likely that more than half of all medical graduates failed to find a job. The growth of the professions (and their increasing political influence) was evident in the composition of parliament, which, especially after the advent to power of the southern-dominated Left in 1876, witnessed a shift in its centre of gravity away from the old landowning elites (represented by the likes of Cavour) towards new cadres of ambitious, upwardly mobile graduates, often of petty bourgeois extraction. One estimate suggested that in 1913 as many as 49 per cent of deputies had been trained as lawyers.

As in the first half of the nineteenth century, the high numbers of law and medical students (57 per cent of those enrolled at universities in 1911–12) posed serious problems of intellectual unemployment. Many entered the civil service, which grew by 68 per cent between 1882 and 1911. Others looked to a career in local politics or perhaps journalism – a fast expanding profession in the later years of the century. Others, however, joined the growing chorus of critics of liberalism. A high proportion of the leading socialists after the 1880s (and sixteen out of the thirty-four parliamentary deputies in 1909) were lawyers; and on the far right, the Nationalists and later the fascists included many struggling journalists, writers, and lawyers, whose frustrations had turned to anger with the entire political system.

The weight of Italy's 'humanistic petty bourgeoisie', steeped in Dante and Virgil, brought up to appreciate rhetoric and forensic skills, and encouraged in general to admire philosophical abstractions more than the concrete, was in part a product of the shortage of openings in the world of business and manufacturing. At the same time, however, this same cultural set was itself a factor contributing to the slow growth of industry. Many commentators noted the aversion of the Italian middle classes to capitalist enterprise and their preference instead for safer forms of investment. Prior to the First World War more than two-thirds of all personal wealth was in buildings, furniture, and land, and less than a quarter in shares, industrial plant, government bonds, and cash deposits. Only in Piedmont and Lombardy was there much interest in the newer forms of wealth.

Italy was certainly not without its industrial culture. In the Veneto particularly, but also in Lombardy and Tuscany, a belief in production was wedded to doctrines of paternalism and class solidarity. This was helped by the strong social presence here of the Church. Lombardy had an important technocratic tradition, in which the engineer figured as the model of the entrepreneur. The Milan Polytechnic, set up in 1864, fostered this tradition and helped to give the engineering profession great respectability. However, such elements of an industrial culture had to struggle to be heard at the national level. Both government and bureaucracy remained dominated by spokesmen of less progressive values, and Italian liberalism as a result risked losing touch with the more vital sections of society.

THE SEARCH FOR A NEW POLITICAL IDENTITY, 1876–1900

The advent of the Left to power in 1876 coincided with a growing loss of faith in moderate liberalism. Cavour's belief that Italian unification would unlock a reservoir of entrepreneurial initiative and talent, long stifled by the old political order, came to grief on the socio-economic realities of the peninsula. The onset of depression from 1873 provided something of a *coup de grâce*. The Right had wanted to confine the role of the state primarily to the maintenance of order and the provision of infrastructures: during the first decade and a half of unity the railway system had grown from 1,829 km to 7,686 km, the telegraph network from 9,860 km to 21,437 km, and 21,000 km of roads had been built. This could not resolve the basic structural weaknesses of the economy, and by the mid-1870s there were calls for a different kind of state intervention.

The Left did not really have a coherent programme. Its disparate ranks were united more by a general opposition to the fiscal and centralising tendencies of the Right than by any consensus about what to do instead. After 1870 the old Left of Garibaldians and Mazzinians had been diluted by new groups, many of them from the South. They saw the state more as an instrument for defending sectional interests than as the embodiment of any putative general will. One important group, for example, behind the victory of the Left in 1876, and which waved in rather transparent fashion the banner of free enterprise, consisted of various financiers who were determined to safeguard the issuing rights of regional banks with which they were connected. In return for this, they were quite happy from 1878 to permit tariffs to be increased on certain industrial and agricultural items.

The manner in which parliament after 1876 was turned into a forum where interest groups haggled with one another for favours, reflected, and at the same time widened, the gap between what critics now referred to as 'legal' and 'real' Italy. The few important laws that the Left passed (and they were confined to a brief period around 1880) were themselves heavily tailored to meet sectional needs. The suffrage reform of 1882, for example, which trebled the electorate to a little over two million (about 25 per cent of the adult male population), ensured that the bulk of the peasantry was excluded by retaining a literacy qualification. This was something that most southern landowners insisted on, and as a result the South ended up with less than one-third of the electorate; by 1895 the figure was just 26 per cent.

The southern deputies formed a powerful bloc in parliament. This was in part because of their numerical strength (two-fifths of the total), but more importantly, perhaps, because it was easier for governments to buy their support than that of the northern deputies, who represented a broader range of socio-economic interests. Most southern deputies asked for no more than a guarantee of the status quo in the South. This they secured through strict policing of the peasantry (with the army sent in when lawlessness was acute), and above all (after 1887) through the concession of a high tariff on wheat, which shielded landowners from the effects of the fall in world grain prices. Middle-class electors were appeased by the periodic allocation of money for public works (which afforded plenty of opportunities for speculative gain), or the granting of jobs or titles.

Agricultural protection (the duty on imported wheat more than trebled in 1887–8) did have a certain economic logic in that it saved Italy from a serious balance of payments deficit, but its main long-term consequence was to accentuate the problems of the South by allowing existing patterns of ownership and production to survive. For many peasants, the outlook was now bleaker than ever. The rise in food prices hit poor consumers hard; and to make matters worse, the government began a trade war with France in 1888. This led to a severe drop in exports of products such as wine, on which a large number of small southern farmers had relied for income. Faced with destitution, many emigrated: between 1881 and 1900 a million and a half peasants settled abroad permanently, mostly in the Americas.

State protection was not limited to agriculture only. During the 1880s governments began to look with increasing favour on industry. This was partly because the arrival of cheap American wheat in Europe after the 1870s made it clear that Italy's economic future did not lie with food exports; and partly, too, because growing international rivalry, above all with France, produced demands for a native armaments industry. In 1884 a state-owned steel plant was created at Terni: by 1889 national output stood at 157,000 tons, compared with less than four thousand tons at the beginning of the decade. Iron production doubled in the 1880s, helped, like steel, by protection. Although the setting up of a metal-making sector was somewhat illogical given Italy's shortage of coal, it did pave the way for a good deal of subsequent industrial development.

Parliament undoubtedly succumbed more and more in the 1880s to

Plate 21 The nation as religion. The monument to Victor Emmanuel II, incorporating the 'altar of the fatherland', erected next to the Capitoline Hill in the centre of Rome between 1885 and 1911. It was supposed to represent the essence of 'Italian-ness'.

pressure from sectional interests; and if the introduction of protective tariffs was somewhat less irrational and self-interested than many commentators suggested, it did nevertheless reflect an increasing tendency among the elites to see government as existing simply to meet their needs. This surrender of principle to short-term expediency became associated with the term 'transformism', the process whereby during the 1880s the old party labels of Left and Right lost their meaning as governments became shapeless amalgams of one-time opponents. In part this development was due to the absence of major reform proposals after 1882: to many, it now seemed logical to bury old differences, and focus collectively on ad hoc issues.

However, transformism was also the result of uncertainty, a feeling that Italy's ruling class needed to close ranks in order to face the growing challenge of socialism. The pessimistic and deeply conservative leader of the Left, Agostino Depretis, a quintessential northern bourgeois, who dyed his long beard white for added gravitas and raised expediency and indecision to fresh heights of political artistry, was worried that 'new social strata' would destroy the institutions: he saw the 1882 electoral reform as a perilous, but necessary, leap in the dark. Marco Minghetti, the dominant figure of the Right, a man of high principles and profound intelligence, was no less fearful. He offered to work with Depretis in their common task of holding back the flood of what he called 'seething demagogy'.

Socialism in Italy drew on a number of different traditions, not all of them readily compatible. Mazzinian radicalism, with its stress on duty, personal dignity, and independence within a collectivist framework, had struck a chord with many urban artisans, particularly in the North, and was an important spur to the establishment of mutual aid societies after the 1840s. These provided sickness relief, pensions, and various other benefits, and filled a gap that the state endeavoured to plug only from the turn of the century. In 1862 Italy had 443 mutual aid societies; by 1885 the figure had risen to almost 5,000. Workers' cooperatives (which flourished from the 1890s) also fed upon a solidarist tradition, though here the ideological inspiration was more often Catholic than Mazzinian.

A much more subversive strand of the working-class movement in Italy was anarchism. The Russian anarchist, Michael Bakunin, came to Italy in the 1860s, and won a lively following among groups of students and artisans, especially in Naples. His ideas of communal autonomy and opposition to the state easily took root in an environment where localism was strong, and resentment at the liberal regime's demands for taxation and military service ran deep. The Paris Commune of 1871 greatly helped his cause: it seemed to offer a working model of spontaneous insurrection and self-government; and the fact that Garibaldi supported it, helped to steer at least part of the old Left (though not Mazzini, who opposed the Commune) towards the anarchist camp.

The split in the International Working Men's Association in 1872 between the Marxists and the anarchists saw Italy ranged firmly on the side of the latter. Marx's idea of a centralised party and state ownership had little appeal in a country of independent-minded peasants and artisans. In the next few years the Italian anarchists gained in strength, above all in the Romagna, where they were organised by an energetic young man called Andrea Costa. However, Bakunin's belief that a revolution could be ignited spontaneously, and then sustained, in the countryside proved unfounded; and two attempts to launch insurrections, one in the Romagna in 1874, the other in Benevento province in 1877, were fiascos. In the second instance, the insurgents met with the near total incomprehension of the peasantry, not least because they failed to speak their dialect.

After 1877 the anarchists turned their attention from insurrection to terrorism, hoping that 'propaganda by the deed' with assassination and bombs would polarise society and generate a revolutionary climate. In 1878 an attempt was made to kill the new king, Umberto I: he was saved partly because his prime minister, an ex-republican, shielded him from the assailant's knife. The government now conducted a crack-down, and many anarchists were rounded up or driven into exile. However, despite this, they remained influential in the 1880s and beyond, particularly in central Italy and in *émigré* circles. It was Italian anarchists who murdered the President of France in 1894, the Spanish prime minister in 1897, the Austrian Empress in 1898, and King Umberto himself in 1900.

From the late 1870s the worsening agricultural crisis caused increasing unemployment, especially in the Po valley, where landless day labourers became both more numerous and desperate. Strikes grew common and were almost invariably violent. The electoral reform of 1882 passed against a background of agitation in the countryside of Cremona, Brescia, Parma, and Mantua; and in the years that followed, to the consternation of the government, the unrest mounted. In 1884 a wave of strikes swept across the entire Po valley. The landowners clamoured for help; they received it in the shape of police and military intervention against workers, the forcible dissolution of peasant leagues and resistance societies, and, in 1887, tariffs.

The strategy of the government was to try and steer the discontent into constitutional channels. It sought to achieve this on the one hand by broadening the country's political base (the 1882 electoral reform), on the other by presenting a resolute and united front in parliament that would give the regime an air of impregnability (transformism). In some ways this succeeded. From the early 1880s revolutionaries, among them Andrea Costa, rejected anarchism and looked instead to build organised parties that would enable workers or their representatives to get into parliament. Costa himself set up the Revolutionary Socialist Party of the Romagna in 1881, and the following year became a deputy. He even agreed to take the parliamentary oath of allegiance, to the chagrin of his less pragmatic friends.

However, the creation of workers' parties did not lead to a rejection of the ideal of revolution. Neither Costa's Romagna party, nor the Lombardy-based Italian Workers' Party (set up in 1885 but suppressed the following year), nor the Italian Socialist Party (1895), renounced the goal of a socialist revolution: the issue was simply how and when the revolution would occur. Nor did the emergence of these parties reduce grass-roots activism. During the 1880s and 1890s a dense network of local leagues and associations sprang up across the Po valley, often headed by middle-class firebrands. These looked to improve conditions of employment and pay, support strikes, and raise political awareness among rural workers. For many employers faced with recession, this often seemed intolerable.

As the tide of 'seething demagogy' continued to rise, Italy's political elite cast around for a means of shoring up the authority of the state. The options were limited. A 'national' platform that would rally the middle classes (let alone the peasants and workers) was hard to locate. The weakness of the economy, aggravated by the recession and overlaid with a deep and growing disparity between North and

South, imparted an urgent note to regional and sectional demands, and made the appearance of a broad-based industrial or agricultural party unlikely. Deputies traded their votes in parliament for funds to build roads, sewers, and opera houses in their constituencies. 'National' issues were generally far less compelling.

One solution dreamed of by some, possibly many, was a reconcilation with the Church. This, they felt, would have given the state legitimacy and provided a powerful ideological shield against the advance of socialism. However, a high proportion of deputies, especially on the Left, remained deeply anti-clerical: the strength of freemasonry among politicians, and indeed among the professional classes in general, reflected this. For its part, the Vatican was also firmly opposed to an agreement. Hostile if essentially needling gestures by successive governments (such as the erection of a statue to the heretic Giordano Bruno in Rome in 1889), kept papal anger alive. Meanwhile, the Church could call upon its own network of parish-based associations (coordinated nationally in the Opera dei Congressi) to spearhead the fight against socialism and liberalism.

The narrow horizons of many deputies, and what could easily be construed as their venality, brought parliament into growing disrepute. This made the problem of the state's authority still more serious. Few writers or journalists were prepared to defend 'transformism', or indeed any aspect of parliament from the 1870s. Giosuè Carducci, the greatest poet of the age, continually decried what he saw as the sordid feebleness of liberal Italy. The dream of Rome, in 1860, he said, had given way to the squalid reality of Byzantium, and a 'farce of infinite pettiness'. The idea of governmental corruption became a regular theme in novels of this period, from *L'Onorevole* (The Honourable Member), by Achille Bizzoni (1895), to Luigi Pirandello's *I Vecchi e i Giovani* (The Old and the Young) (1913). Gabriele D'Annunzio, in *Le Vergini delle Rocce* (The Virgins of the Rocks) (1896) referred to a 'wave of vile greed ... ever more stinking and swollen', engulfing the piazzas of Rome, 'as if the sewers had vomited'.

If denouncing corruption became something of a cliché at this time (fed, no doubt, by the huge growth in the newspaper industry in the 1880s and 1890s, and the resulting demand for sensational copy), there was also a great deal of substance to the charges. A succession of major scandals rocked the establishment in the 1890s, causing many to believe that the entire edifice of the state was in danger. The scandals centred on the banks. In the boom of the 1880s a number became heavily overcommitted, and when the bubble burst in 1887 they were in crisis. One, the Banca Romana, resorted to printing money illegally; but in 1893 it collapsed. Enquiries showed that banks had been in the habit of granting unsecured loans to politicians, and it was clear that these were made in exchange for overlooking irregularities such as those at the Banca Romana. Among the casualties of these findings was Giovanni Giolitti, who resigned as prime minister. His successor, Francesco Crispi, was also involved, but he refused to stand down.

Crispi was the dominant political personality in Italy during the last years of the century. As a former disciple of Mazzini who had fought with Garibaldi in Sicily, he, more than anyone perhaps, felt that the glorious nation of which he had dreamed in 1860 had been betrayed with pettiness and corruption. In the 1880s he attempted to stop the drift into transformism by reinstating clear party lines and rebuilding the Left: he failed, in part because he was too headstrong a character for most of his colleagues. In 1887, when Depretis died, he became prime minister, and immediately set about trying to restore the authority of the state. His policy consisted of limited democratic reforms (for example in local government), giving more power to the executive, and engaging in an aggressive foreign policy.

Crispi's energetic reform programme and warmongering arose from a belief that Italians had failed since 1860 to develop a sense of loyalty to the country's institutions and to think in 'national' terms. The growth of social unrest and the inability of parliament to subordinate private or local interests to those of the nation had convinced him of the urgency of 'political education' if Italy were to avoid moral, and possibly real, disintegration. He set out (as a good ex-democrat) to make patriotism a secular religion, propagating what he called a 'cult of sacred memories' linked in particular to the heroes of the *Risorgimento*, and especially Garibaldi and Victor Emmanuel II. Above all, he looked to mobilise the nation through war; for, as many nineteenth-century Italian patriots had recognised, success in war was one of the surest ways of generating a sense of nationhood.

Crispi's two periods in office (1887–91 and 1893–6) coincided with

Table 8 *Italy's foreign trade (percentage of value)*

	Exports				Imports			
	1886	1913	1922	1938	1886	1913	1922	1938
France	44	9	15	3	23	8	7	2
Germany	10	14	11	21	9	17	8	27
United Kingdom	7	10	12	6	18	16	13	6
USA	5	11	11	7	4	14	28	12
Others	34	56	51	63	46	45	44	53
Total	100	100	100	100	100	100	100	100

Note the importance of France as a trading partner in 1886 and the increased importance of Germany in 1938.
Source: V. Zamagni, *Dalla periferia al centro* (Bologna, 1990).

what one observer called 'the blackest years of the Italian economy'. Crispi himself was partly to blame for this. He had little time for economics, regarding Italy's problems as more moral than material in character; and his belligerent foreign policy raised the spectre of war and undermined business confidence. Investment in industry, which had been so vital to the boom of the early 1880s, dried up, while the tariff war with France, provoked by Crispi for largely political reasons, resulted in a dramatic slump in exports. The value of trade between France and Italy fell from an average of 444 million lire in 1881–7 to just 165 million in 1888–9. Only a small percentage of this lost trade could be made up elsewhere (see Table 8).

Crispi's chief interest was in foreign affairs. He claimed that France was incorrigibly hostile to Italy – for historical and geopolitical reasons, and because of Italy's dispute with the Vatican – and would seek any pretext to attack. However, this was mainly a projection of his own aggressive ambitions. He believed (and here Mazzini's influence was evident) that Italy could only achieve its full potential as a nation at the expense of France: both countries were natural rivals in the Mediterranean; and as long as France, with its great military and revolutionary tradition, could lord it morally over Italy, Italians would never develop a sense of their own worth. 'We are crushed by the French Revolution', he once wrote: 'It presses on our spirits still . . . and prevents us from walking in the footsteps of our fathers. We need to break this moral chain.'

Since 1882 Italy had been allied to Germany and Austria under the Triple Alliance. This was a defensive alliance, but Crispi wanted to put it to a more aggressive use, believing, wrongly, that Bismarck was prepared to do the same. Despite the recession and falling revenues from taxation, he stepped up military spending to its highest level since unification, maintaining that France was planning an invasion; and twice, in 1888 and 1889, he told astonished ministers (and Bismarck) that such an invasion was imminent. (The second of these was due to coincide, he said, with the centenary of the fall of the Bastille.) Bismarck, however, refused to take the bait, and no war ensued; and by the time he fell from power in 1891, Crispi had to admit that his foreign policy had largely failed.

Nevertheless, Crispi's first ministry did succeed in raising the prestige and authority of the executive, and imparting a new sense of direction to government. For some years, critics of parliament had urged this. Pasquale Turiello, in an influential book of 1882, claimed that an authoritarian and militaristic state was needed to pull the nation together: representative government was disastrous in Italy, as it simply mirrored the divisions in civil society. The famous sociologist Gaetano Mosca shared Turiello's disdain for the Chamber of Deputies: it was an amalgam of private interests, he said, 'whose sum is far from constituting the public interest'. Many writers suggested that one possible answer to Italy's political problems would be for the crown to take the initiative from parliament and elevate itself into a strong unifying force.

When Crispi was recalled as prime minister at the end of 1893, the need for strong government seemed more urgent than ever. The banking scandal had recently erupted; the economy was in trouble; the socialists had set up a national party; and in Sicily, a movement of economic organisations called *fasci*, launched the previous year by local intellectuals, which aimed to mobilise the peasants and improve their pay, had grown violent and threatened in the view of many to spark off a more general working-class revolt. Crispi dispatched 40,000 troops to Sicily, and the *fasci* were crushed: he claimed (quite absurdly) that the rioting had been part of a plot by France and Russia to overthrow the state. The leaders were arrested and sentenced to long terms in prison; the Socialist Party was suppressed;

Plate 22   Francesco Crispi (*right*) meeting Bismarck at Friedrichs-
ruhe, Germany, 1887. Crispi was extremely proud of his friendship with Bismarck, but failed, despite repeated endeavours, to
lure him into a war against France.

and the electoral registers were 'revised', and more than a quarter of
all Italian voters (most of them poor) were disenfranchised.

Crispi, however, was not a simple reactionary. He sought to

destroy the threat of socialism (or 'anarchism' as he chose to call it) with reforms as well as repression, and even introduced a bill to split up the larger Sicilian *latifondi* and lease them out to peasants, a move that bitterly angered many southern landowners and greatly weakened Crispi's position in parliament. Crispi's efforts to safeguard the state for which he had fought in 1860 raised a growing storm of protests from all quarters, and when at the end of 1894 he was accused in the Chamber of Deputies of involvement in the Banca Romana scandal, he became convinced that it was no longer possible to pursue the 'national' interest through parliament: it was too riven with factionalism and what he called 'micromania'. In December he prorogued parliament, and for most of 1895 ruled by decree. He prorogued it again in January 1896.

Crispi's drift towards authoritarianism was in part just self-serving; but it was also sanctioned by a tradition on both Left and Right that stretched back well into the *Risorgimento*. Much of Cavour's pro-gramme in the 1850s had been implemented with little reference to parliament, and Garibaldi had advocated (and indeed practised) dictatorial rule as the best form of government in times of emergency. To this tradition Crispi added a juridical justification: nations, he asserted (in what was really just a logical extension of Mazzini's idea of the nation as divinely ordained), had an existence prior to the individuals composing them (*natio quia nata*, in his rather cryptic Latin phrase), and thus had rights of their own – in particular the right to self-preservation. Hence, recourse to dictatorship was accept-able if 'the nation' were in danger.

In a bid to save 'the nation' as well as his own reputation (he found the two hard to disentangle), Crispi looked to foreign policy. In particular he wanted a victorious war in Africa, something that even his old mentor, Mazzini, had felt to be in keeping with Italy's 'mission' in the world. During the 1880s Italy had occupied the port of Massawa on the Red Sea coast, but attempts to push inland and win control of local trade had not met with much success. Early in 1887 500 Italian troops were massacred at Dogali. This was followed in 1890 by the revelation that a treaty signed with the Emperor of Abyssinia, which it was thought had made Ethiopia into an Italian protectorate, had in fact done no such thing due to a mistranslation in the text. Crispi was mortified. When he returned to office in 1893 he set out to avenge the humiliation; but his importunity led only to the most disastrous defeat ever inflicted on a colonial power in Africa when, on 1 March 1896, 5,000 Italian soldiers were killed at the Battle of Adua.

Adua brought about Crispi's fall from power, but it did not bring an end to the air of crisis surrounding the institutions. Socialists, radicals, and republicans clamoured more loudly than ever against the government. In 1897 a leading liberal, Sidney Sonnino, appealed to the king to take the initiative against parliament and return to the strict letter of the constitution: 'Your Majesty . . . The nation looks to You.' Umberto refused to act. In May the following year, however, when serious rioting broke out in Milan, he took a more resolute line, authorising the introduction of martial law. The army opened fire on demonstrators killing at least eighty, and various 'subversive' parties and associations (Catholic ones included) were dissolved and their leaders imprisoned. To add insult to injury, the king decorated the general who had headed the operations for the services he had rendered 'to our institutions and to civilisation'.

In 1899 the government, headed by a Piedmontese general, Luigi Pelloux, tried to push through a package of measures limiting press freedom and curtailing rights of assembly and strike. The extreme left organised a filibuster to block them, and emerged, ironically, as staunch defenders of the constitution. Many argued from this that the 'subversives' were much less of a threat than had often been supposed and might even, in due course, be 'transformed' into government supporters. A new breeze of liberal optimism began to stir, fanned by signs that the economy had moved out of recession. Pelloux dropped his authoritarian package; and even the murder of the king by an anarchist in the summer of 1900 did not trigger a right-wing backlash. For the time being at least, strong government was off the agenda.

7

Giolitti, the First World War, and the rise of Fascism

ECONOMIC GROWTH AND THE IDEALIST REVOLT

The crisis of the 1890s had brought Italy's political system to the brink of collapse. Crispi contemplated a presidential alternative. An elected Chamber, he told the queen in 1895, was unworkable, and suggested that it should be replaced with a non-elected and purely consultative Senate. In 1897 he again voiced his profound disquiet, and urged the adoption of the German model: 'Whenever parliament is involved in government, it leads to the abyss ... The king does not rule, he is ruled ... If we carry on with the present system, we will have a revolution.' Many felt that a revolution, or at least some form of fundamental political or spiritual regeneration, was in fact the answer. Marxism swept the universities in the 1890s and became the dominant creed of intellectuals; and even Gabriele D'Annunzio, Italy's leading exponent of decadentism, crossed the floor of the Chamber of Deputies in 1900 to join the Socialists: 'As a man of intellect, I go towards life', he declared.

The atmosphere of crisis brought to a head the uncertainties about Italy's identity that had been in the air since the 1870s. Crispi's heroic vision of national greatness was rooted largely in the past, in the *Risorgimento*; others preferred to look to an imagined future. The upturn in the economy from the end of the century opened up an alternative path, and for a while rekindled the dream of Cavour and the moderates that the country's liberal institutions could be legitimated through a growth in material prosperity. 'We are at the

Table 9 *Average annual growth of GDP, population, and per capita product 1896–1913*

Country	GDP	Population	Per capita GDP
Austria[a]	2.5	1.0	1.3
Belgium	2.0	1.0	1.5
France	1.9	0.2	2.0
Germany	3.2	1.4	1.8
Japan	2.8	1.2	1.6
Italy	2.8	0.7	2.1
United Kingdom	1.7	0.8	0.9
United States	4.3	1.9	2.4

Note: [a] 1919 borders.
Source: Estimates from A. Maddison, *Phases of Capitalist Development* (Oxford, 1982).

beginning of a new historical period', proclaimed Giovanni Giolitti confidently in February 1901. Giolitti was to dominate Italian politics in the decade and a half leading up to the outbreak of the First World War. Like Cavour, he put his faith in economic modernisation; but unlike him, he looked to industry rather than agriculture to lead the way forward.

The surge in the Italian economy between 1896 and 1914, following decades of sluggishness, was remarkable. For the first time since 1860 the rise in GDP greatly exceeded the growth in population: the average increase in per capita GDP during this period was 2.1 per cent annually, compared to 0.9 per cent for the United Kingdom, 1.8 per cent for Germany, and 2.0 per cent for France (see Table 9). Income levels on average rose faster than at any other time between 1860 and the 1950s, and many Italians had their first experience of what it was to live above the threshold of subsistence, afford a more varied diet, and even to have a surplus left over to spend on consumer goods and services. One measure of the new affluence (though also of growing aspirations) was the rise in primary school attendance. In Sicily, it leapt from 55 per cent in 1901–2 to 74 per cent five years later.

Most of the economic growth in the 'Giolittian period' (as the years 1901–14 are often known) occurred in industry. Sectors such as

engineering and chemicals led the way. Fiat was founded in Turin in 1899, and in the next few years a plethora of other car manufacturers emerged in northern Italy helped, from 1903, by duty-free imports of iron and steel. They included Isotta Fraschini (1904), Lancia (1906), and Alfa (the result of a British initiative of 1906). Pirelli grew rapidly into Italy's first major multi-national company, a pioneer in rubber production and the world's leading manufacturer of insulated cables. Montecatini spearheaded the burgeoning chemical sector: output of one of the key industrial chemicals, sulphuric acid, went up by 10.6 per cent per annum between 1896 and 1913. Another 'new industry' of sorts was sugar beet, which was created from almost nothing in the 1890s with strong government support: sugar production leapt from under 6,000 tons in 1898, to more than 130,000 tons five years later.

Although the fortunes of Italian manufacturing were to depend heavily in coming decades on 'new' industries such as engineering, that grew to prominence in these years, the importance of these industries should not be exaggerated. The Giolittian boom was created in large measure by a sustained, and sometimes major, growth in traditional sectors, especially textiles. Cotton and silk both flourished: the number of cotton spindles almost doubled between 1900 and 1908, from 2.1 million to 4 million, while the silk industry succeeded in retaining a third of the entire world market until the First World War, aided by new developments in dyeing and weaving. The wool industry found life rather more difficult: it was badly affected by strikes and failure to modernise. The continuing relative importance of textiles in Italy is shown by the fact that in 1911 they still accounted for a quarter of all manufacturing jobs.

The often dramatic growth in Italian industry in the Giolittian period was the result of a number of factors. The general upturn in world demand was undoubtedly of prime importance. These were the years of the *belle époque* in Europe, of conspicuous consumption and growing middle class affluence: 'What an extraordinary episode in the economic progress of man', declared Keynes in 1919 of the pre-war era. However, Italy's ability to benefit from the expanding international market was not a foregone conclusion, and depended on other more specific factors. These included a huge rise in foreign earnings, partly from tourism but above all from remittances: more than six million Italians emigrated between 1900 and 1910, and the money they sent home to their families helped maintain Italy's balance of trade and effectively paid for the imports of new plant and machinery on which much of the boom was built.

Another important factor behind the industrial boom was the reorganisation of the banking sector after the scandals of the 1890s. In 1894 steps were taken to ensure that in future the printing of money would be more tightly controlled by the Treasury, a move which irritated the shareholders of the banks of issue, who were worried about their profits, but which guaranteed the economy as a whole a new degree of financial stability. 1894 also saw the creation in Milan of the Banca Commerciale Italiana, with foreign, and mostly German, capital. This was the first of four 'mixed' banks in Italy, that proved vital to the funding of so many initiatives in the Giolittian period. 'Mixed' banks were based on a German model and provided venture capital in situations that other banks might have regarded as too unsafe. They monitored closely the firms they invested in, and had representatives on the company boards.

One of the areas in which the Banca Commerciale Italiana invested heavily was electricity, and the rapid growth of this sector in the 1890s enabled Italy to overcome some of the relative disadvantages it had suffered from in the past due to its lack of coal. Much of the credit for this must go to Giuseppe Colombo, whose awareness of the potential offered by the huge Alpine rivers in the north for hydro-electricity led to the inauguration in Milan in 1883 of Europe's first central generating plant, which lit La Scala opera house, the Galleria, and the surrounding streets. In 1890 Italy produced 11 million kWh of electricity. Thereafter, the industry grew by leaps and bounds, and by 1913 it had a capacity of over 2,000 million kWh, more than France and only a little less than Great Britain. It was this electricity that powered many of the new factories of Liguria, Piedmont, and Lombardy.

The major boom in industry during the Giolittian period was not matched in agriculture. Production in this sector probably rose by about 2 per cent annually, helped by the end of the trade war with France and above all by increased demand from the home market. Technical innovation certainly occurred: new machinery was introduced along with fertilisers and pesticides; and up-to-date instruction was provided by peripatetic bodies known as the *cattedre ambulanti*. However, most of these developments had already begun back in the 1880s in response to the depression; and most were confined to the Po valley. One important new initiative after 1900 was a set of state-funded land reclamation projects. These differed from earlier projects in taking an 'integral' approach, addressing several related problems (such as drainage, irrigation, and deforestation) simultaneously in a designated area. Huge sums were spent on such schemes (the majority in the South), but with only modest results.

The main changes in southern agriculture during this period came about as a result of emigration. In the first fifteen years of the century some four million people (for the most part young rural labourers) left the South to work abroad, principally in the United States (cf. Table 2). They were attracted by the high wages (relatively speaking) to be had on the construction sites or in the factories of America, and by the increasingly cheap transatlantic fares: in 1900 it cost less to go from Palermo to New York than to Paris. The money they saved allowed many peasant families to free themselves from long-standing debts and fulfil their dreams of buying a plot of land back home. Contemporary commentators hoped that this might be an answer to the southern question; but many of the new holdings proved too small or of too poor quality to be viable, and their owners were often soon forced to sell up.

The limits of the Giolittian boom are in many respects as important as the changes. Italy remained an overwhelmingly rural society: according to the 1911 census, almost 59 per cent of the workforce depended on agriculture, and many others were employed on the land part-time. The cities, especially in the north-west, grew; but a high proportion of immigrants from the countryside took up jobs in construction or in domestic service, not in factories, and overall the industrial labour force increased by only about 500,000 in the period 1901–11. Despite the enormous exodus of peasants overseas in these years, the Italian countryside remained hugely overpopulated: according to one estimate, Italy's total agricultural output in 1908–11 could have been obtained using less than half the actual rural workforce, fully employed.

Most Italians, particularly in the South, which scarcely felt the

Plate 23   Emigrants from southern Italy arriving at New York. A photograph by Lewis W. Hine, c.1905. Most Italian emigrants went abroad with the idea of returning home when they had saved enough money; many ended up settling permanently.

impact of the Giolittian boom, continued to live close to the margins of subsistence. Even industrial workers, whose standard of living was probably a good deal higher than many peasants', earned on average in 1911 only about 435 lire a year, of which perhaps 350 would have been spent on food. The principal beneficiaries of the economic boom were probably the middle classes, whose share of the total private wealth according to one estimate went up from 25 per cent to 36 per cent between 1890 and 1914. In 1904 the directors of Ansaldo were paid from 10,000 to 60,000 lire a year, the engineers 3,900 lire, and the book-keepers and secretaries around 1,700 lire. In 1910 civil servants earned on average a little over 2,000 lire, and professors 2,440 lire.

However, the affluence of the middle classes did not mean that Italy's old problem of intellectual under-employment had been resolved. The restricted economic opportunities in the South especially made the allure of a higher degree and a secure job in the civil service or the professions, seem all the greater. From the end of the century southerners started to colonise the bureaucracy in rising numbers. The result (despite a big expansion of the civil service) was continued, perhaps increasing, pressure on the pool of safe middle-class posts. The ranks of those whom one deputy described in 1899 as 'the disillusioned of the universities ... fed on Greek and Latin but dying of hunger, who together constitute that new type of intellectual proletariat, far more wretched and menacing than the economic proletariat', remained formidable.

This was partly, perhaps, why the Giolittian period was intellectually so turbulent, and why Italy's first real taste of economic modernisation led to such ambivalence and uncertainty. The dominant cultural figure of the age, the wealthy philosopher and historian Benedetto Croce, recoiled from materialism and its attendant doctrines – positivism, socialism, and even democracy – afraid that the pursuit of mammon would corrode the fabric of society, unsettle the masses, and deprive the educated of their political and moral leadership. From 1903 Croce and his followers (among them the Sicilian philosopher Giovanni Gentile) embarked on a crusade to win over the middle classes to 'idealism' and to disabuse them of positivism, the creed that had been so fashionable in Italy in the 1890s and had underpinned the advance of socialism, but which was now dismissed condescendingly as merely 'a revolt by slaves against the rigours and austerity of science'.

Croce's 'neo-idealism' was symptomatic, both in its hostility to socialism and in its aggressive elitism, of a broad current of anti-modernist, anti-democratic thought that ran through the Giolittian period. Young middle-class men, whose skills were intellectual rather than practical, and whose financial situation was precarious, resented the new favours being accorded to technocrats and industrial workers, and off-loaded their anger in print. The early years of the century witnessed a succession of radical journals, whose political emphases differed but whose common theme was hostility to materialism. *Leonardo*, for example, started in Florence in 1903, carried in its first number a characteristic attack on the wireless telegraph: 'To send messages without wires seems something almost god-like to fools; but what else is it but the substitution of one material method for another?' Such technical discoveries, it said, might make life quicker, 'but not more profound'.

These journals drew together many of the leading Italian intellectuals of the period and aimed, with increasing self-consciousness, to construct a kind of 'intellectuals' party', whose task would be morally to regenerate Italy and forge a new ruling elite. This was true above all of *La Voce*, founded in 1908 by Giuseppe Prezzolini, whose contributors included Croce and Gentile, the historian Gaetano Salvemini, the economist Luigi Einaudi, the radical priest Romolo Murri, the writer Giovanni Papini, and the poet-artist Ardengo Soffici. It did not speak with a single voice, but it was almost consistently critical of Giolitti and of what it saw as the moral decadence of the political classes ('a superior conception of life and of individual morality forces us to despise that entire pack of men', as one contributor wrote in 1910). It urged a spiritual revolution in Italy, by one means or another (and this is where the disagreement lay), but if need be, through war.

The anti-materialism of the angry young men who wrote in these journals did not always entail a rejection of modernity. What they disliked was not so much the process of industrialisation or change itself, but more the spirit behind it – the assumption (of which the one-time accountant, Giolitti, seemed to them the living embodiment) that the supreme end in life was a comfortable bourgeois existence, free from wants and dangers. In the case of the Futurists – a group of mainly Milan-based artists and writers, led by the flamboyant figure of Filippo Tommaso Marinetti, who from 1909 onwards proclaimed their irreverent vision of the world in a set of 'manifestos' – modernity, or more precisely the modern machine, was glorified; not because aeroplanes or cars made life more comfortable or easier, but on the contrary, because they made it more exciting, insecure, and dangerous.

The influence of journals such as *La Voce*, or groups such as the Futurists, is hard to gauge, and ought not perhaps to be exaggerated. However, the fact that Giolitti failed (and indeed hardly tried) to build a platform of intellectual support for his policies undermined his authority, not least with the middle classes, who were often unable to see the logic of what he was doing; and as the First World War approached, and Italy's economic situation deteriorated, and the threat of socialism seemed greater than ever, so the angry young men of *La Voce* and Futurism were left virtually unchallenged on the moral high ground and found themselves attracting increasing interest and sympathy. Their ideas – initially intemperate, and clearer as to what they loathed than as to what they wanted – started to crystallise into coherent political programmes; and it was from these that fascism derived a good deal of its substance after 1918.

GIOLITTI'S POLITICAL EXPERIMENT

Giovanni Giolitti had been only eighteen in 1860 and had taken no part in the *Risorgimento*. This left him perhaps freer, psychologically, than many of his predecessors to contemplate new social and political directions for Italy. He came from Piedmont, and until the age of forty had worked as a civil servant, rising to the position of Secretary General at the Court of Accounts. By temperament he was dispassionate and pragmatic. He disliked rhetoric, and on a rare occasion when he ventured a quotation from Dante in a speech, there was an audible gasp of surprise in the Chamber. His low-key approach to politics, however, savoured to many of cynicism; and certainly he seems to have felt that most Italians had their price and could be bought off. He had little time for scruples, and once defended the way in which he interfered in elections by claiming it was pointless to try and dress a hunchback in a normal suit of clothes.

It was this lack of moral vision that troubled many of Giolitti's critics. As Gioacchino Volpe, an eminent historian whose worries about the limits of liberalism impelled him first towards the National-ist Party and later towards fascism, wrote: 'Giolitti never seemed to have ... any higher goals beyond the here and now, beyond the attainment of order and personal well-being ... He never called upon the power of emotions to engender faith and draw others behind him ... He could never conjure up the mirage of a great nation, that myth that inspires men to action ... The present, with all its restrictions, and whatever could be realised straight away, were the only things that concerned him. It was all a question of science, rationality, and common sense, with the advantages and short-comings that the excess of these entails.'

If Giolitti seemed to lack ideals, he was certainly not without political vision. He had witnessed the attempts of Crispi and Pelloux in the 1890s to halt the advance of socialism with authoritarianism, and had concluded (though rather late in the day: like many other liberals he had at first supported Pelloux's package of repressive measures) that another tack was called for. With the economy picking up, he aimed to channel some of the new wealth towards the working classes and thereby lure the Socialist Party away from revolutionism and towards cooperating with the government in a more moderate, reformist direction. The pay-off for employers would have been a less militant work force, and also a more productive one: 'It is irrational', he said in his memoirs, 'to think low wages help industry. Low wages mean a poor diet; and an underfed worker is both physically and intellectually weak.'

Giolitti's approach to the working classes was reminiscent, in spirit at least, of the Enlightenment; but his Piedmontese origins ensured that his principal concern was more with the stability and strength of the state than with social justice. 'Keeping wages down might serve the interests of the industrialists', he wrote, in a remark that revealed something of his priorities, 'but it could not be in the interests of the state ... [It] is unjust, and even more than that, an economic and a political mistake.' Central to Giolitti's strategy was the government's neutrality in labour disputes, a radical break with earlier practice, for the police and army had in the past been extensively used to dissolve strikes and intimidate workers. Giolitti wanted levels of pay to be established freely by 'the law of supply and demand'; more importantly, he wanted the working class to feel that the state was not its enemy.

Giolitti was assisted in this strategy by the attitude of key sections of the Italian Socialist Party (PSI), who had concluded (using a Marxist analysis) that Italy could not possibly have a socialist revolution unless it first underwent a process of industrialisation and created a modern bourgeoisie and a factory proletariat. The idea of 'modernisation', indeed, became a shibboleth for many party intellectuals, and seemed at times to drown out the putative goal of revolution. This was especially true of the party's parliamentary delegation, thirty-two strong in 1900; and Giolitti was the man to whom these deputies turned: 'He has understood us . . . Oh, if only he were to embark upon the economic restoration of the country . . . and fashion the heart of a mighty country that was truly modern and capitalist', said one of their number, Claudio Treves, 'what glory for him, what gratitude!'

Giolitti's policy of government neutrality led in the first years of the century to a wave of successful strikes and a dramatic increase in trade unionism. By 1902 nearly a quarter of a million industrial workers were enrolled in socialist-led unions. For the most part, these were national 'federations' of local craft-based unions. The 'Chambers of Labour', the most distinctive, and in many ways most important, institutions in the Italian labour movement, also enjoyed a rapid expansion: from fourteen in 1900, their number rose to 76 two years later. The Chambers were generally run by skilled workers or artisans, and were not only employment centres, but also served to provide leisure and education facilities and to propagate socialist culture and morality. Some even had their own shops or housing cooperatives.

Giolitti did not confine his goodwill towards the working classes simply to non-intervention in strikes. He also introduced Italy's first serious programme of social reforms. In 1902 a law banned children under twelve from employment and restricted the working day for women to eleven hours; and in 1907 a compulsory day of rest, once a week, was instituted. Among other measures were a prohibition on night-work in bakeries, the creation of a Maternity Fund (1910), and the establishment of sickness and old-age funds for certain

Plate 24   Giovanni Giolitti in a photograph of 1908.

professions. A voluntary national insurance scheme had already been set up in 1898, but attempts to expand it ran foul of vested interests, and little progress was made here until after the war. Public works were much less contentious: by 1907 the government was spending 50 per cent more on them than in 1900.

The expansion of the working-class movement, the increase in strikes, the growth in state intervention and public expenditure, and the benevolence of Giolitti towards the Socialists, tested the attitudes of Italian employers to the limits. Some leading industrialists, including Giovanni Agnelli, Camillo Olivetti, and Giovan Battista Pirelli, were sympathetic to the Giolittian experiment. Travel, and in certain cases study abroad, had given them a modern vision of capitalism, with a taste for risk and planning, a belief in profit, and an acceptance that the conflict between capital and labour was a component of, if not a spur to, progress. This, however, was not a common view. Most Italian employers remained wedded to the idea that the government should further their interests through favours and concessions, and not worry about the workers.

The scepticism of many industrialists towards Giolitti remained muted as long as the economic boom continued and profits held up. Between 1897 and 1907 wages in industry rose in real terms by around 2.2 per cent per annum, while per capita productivity increased by nearly 3.0 per cent. After 1907, however, and above all after 1912, the speed of economic growth slowed fast, and with profit margins falling, manufacturers responded by organising cartels and stepping up pressure on the government for orders and contracts. Giolitti's benevolence towards the workers now rankled with them more than ever. Italy, they argued, as a latecomer on the industrial scene, could not hope to emulate Britain or Germany in their labour relations without seriously damaging both output and competitiveness. Production must take precedence over social justice, it was claimed. Otherwise Italy would remain an impoverished second-rate power.

The growing hostility of Italian employers towards Giolitti weakened him politically; but his programme was already foundering on internal contradictions. For one thing, the neutrality of the state in labour disputes was easier to promise than to secure: violence often erupted during strikes; who provoked or started it – police or workers – was almost inevitably hard to establish, and led all too easily to mutual recriminations. Moreover, the fact that Giolitti relied very heavily on southern deputies for his majority in parliament meant that he was forced to pursue a dual policy: in the North industrial modernisation, in the South the preservation of the *latifondo* economy, with absentee landlords, feudal residues, and harsh, often inhuman, labour relations.

These inconsistencies would not have mattered so much if the Socialist Party had been unanimous in its support for Giolitti's programme. But it was not. The party was divided between reform-ists – such as Claudio Treves and Filippo Turati, high-minded men of university education and austere principles, whose faith in positivism and belief that society evolved according to strict scientific laws were combined with a deep and generous humanitarianism – and militant revolutionaries, intolerant of 'collaborationism', and influ-enced by new currents of thought which gave primacy to the irra-tional in politics: will, intuition, violence, and myth. Among the revolutionaries, the syndicalists were especially strident: they wanted a seizure of power through a general strike, and the fusion of economic and political power in workers' syndicates or unions.

The inability of Giolitti to stop the police opening fire on strikers – over two hundred were killed or wounded between 1900 and 1904 – dealt a crucial blow to his political strategy. The revolutionaries in the Socialist Party denounced these so-called 'slaughters' and up-braided their reformist colleagues for thinking that anything good might come from a collaboration with Giolitti. In 1904 the revolution-aries were victorious at the PSI party congress; in 1908 the reformists won back their majority; but in 1912 they lost it again to the revolutionaries, now dominated by young firebrands such as Benito Mussolini. Giolitti was thus unable to 'transform' the Socialists; indeed his attempts at courting the left ended up, it seemed, polarising Italian politics more than ever.

Among those who were most hostile to Giolitti's strategy were a group of dissident young writers and journalists, collectively known as the Nationalists. They started in the early years of the century in Florence, and used the medium of literary journals to express their hostility to the Italian bourgeoisie and the liberal parliamentary system, all of which they regarded as too effete and corrupt to save the nation from the threat of socialism. Giolitti's pragmatism and lack of ideals, and his view that extremism could be bought off with reasonableness, seemed to them symptomatic of the failure of Italy's ruling class. They urged a more vigorous authoritarian government, to inspire the masses, extinguish class warfare, and lead the nation forward to greatness.

The Nationalists were by no means a coherent group: they were

Plate 25   The masses mobilised. Agricultural labourers and their families in front of the trade union headquarters of Coccanile di Copparo, Ferrara, during a strike in 1910. Ten years later such buildings were ransacked by the fascists.

united more by a common radicalism of tone than by any strict uniformity of ideas, and not all were properly speaking anti-liberal. However, one theme recurred with great regularity in their writings: the value of war as an instrument for galvanising the bourgeoisie and creating a sense of collective purpose. Italians, they felt, needed to realise that the nation was prior to the individual; and the individual must learn to subordinate his selfish material desires (and socialism was the acme of materialism; and Giolitti its handmaid) to the interests of the nation as a whole. A war would teach Italians how to die for an ideal. It would also purge the bourgeoisie of what the sociologist Vilfredo Pareto called 'its stupidly humanitarian sentiments', and forge a new ruling elite.

Italy's growing economic problems after 1907, and mounting unease at Giolitti's attitude to the Socialists, gained the Nationalists a new audience. Industrialists in particular found their views attractive. A more robust approach to the Socialists was welcome to them; so, too, at least for some, was the prospect of higher military spending; and so, too, was the idea of equating the 'national interest' with greater production. International instability, and the threat of a

European war sparked off by the crisis in the Balkans or colonial rivalry in Africa, added to the Nationalists' appeal, and at the end of 1910 a major congress was held in Florence, which brought together a galaxy of Nationalists of varying political and intellectual hues. It also gave birth to the Italian Nationalist Association, which in the next few years helped transform Nationalism into a major political force in Italy.

The most vocal figures at the Florence congress were the advocates of war. Enrico Corradini, a former seminarist, and minor playwright and novelist who from the beginning of the century had been the leading spokesman for the Nationalists, set the tone with his opening address. Italy, he declared, was 'a proletarian nation morally and materially'; and just as the working classes had been spineless and divided before socialism taught them the value of conflict, so the Nationalists must now teach Italians the virtues of 'international struggle': 'What if that means war? Well, let there be war! And let Nationalism stir up in Italy the will for victory in war.' War, he said, was the path to 'national redemption'; it was a 'moral order', a way of creating 'the inexorable necessity of a reversion to the sentiment of duty'.

The growing atmosphere of belligerency in Italy provided the backdrop for Giolitti's extraordinary decision in September 1911 to invade Libya. His motives were mixed. He was worried, it seems, after the Moroccan crisis in July, about a possible French invasion of Tripolitania; and he was keen to protect Italian economic investments that had been building up in Libya in recent years. More important, though, were domestic considerations. A successful war, he hoped, would appease Nationalist opinion; it might also constrain the Socialists (or at least their parliamentary deputies) to decide where they stood – with or against the government; and the signs were that some reformists were now fully prepared to enter the cabinet, if need be at the price of splitting their party.

Giolitti's political calculations went badly wrong. The invasion was tolerably successful – though it was hugely expensive and left Italy saddled with a colony that it could never fully control (tens, perhaps hundreds, of thousands of Arabs were to lose their lives in Libya during the next thirty years resisting Italian rule). The Nationalists gave Giolitti no credit for the war: they claimed it had been mishandled – and used it as a further stick with which to beat Italy's ruling class and the parliamentary system. The Socialists denounced the invasion; and any prospect of their being 'transformed' and led into the constitutional fold now vanished. A few reformists left the party; most stayed, to suffer the taunts of the revolutionaries who felt that their mistrust of Giolitti was finally vindicated.

The Libyan war destroyed the Giolittian system. The extremes of both left and right grew in prestige and size, and drew sustenance from the moral bankruptcy of the liberal centre. The Nationalists started to crystallise into an anti-system party; and by 1914, thanks largely to the work of a brilliant lawyer, Alfredo Rocco, they had formulated a blueprint for a new type of state that would minister to the needs not of the individual but 'the nation', and in which all 'producers' (managers as well as workers) would be disciplined in monolithic trade unions. The PSI was now led by the revolutionaries; the syndicalists were 100,000 strong by December 1913; and even the anarchists started to enjoy a resurgence, and took part in a series of violent riots and strikes that rocked Italy during what was later called 'Red Week', in June 1914.

Having failed to broaden the base of legitimacy by 'transforming' the Socialists, Giolitti looked instead to the Catholics. From the early years of the century relations between the government and the papacy had steadily improved: with the rise of socialism, liberalism had come to seem the lesser of two evils and a potential ally, even, in the war against materialism. In 1904 the papal ban or *non expedit* was relaxed for the first time, and Catholics allowed to vote if it meant keeping out a Socialist. In the 1909 elections the *non expedit* was dropped in about 150 constituencies, and the turnout in such strongly Catholic areas as the Veneto rose quite dramatically. A few Catholic deputies now even sat in parliament, though the Vatican made it quite clear that they were not in any sense spokesmen for Church opinion.

This rapprochement of Church and state was entirely pragmatic and was never official; it could not be unless the Roman question were solved, and neither Giolitti nor his more radical supporters were prepared to make any concessions on that score. Giolitti, indeed, once said that Church and state were as 'two parallel lines, which should never meet'. The result of such rigidity of principle was that the liberals failed to tie the huge organisational structure of Catholicism firmly to the state. In the 1913 elections the Catholic Electoral Union (the body set up by Pius X to mobilise the vote of the faithful) backed liberal candidates in exchange for certain pledges; but the deal was meant to be secret, and when news of it leaked out Giolitti faced a revolt in parliament, and his government collapsed. Giolitti himself denied the existence of the deal, so dashing any hopes that Church and state might now be able to embark on some kind of formal alliance.

Giolitti had needed the Catholics in the 1913 elections, for the year before a new electoral law (conceived initially as a bait to lure the Socialists into government) had been passed which granted the vote to almost all adult males. One of the hopes was that the enlarged rural vote could be used as a conservative counterweight to the cities; and the fact that the tally of government deputies fell by only about 60, to 318 deputies out of 511, while the number of PSI deputies went up, undramatically, from 41 to 79, seemed to vindicate this. However, the liberals had depended on organised Catholicism for their relative success. They themselves had no party machine of any kind with which to confront the new mass electorate; and the old tools of clientelism and prefectural interference were unsuited (at least in their current form) to securing the working-class, or even the petty bourgeois, vote.

Above all there was still the problem of what the liberal state stood for in Italy. The Giolittian period had coincided with a major surge in the economy; but the great mass of the population, particularly in the South, had been untouched by the changes; and even those parts of the urban (especially northern) middle classes who had profited were bound to feel sceptical by 1914, given the militancy of socialism, as to the political wisdom of economic 'progress'. Without its material claims, however, what could Italian liberalism represent? 'We cannot offer Paradise in heaven, unlike our Catholic colleagues', declared a leading liberal, Antonio Salandra, in 1913, 'nor can we offer Paradise on earth, unlike our socialist colleagues.' Instead, he claimed, 'the very essence of Italian liberalism is patriotism'; and it was in accordance with this belief that Salandra led Italy into the war in May 1915.

ITALY AND THE FIRST WORLD WAR

The outbreak of the First World War in the late summer of 1914 was not met in Italy with any general demand for intervention. Italy was still, in theory at least, an ally of Germany and Austria–Hungary under the Triple Alliance, first signed in 1882 and then renewed at more or less regular intervals thereafter; but because Austria declared war on Serbia without consulting Italy, in contravention of the terms of the treaty, the Italian government decided it was under no obligation to the Central Powers and for the time being remained neutral. This accorded, it seems, with the general mood of the country; but it did not satisfy everyone. Some maintained that if Italy stayed neutral it would be excluded from any future territorial settlement; and in the Balkans especially, that might prove disastrous. Others felt strongly that Italy ought to enter the war for domestic reasons, that somehow or other war would be the making of the nation.

Among those most strongly in favour of joining the war – although they often disagreed as to which side Italy should support – were the various groups of intellectuals who had been identified since the beginning of the century with the 'revolt against positivism', and who had strongly opposed Giolitti. The Futurists had already declared in a famous slogan that 'war [was] the only cure for the world'; and Marinetti greeted the outbreak of fighting in 1914 as 'the most beautiful Futurist poem yet'. The Nationalists regarded Italy's entry into the war as a means whereby 'the nation' could assert itself against parliament and, if necessary, 'destroy [it], overturn the benches of the embezzlers, and purify, with fire and steel, the procurers' dens'. Many intellectuals saw the war as a chance to forge a national community and complete the work of the *Risorgimento*.

Nor was support for intervention limited to the political right. On the left were various elements who also felt that Italy should enter the fray. The democrat and ex-socialist Gaetano Salvemini thought the experience of a war would make ordinary Italians more politically aware and hence more assertive, and so finally break the power of the old elites, especially in the South. Further to the left, a number of syndicalists and anarchists felt that entry into the war might generate the right conditions for a revolution, a view also shared by a few within the PSI, notably the editor of the main party newspaper, the brilliant but volatile journalist, Benito Mussolini. In October 1914 Mussolini publicly came out in support of intervention; and was promptly expelled from the party.

The 'interventionists' were highly vocal and ready to use almost any means to push the country into war. However, they were never anything but a minority. The PSI stuck resolutely to its demands for neutrality – the only west European socialist party to do so. Catholic opinion was in general against intervention; so, too, were a majority of liberal deputies. Giolitti maintained in a famous phrase that Italy could secure 'quite a lot' by negotiating with the other powers to stay neutral. Businessmen were for the most part afraid of the disruption that a war would cause, though they were also concerned that if Italy stayed out of the war she might end up deprived of vital imports of raw materials, above all from France and Britain.

In the end, Italy was propelled into the war as a result of secret deals made by the prime minister and the foreign secretary behind the back of parliament, and without the army or even, apparently, the king being privy to the negotiations. When, at the beginning of May 1915, it became clear that Italy had been committed to the war on the side of Britain and France, there was an outcry. Some 300 deputies left their visiting cards with Giolitti as a sign of support for non-intervention. But it was too late. To back down now would have entailed a disastrous loss of face. The Futurists and Nationalists, and other interventionists, including Mussolini, staged a series of noisy pro-war rallies: the 'nation' had spoken. The king submitted to the inevitable, and Italy entered the war.

The events of May 1915 were in retrospect to seem a turning point in the history of liberal Italy. Mussolini, Gabriele D'Annunzio, and the other leading supporters of intervention took the credit for Italy's entry into the war; and it was achieved, they claimed, in defiance of parliament and other enemies of the nation, above all the Socialists. It was, they said, a revolution: 'real Italy', the Italy of the piazzas, of heroic ideals, and patriotism, had triumphed over 'political Italy', the Italy of venal, selfish, and cowardly politicians. In truth, though, the overwhelming mass of Italians had greeted intervention with silence; a silence that probably signified not so much hostility or even indifference, but resignation.

During the next three and a half years some 5 million Italians were conscripted into the army, and more than 600,000 of them were killed fighting in the trenches high up in the Alpine foothills of Friuli and Trentino. The majority of the front-line soldiers were peasants, primarily from the South; and for most of these, Italy's mission to secure from Austria the 'unredeemed' territories of the South Tyrol and Istria must have seemed irrelevant. Conditions in the army were severe, even by contemporary standards: rations were poor, pay extremely low, and leave restricted to just fifteen days a year. Discipline was also harsh: decimation was encouraged when individual culprits could not be found; and between 1915 and 1919 nearly 300,000 soldiers were brought before courts-martial, mainly for desertion.

Morale was low, and this contributed to Italy's humiliating defeat at Caporetto in October 1917 – militarily and politically the most damaging episode of the war, when the Veneto was overrun, and some 300,000 Italian soldiers taken prisoner. However, not everybody's experience of the war was negative. Among the younger officers in particular (and especially those, like Mussolini or Marinetti, who had been active in interventionism), there was often a strong (and apparently sustained) feeling that the war was both worthwhile and heroic. This attitude was in large measure political. It stemmed from a need to vindicate the decision to enter the war; and it was also a posture against the neutralism of the PSI and the equivocal stance of many liberals.

Herein lay the political tragedy of the war. Far from healing the rifts that had so threatened the stability of liberal Italy before 1914, the experience of 1915–18 served to fragment the nation more than ever. The PSI was now irredeemably beyond the constitutional pale; mistrust and hatred of the Vatican was fuelled when the pope called the war a 'useless slaughter' (some generals felt he should be hanged); and the government was widely condemned for failing to clamp down on defeatists (the PSI). Moreover, the fact that the army insisted on prosecuting the war without interference from politicians (from August 1916 politicians were banned from the war zone entirely) meant that parliament would derive little credit or prestige from victory; yet the military also blamed the government when things went wrong.

Plate 26   The Futurists in peace and war. Above, the artists
Carlo Carrà and Umberto Boccioni (seated), and behind them,
left to right, the writers Palazzeschi, Giovanni Papini, and
Marinetti, in 1914. Below, Marinetti (*left*) and the artists Antonio Sant'Elia (killed 1916), Luigi Russolo, and Mario Sironi, at
the front in the north-eastern Alps, 1915–16.

The government (and parliament) thus had the worst of both worlds, and despite some vigorous initiatives undertaken by the new prime minister, Orlando, after Caporetto, Italy's ruling class, and its liberal institutions, emerged from the war with their reputations probably more tarnished than enhanced. This was unfortunate and also in many respects unfair, for the manner in which the country had coped with the production demands imposed by over three years of fighting was little short of miraculous. Italy had begun the war, for example, with just 600 machine guns: it finished it with 20,000; by 1918 it had more heavy guns in the field than Britain; and its aircraft industry had developed from virtually nothing in 1914 to producing some 6,500 planes in 1918, with a workforce of 100,000.

This astonishing achievement was the result of state planning and regulation on an unprecedented scale. Any firm seen as necessary to the war effort was designated 'auxiliary'. Its prices and its production targets were then fixed by a government committee, and its workforce subjected to military discipline. The distribution of raw materials, particularly coal, was carefully monitored. By the end of the war Italy had almost 2,000 'auxiliary' firms, the majority in the northwest. Some of them had expanded almost out of recognition. Fiat, for example, had 4,300 workers in 1914 and produced 4,800 vehicles; in 1918 it had over 40,000 employees and produced 25,144 vehicles. Ansaldo's workforce rose from 6,000 to 56,000; and its massive output in the war included 3,000 aircraft, 200,000 tons of merchant shipping, and 46 per cent of Italy's artillery.

Such huge economic expansion was the result of war; and adjusting to peace proved profoundly difficult. It was not only a question of falling government orders and the problems of converting from a primarily military market to a civilian one. Expectations had also changed, making a return to pre-war economic relations very hard. The feeling of having contributed vitally to the war gave many workers a new sense of political worth, and after 1918 they reacted to the threat of unemployment and a drop in the standard of living with exceptional militancy. Many employers, for their part, had grown used to strong state support; and a resumption of governmental neutrality produced feelings of indignation and even betrayal.

More important than these economic changes, however, was the

Plate 27   The domestic front: women street cleaners in Milan.
As in other European countries, the economic mobilisation of
women during the First World War encouraged demands for
their political emancipation. These demands were not met.
However, fascism was to be more attentive to women than the
liberal state.

myth that the First World War engendered. The fact, not merely of
surviving, but of actually winning the war – in October 1918, exactly
a year after the humiliation of Caporetto, the Italian forces threw
back the Austrians in a final drive across the River Piave to Vittorio
Veneto, where they proclaimed victory – meant that a whole set of
political and moral values acquired a new aura of legitimacy, and
could mount a powerful challenge to Italy's much battered liberal
identity. The war was held up as a triumph for the ideals of May
1915, ideals that certainly had a positive dimension (for example in

patriotism, or the craving for vigorous leadership), but whose principal manifestations were negative: the loathing of socialism, equality, materialism, parliament, humanitarianism, democracy, and pragmatism.

THE COLLAPSE OF THE LIBERAL STATE

When the First World War began none of the belligerents knew quite what principle they were fighting for. Salandra, indeed, had negotiated Italy's entry under the unfortunate slogan, 'sacred egoism'. By November 1918 the situation was very different: by accident rather than design, the winners turned out to be democracies, the losers (including Russia) autocracies; and the war had thus, it seemed, been fought in defence of democracy. Italy, an erstwhile ally of imperial Germany and Austria, was now bracketed with Britain, France, and the United States, and it no longer had any political or moral justification for resisting demands for the full 'representation of the people'. In December 1918 the government conceded universal male suffrage. This was followed in August 1919 by a still more unmanageable concession, that of proportional representation.

The liberals had been pushed into an untenable position. Without an organised party to mobilise the electorate, they were at a huge disadvantage compared to the Socialists, with their Chambers of Labour, local leagues, and trade unions. Nor could they rely (as Giolitti had done in 1913) on the Church, for early in 1919 a new Catholic party, the Partito Popolare Italiano (PPI), was founded, which, though not strictly speaking 'confessional', was nevertheless run by Catholics, with a specifically Catholic programme. It appealed largely to the peasantry (small peasant proprietors in particular) and was led by a priest, Don Luigi Sturzo. It had no reason to feel beholden to the liberals. The crisis facing the government was clear in the elections of November 1919: the Socialists won 156 seats and the *Popolari* (as members of the PPI were commonly known) 100, while the liberals and their allies were reduced to under half the Chamber.

Had the government been able to take full advantage of victory, it might have fared better. However, the Italian delegation at the Paris peace conference demanded more than it might reasonably have hoped to gain, and ended by being severely rebuffed. Italy won

Trent, the South Tyrol, and Istria; it failed to secure Dalmatia and
the Italian-speaking port of Fiume (Rijeka); and the prime minister,
Orlando, walked out of the conference in disgust. The way was now
open for the Nationalists and other interventionist groups to de-
nounce what they called the 'mutilated victory'. They had already
been inclined to argue that Italy had won the war despite its political
leaders; now, it seemed, the government could not even win the
peace. Their anger mounted after June 1919 when Orlando was
replaced as prime minister by Francesco Saverio Nitti, whose conciliatory approach to the Allies earned him the soubriquet *Cagoia* ('vile
coward') from Gabriele D'Annunzio.

In September 1919 D'Annunzio marched into Fiume in a military
coup organised by the Nationalists and supported by a number of
generals and industrialists. For over a year the city remained occupied. Nitti shrank from sending in the army, partly for fear of a
mutiny: this added to the growing moral bankruptcy of the liberal
state. Left to its own devices, Fiume became an experiment in
alternative government, with a constitution drawn up (though not
implemented) by revolutionary syndicalists, and a new political language whose essence was passion and theatrical effect. D'Annunzio
improvised speeches from balconies and roused his audiences to
frenzies with meaningless chants and slogans. It was only fitting that
such an outlandish manifestation of the 'revolt against reason' should
be suppressed by Giolitti: in December 1920, as prime minister for
a fifth and final term, he ordered in the navy, and D'Annunzio
surrendered.

Watching D'Annunzio at Fiume with some jealousy was Benito
Mussolini. He had spent much of the war (after a spell at the front)
in Milan editing *Il Popolo d'Italia*, the newspaper he had set up after
being expelled from the Socialist Party. His sympathies were still
with the left; but the problem that he and other exiles from the PSI
faced was where to find a political following. In 1918 he altered the
masthead of his newspaper to, 'Combatants' and Producers' Daily':
the term 'producers' had strong syndicalist and Nationalist overtones,
and suggested that Mussolini was trying to detach himself from the
Socialists and move closer to these other interventionist groups.
However, when in March 1919 he launched a new movement, the
Fasci di Combattimento, in Milan, its programme was still close to

Map 6   Italy since 1919.

that of the PSI: the abolition of the Senate, a constituent assembly, confiscation of war profits, and land for the peasants.

Mussolini and the assortment of Futurists, syndicalists, and Nationalists who supported him at this time, were politically at sea. They shared a belief in the war and loathed parliamentary liberalism; but they had no clear platform, and certainly not one that differed markedly from the Socialists. Mussolini's predicament was made clear in the elections of November 1919: no fascist deputy was returned, and even in his home town of Predappio in the Romagna, Mussolini failed to win a single vote. In this situation, the only option was to move to the right, and in the course of 1920 many of the most conspicuous left-wing elements of the fascist programme were dropped. What remained was an emotive mixture of strident patriotism, justification of the war, concern for national greatness, and, linked to all these, a growing aversion to the Socialist Party. Fascism now began to attract the attention of the more conservative sections of Italian society.

However, the growth of the fascist movement in the second half of 1920 was due to factors beyond Mussolini's control. Above all, it was linked to the threat (or rather, perceived threat) from the Socialist Party. The PSI ended the war estranged from the state, vilified by the interventionists, and more committed than ever to the rhetoric of revolution. Its confidence was increased by the victory of the Bolsheviks in Russia in 1917. The reformists were drowned out by the militants, who agitated among factory workers and day labourers and kept alive their hopes of an impending collapse of the system with a succession of violent strikes, factory occupations, and clashes with the police. A wave of food riots swept across northern and central Italy in the summer of 1919, and shops were looted, trees of liberty planted, and local republics declared. Over a million people went on strike in 1919; the following year the figure was even higher.

Much of this militancy stemmed from the economic crisis that faced Italy after 1918. Unemployment soared, reaching 2 million by the end of 1919, as troops were demobilised and wartime production was scaled down. Inflation also rose: the wholesale price index leapt by nearly 50 per cent between 1918 and 1920. This had devastating consequences for rentiers and those (like civil servants) on fixed incomes. In the countryside, landlords, many of whom had suffered as a result of a wartime freeze on rents, were confronted by angry ex-servicemen demanding land. After the disaster at Caporetto the government had repeatedly promised 'land to the peasants' in order to raise morale. The landowners now paid the price; and the government even sanctioned 'illegal' occupations of estates with two decrees, in 1919 and 1920, that guaranteed the peasants security of tenure.

Employers, faced with new and terrifying levels of militancy, looked to the government for help; but the government refused to take a stand – partly out of fear, but partly also from a belief that a revolution could be averted through compromise. This approach reached its climax with the so-called 'occupation of the factories' in September 1920, when for nearly four weeks almost half a million workers took over their plants and shipyards, expelled the managers, and ran up the red flag. Giolitti failed to send in troops, and even harried the factory owners into making concessions. Moreover, he agreed to set up a commission to draft a bill that would make it mandatory for trade unions to be able to inspect company books. For many employers this was the final straw, the ultimate act of government betrayal; for many, too, it seemed that the revolution had finally come.

It had not; and in many ways September 1920 marked the high point of post-war labour militancy. In the local elections of October–November the Socialist vote fell back slightly, although the PSI did make some notable gains, above all in rural areas of the Centre and north-east: in Ferrara the red flag was hoisted over the town hall, the old Castello Estense, and slogans, including 'Viva Lenin!', were scrawled on its walls. However, despite the rhetoric and the militant posturing, the national leadership of the PSI failed to press seriously for a revolution. Serrati, the party's dominant figure, had grave doubts (in private) about the maturity of Italy's working class; and he felt, probably rightly, that the Allies would have intervened to crush a socialist insurrection. The result was a fatal gap in intentions between grass roots and the top.

Without a national strategy, the unrest of the 'red biennium' of 1919–20 was perilously uncoordinated. In some areas, the syndicalists were dominant; in others, the anarchists made the running. In Turin, a talented group of young university graduates led by Antonio Gramsci carried out an experiment with elected 'factory councils' intended as building blocks for a new worker-run state; but the experiment did not translate to other cities. The absence of coherent leadership deprived the workers' movement not only of direction but also of resilience, and when in the second half of 1920 the Italian economy went into severe recession, many rank and file supporters began to peel away, frightened lest continued militancy result in victimisation by landowners or manufacturers, desperate now with prices and profit margins falling to cut their costs.

It was against this background that the fascist movement suddenly took off at the end of 1920. Para-military groups or 'squads', usually led by ex-junior officers, and backed very often by the local military and police, sprang up across northern and central Italy. They began in Istria and Friuli, carrying out 'patriotic' raids on Slav-speaking councils and institutions; but from the late autumn onwards they turned to a greater 'national enemy', the Socialists, whose insidiousness had been magnified in the eyes of many by the recession, the occupation of the factories, and the recent administrative elections. By the spring of 1921 fascism had become a mass movement. Its strongholds were in the Po valley (in towns such as Ferrara, Bologna, and Cremona) and Tuscany. These were the areas in which peasants and rural labourers had been most organised and militant.

The squads were composed of young men, often barely out of their teens. Many were students of petty bourgeois extraction; many, too, were smallholders and sharecroppers angered by the PSI's policy of land collectivisation; and many had served in the war. They claimed to be restoring law and order and saving Italy from the clutches of Bolshevik tyranny. Those who had been the victims of Socialist agitation and abuse (and they included vast swathes of the petty bourgeoisie, particularly public employees, whose level of income had dropped dramatically in 1919–20, both in real and relative terms), agreed. The squads were in their view simply doing what the liberal governments had lacked the resolve to do. Beating and killing socialists, burning and ransacking Chambers of Labour and PSI headquarters, and forcing opponents to drink castor oil, were easily seen as acts of zealous patriots saving the nation.

In the space of a few months the entire edifice of the working-class movement in Italy collapsed. The leaders of the PSI stood passively by. Some of them even helped the fascists by splitting the

Plate 28 Civil war, 1920–2. Above, a typical fascist squad: the *Disperata* squad of the *fascio* of Ponte a Egola, Florence. Below, their enemies: socialist 'Red Guards' during the occupation of the factories, September 1920.

party at the worst possible moment: in January 1921, at the Livorno
congress, Antonio Gramsci and a number of his friends walked out
of the conference hall in disgust and founded the Italian Communist
Party (PCI). Only a minority of the PSI followed, and the Communists won just fifteen parliamentary seats in the May elections. They
were little more than a marginal force, distinguished by the quality
of their leaders not the size of their support. Their main political
contribution was negative. They added to the PSI's already severe
demoralisation; and they furnished the fascists with some excellent
propaganda: Italy now had a real 'Bolshevik' enemy in its midst.

The eruption of the fascist movement in the winter and spring of
1921 surprised Mussolini as much as anyone. It also alarmed him.
The earliest fascists had been syndicalists, Futurists, and dissident
Socialists, with radical leanings. The *squadristi*, by contrast, appeared
crudely reactionary and were in effect tools in the hands of the local
landowners or businessmen, who sponsored them. They were inspired
by little more than a blind hatred of socialism and a love of violence.
In addition, they were hard to control. Their prime allegiance was to
the squad leaders or *ras* – rebellious, ebullient characters such as
Roberto Farinacci in Cremona, Italo Balbo in Ferrara, and Leandro
Arpinati in Bologna – and Mussolini struggled throughout 1921 to
impose his own authority. He even tried in the summer to make a
formal peace with the Socialists; but the *squadristi* rebelled and
threatened to depose him in favour of D'Annunzio.

The growth of the fascist movement in 1921 and 1922 depended
crucially on the attitude of the authorities. The police and the army –
who had been constant targets of Socialist abuse and violence during
the 'red biennium' – willingly lent a hand to the *squadristi*, furnishing
them with weapons and transport or, more importantly, turning a
blind eye to their criminal brutality. They felt disinclined to heed
government directives requesting that the law be enforced impartially.
Anyway, the government was itself manifestly sympathetic to the
movement (if not to its excesses): in the elections of spring 1921
Giolitti allowed Mussolini and the fascists to join the list of government parties. He hoped this would be a way of tempering their
extremism (which he was inclined to dismiss as a neurotic by-product
of the war) and absorbing them into the system.

In fact, the elections of 1921 simply compromised the government and allowed the fascists to act with greater impunity than ever. Henceforth, any prefect or policeman who thought fit to oppose the *squadristi* could expect a telegram from the Minister of the Interior informing him that he was being transferred or suspended. Moreover, thanks to Giolitti the fascists now had thirty-five deputies in parliament, quite needlessly; and the Chamber was even more riven and unworkable than before, with the PSI and the Communists gaining 138 seats, and the *Popolari* 107. For the next eighteen months Italy had a succession of pitifully weak governments, whose lack of authority was continually exploited and added to by the *squadristi*, who rampaged almost unchecked across northern and central Italy. By the early summer of 1922 the fascists claimed 300,000 members; and elated by their success, many called for a revolutionary seizure of power.

The lawlessness of the squads was both an asset and a liability for Mussolini. On the one hand it gave him great political leverage at the centre: he could promise to tame his followers in return for being given a share of power. On the other hand he had to show that he really could control the movement; and that was not easy. Local fascist bosses such as Balbo or Farinacci certainly acknowledged Mussolini's political skills and his virtual indispensability as a national leader; and they agreed in October 1921 to allow the 'movement' to become a party, the Partito Nazionale Fascista (PNF), which left Mussolini in a position of greater formal authority. However, the *ras* also knew their own strength: without the unruly *squadristi*, Mussolini would have lacked political muscle and would have been in no position to negotiate – as he was increasingly able to do during 1922 – the terms on which he would enter a coalition government.

Mussolini was thus forced to walk a political tight-rope. He had to reassure men such as Giolitti and Salandra that he had little sympathy for his followers and their subversive demands, and that when in power he would do his utmost to curb them; at the same time he was forced to placate his rank and file by alleging that his negotiations with the liberals were just a tactical ploy, a Trojan horse with which to penetrate the enemy citadel, which, once inside, he would set about destroying. Mussolini's own preference may well have been for a peaceful and altogether constitutional entry into government – the offer, perhaps, of a few fascist ministers in a coalition led by Salandra. But the *squadristi* felt otherwise: they wanted their revolution. At a mass rally in Naples on 24 October, 40,000 of them called for a march on Rome.

The idea of a march on Rome was pregnant with historical associations. For Mazzini, Garibaldi, and their democratic followers it had been both a symbol of national regeneration and the means whereby 'the people' would take Italy for themselves and inaugurate a new era of spiritual greatness. However, the fascist March on Rome, held on 28 October 1922, was far from glorious. Three straggling columns of ill-armed young men converged on the capital in pouring rain. A number of post offices, police stations, and prefectures were seized. Mussolini remained in Milan, well away from the action and close to the Swiss border: he seems to have had little faith that the gamble would succeed. But the king (for reasons that remain obscure) lost his nerve and refused to sign a decree authorising the army to open fire and disperse the rebels; Mussolini was summoned to Rome, and at thirty-nine became Italy's youngest ever prime minister.

8

Fascism

The March on Rome did not seem to most contemporaries to mark a watershed. No riots or demonstrations broke out; the routine of daily life continued uninterrupted; and the press reported the events as if they were just one more dramatic episode in Italy's chaotic and violent post-war drama. The general mood was, if anything, one of relief – a sense that the confusion and uncertainty of the last few years was now over and normality about to return. Most observers anticipated that the *squadristi* would be absorbed into the system; and many believed that this would provide a badly needed injection of spiritual energy, that would strengthen the institutions and narrow the gap between 'real' and 'political' Italy. Politicians such as Giolitti were quietly dismissive of Mussolini, whose plebeian manner and evident insecurity encouraged them to think that he could be manipulated without difficulty, used, and then discarded when he had served their turn.

Mussolini was appointed prime minister in an essentially constitutional way, but in deference to the rank and file a 'victory' parade of *squadristi* was held through the streets of Rome in order to foster the illusion of a *coup d'état*. This schizophrenic start set the tone for the following two years. Mussolini had to alternate between appeasing the establishment (on whom he depended for continuance in office) and reassuring the provincial fascist bosses and their followers that he was still a subversive. However, for all their intemperance of language, it was not evident what the radical or 'intransigent' fascists wanted in place of the liberal regime. They knew what they loathed and what they aimed to destroy, but few of them had any constructive political ideas. Fascism was without a distinctive programme.

In this situation, Mussolini bowed to the prevailing calls for a return to stability, order, and normality. His government was to be one of national reconciliation: three cabinet posts went to fascists, the rest to liberals, *Popolari*, a Nationalist, the philosopher Giovanni Gentile, and two leading figures in the armed forces. He quickly set about disciplining the *squadristi*: in January 1923, in a move of brilliant ambiguity, he created the fascist Militia (MVSN). This was ostensibly 'to safeguard the fascist revolution' but its main political purpose was to bring the rank and file party members (who were to form the bulk of the Militia) under centralised command and to curtail the power of the local *ras*, such as Roberto Farinacci. The clamourings of these squad leaders for revolution and their persistent recourse to violence threatened to destroy Mussolini's credibility with the establishment.

Mussolini's drive for conservative respectability was extraordinarily wide-ranging. He annulled the decrees sanctioning the peasant seizures of land after the war, to the particular delight of the southern *latifondisti*. In deference to the Church, crucifixes were restored to certain public places and large sums of public money earmarked for repairing churches damaged in the war. In 1923 a major education reform act made religious instruction compulsory in elementary schools; it also accentuated the division between middle-class *licei*, with their stress on the humanities, and working-class technical schools. Foreign policy was equally conservative: the pragmatic settlement of Italy's claims in Dalmatia in 1924 was widely applauded by the liberal establishment; and so too (more curiously) was the bombardment of Corfu in 1923 following the murder of an Italian boundary commissioner.

Arguably the most important step in Mussolini's search for respectability came with the absorption of the Nationalists into the PNF in February 1923. The Nationalists – who were elitist, monarchist, socially conservative, and hostile to parliament – lacked a large mass following, but from a political point of view they were enor-

Plate 29   Mussolini with two fascist bodyguards during a visit to
London in December 1922. His brusque manner and somewhat
uncouth behaviour did not go down well in diplomatic circles.
Mussolini often cultivated a demonic stare in photographs.

mously influential, for they had support in the highest places: among
army generals, academics, top civil servants, wealthy businessmen,
and at court. They were thus a perfect complement to fascism with
its broad base among the petty bourgeoisie and parts of the peasantry,
but relative shortage of 'quality' personnel. The merger proved
crucial to the development of the regime: it brought the talents and
ideas of men such as Alfredo Rocco and Luigi Federzoni, who after
1924 were to be the chief architects of the fascist state.

The fascist party itself was not wholly devoid of intellectual
content. The majority of *squadristi* may have been boorish and
anarchic (as their slogans and chants – such as 'me ne frego', 'I don't
give a damn'– suggested); but some, and especially those who had

joined the movement at the beginning in 1919, had been strongly influenced by syndicalist ideas and looked to cast fascism in a radical mould. They wanted an end to the class war, and aimed at a new kind of state, built upon 'corporations' or 'syndicates', in which workers and employers would cooperate to further the economic interests of the collectivity. Private enterprise was to be strictly regulated and made subordinate to national needs. This syndicalist strand of fascism was most apparent in the PNF's trade union movement, which developed into a powerful political force after 1922, thanks primarily to the committed leadership of Edmondo Rossoni.

The persistence of radicalism within the fascist party was not necessarily to Mussolini's disadvantage – unless it got badly out of hand. Indeed, as long as Mussolini appeared genuinely eager to restore Italy to 'normality', his liberal allies were prepared to grant him all the assistance he needed in the fight against subversion, wherever it came from. The most striking example of this was the Acerbo bill of 1923, which proposed that the party list that received the largest number of votes in an election, provided it gained at least a quarter of all votes cast, should automatically be given two-thirds of the seats in parliament. This was an extraordinary measure; and the fact that it was passed with the support of Giolitti, Salandra, and Orlando bore witness to the enormous hostility that many liberals felt to the existing electoral system, which had permitted the socialists to swamp the Chamber and saddled Italy with a succession of weak administrations.

The only constitutional party that did not support the Acerbo bill was the Catholic PPI. They had a profound problem with fascism: while many of the upper clergy, including the pope, were sympathetic to Mussolini (not least because of his concessions on education), a large number of parish priests and local PPI supporters were deeply hostile, since they, and the Catholic unions and cooperatives they ran, had often been targets of fascist violence. The result was a fatal split in the party. Don Sturzo, the PPI leader, tried desperately to hold it together; but Mussolini exploited the rift with skill, expelling the *Popolari* from his cabinet and pressing the party into opposition. Frightened of a breach with Mussolini, Pope Pius XI made clear his dissatisfaction with Don Sturzo; and Don Sturzo, as a priest, had no option but to resign. Henceforward, the PPI was a broken force.

Armed with the Acerbo Law, Mussolini could face the elections of April 1924 with confidence. The government list of candidates comprised fascists, ex-Nationalists, right-wing liberals (including Salandra and Orlando), and even a few *Popolari*. The *squadristi* were instructed not to use violence against the opposition, as the elections were to be an irreproachable demonstration of the government's respectability and of the broad support it enjoyed. In the event, widespread violence did occur, though it is questionable whether it had much material effect on the result, which depended to a large degree on such time-honoured instruments as clientelism and intervention by the prefects. The government won 66 per cent of the vote, and was thus entitled to two-thirds of seats regardless. A little over half of the new deputies were fascists.

Mussolini's bid for respectability appeared to have worked; and so, too, it seemed, had the liberals' aim of drawing Mussolini into the constitutional fold. Socialism was no longer a threat (the PSI had been reduced to under 5 per cent of the vote, the PCI to less than 4 per cent); nor were the Catholics; and with the post-war economic crisis receding and prosperity returning, many must have felt that Italy was about to embark on an era of political calm. The *squadristi*, however, thought otherwise. They expected Mussolini to use his majority in parliament to destroy the liberal system and deliver the long-promised revolution into their hands. Early in June 1924 a group of PNF extremists kidnapped and killed the reformist Socialist deputy Giacomo Matteotti, who a few days before had delivered a damning speech in parliament cataloguing fascist violence in the recent elections. Mussolini's credibility was now on the line.

Mussolini denied involvement in the murder, despite certain suggestions to the contrary. However, the extent to which he was or was not personally responsible for the killing was not really central to the crisis that now unfolded. At issue, rather, was the character and purpose of fascism: was it a constitutional or a subversive force? Mussolini faced a very awkward dilemma. To disown the *squadristi* and all their violence would have been to cut himself off from his most committed followers and leave himself at the mercy of the liberal establishment; but not to do so would have meant accepting that fascism was criminal. He was trapped. He tried to appease his liberal allies, making the ex-Nationalist Luigi Federzoni Minister of

A Concise History of Italy

the Interior, and subjecting the Militia to military discipline; but these moves only infuriated the *squadristi* without convincing the growing ranks of Mussolini's opponents.

Fortunately for Mussolini, the opposition parties had responded to news of Matteotti's kidnapping by simply walking out of parliament in protest. He was therefore unlikely to be defeated on a vote in the Chamber. This gave the king a perfect pretext for not dismissing him. However, as the crisis deepened, and as the press brought into the open more and more evidence of the involvement of senior fascists in crimes, so Mussolini's position came to seem increasingly precarious. By mid-December Giolitti and Orlando had gone into opposition; and Salandra was about to join them. Two days after Christmas the so-called 'Rossi memorandum' was published in an opposition newspaper, a damning indictment of Mussolini's role in Matteotti's killing. The government appeared to have no choice open to it except resignation.

However, if Mussolini went, the *squadristi* would have been in dire trouble. They would have lost their jobs in the Militia or in local government; and many of them might also have faced prosecution. On 31 December a group of leading Militia members delivered an ultimatum to Mussolini: either he act against the opposition or they would unleash a reign of terror. Mussolini was stymied: his only option now was to risk declaring a dictatorship. On 3 January 1925 he entered parliament and challenged his enemies to indict him: 'If fascism has been a criminal association ... the responsibility is mine', he declared. Neither the king nor the opposition moved. They were no doubt afraid of civil war; and they were probably unclear as to exactly what Mussolini's intentions were. Their indecision cost liberal Italy dearly.

PARTY AND STATE

The speech of 3 January 1925 is often seen as a watershed, the moment when the liberal parliamentary system in Italy finally expired and gave way to the fascist dictatorship. In reality, however, the fascist regime did not come into being overnight; nor did it ever achieve a final definitive form. In the absence of any clearly devised programme or ideology, it developed in a rather haphazard way, reacting, often pragmatically, to pressure from internal interest groups or responding to specific economic and political circumstances. Mussolini sought to make a virtue of this: fascism was all about spontaneity, intuition, and impulse, he claimed. But the main reason for the eclecticism was that Mussolini, like his predecessors, was never in a strong enough position to behave with any real coherence or consistency.

Just as the fascist regime emerged in an ad hoc manner and never assumed a definitive form, so the liberal state was never really abolished. In fact, continuity was more striking than change. The *Statuto* remained as Italy's constitution; the king was still head of state and commander of the armed forces; and the machinery of administration was preserved almost untouched. The bureaucracy was not subjected to a systematic purge and was dominated, as before, by career officials: between 1922 and 1943 only about one third of all prefects were 'political' appointments from outside the traditional corps. The police and *carabinieri* were similarly unpoliticised: from 1926 until 1940 the police were headed by a conservative career prefect, Arturo Bocchini, whose outlook was staunchly utilitarian rather than ideological.

The limited 'fascistisation' of the state after 1925 reflected the extent to which Mussolini still depended on the traditional elites. Formally, he was no more than prime minister; and just as King Victor Emmanuel had appointed him premier in 1922, so he could always dismiss him (as in fact he did in the end) if the pressure to do so became sufficiently strong. As a result, Mussolini dared not alienate the establishment; and though much of the rhetoric and imagery of the regime were heavily radical, the substance was profoundly conservative. Furthermore, the rank and file fascists were hardly qualified to take over the machinery of the state. Very few of them had any administrative experience or training; and many would perhaps have been better suited, temperamentally and intellectually, to a brawl than to office work.

The need to achieve an accommodation with the traditional elites meant that Mussolini's main task after 3 January, as before, was to destroy the power and independence of the fascist squads. His strategy was imaginative. In February he appointed the leading 'intransigent', the Cremona *ras* Roberto Farinacci, secretary of the

PNF. On the face of it, this seemed a victory for the *squadristi*; but it was a poisoned chalice, for Farinacci was being asked to behave 'responsibly' and discipline the party – something he found almost impossible to do. In October the Florentine *squadristi* rioted and murdered eight liberals. Farinacci tried to excuse their behaviour as the result of 'legitimate exasperation'. Mussolini rebuked him violently; and a few months later he felt strong enough to deliver the *coup de grâce*, and sack him.

The man who replaced Farinacci as PNF secretary, Augusto Turati, was a far more accommodating character. In line with Mussolini's wishes, he conducted a thorough purge of the party, expelling some 60,000 members (mostly young *squadristi*) between 1926 and 1929. In many places the local party section was completely reconstituted using 'respectable' people. These included a high percentage of public employees (lesser civil servants, schoolteachers, post office clerks), for whom membership of the PNF was now made virtually obligatory – in 1933 it became completely so. The leaders of the party at local and provincial levels tended after 1926 to be professionals or landowners, men who in the earlier 1920s were liberals and quite probably anti-fascists too. In the South, aristocrats often took over the key posts.

The political emasculation of the PNF was sealed by a new party statute in October 1926, which introduced rigid centralisation. Henceforth all posts were to be appointed from above, which meant that the organic link between a local *ras* and his followers, the source of so much squad violence in the past, could now be severed. The following January Mussolini resolved the question of the relationship between state and party at a provincial level in favour of the state. The prefect, he declared, was to be supreme: 'All citizens and particularly those who have the great privilege and honour to be members of the fascist party, owe respect and obedience to this highest political representative of the fascist regime.' The state had thus taken over fascism, and not (as many had feared, and Farinacci hoped) vice versa.

The main reason why Mussolini felt able to curb the *squadristi* was because by 1927 he had broken the back of the constitutional opposition. This was achieved with remarkably little trouble. Those politicians who had walked out of the Chamber of Deputies in protest at the murder of Matteotti were debarred from returning; but the PPI was already moribund, and the PSI had split into squabbling factions; and the various liberals and radicals, such as Giovanni Amendola, who still attempted to resist fascism, were impotent without the backing of the king, and soon gave up. The formal suppression of the opposition came in October 1926. Following a series of attempts on Mussolini's life, all opposition parties were banned, and a new law – 'for the defence of the state' – made it illegal for them to be reconstituted.

The press, too, was shackled. In the wake of the speech of 3 January 1925 the law on censorship was strengthened, and newspapers carrying criticisms of the government were liable to be sequestrated. However, conformity was achieved in most cases without coercion. The industrialists who owned the principal newspapers were keen to avoid a clash with Mussolini, and sacked offending editors and replaced them with others who were politically safe. Journalists knew that if they stepped out of line they too would be fired. The result was a press that was uniformly bland in its political reporting. Its tone was hyperbolic, with glowing coverage of the government's actions and fulsome accolades to Mussolini. 'Fascistisation', however, did little damage to sales, partly no doubt because of the popularity of the sports and cultural pages.

That Mussolini could establish a one-party state and eliminate the forces of opposition with such relative ease, showed the extent to which the old liberal parliamentary system had forfeited its claim by the mid-1920s to moral authority. It also reflected the fact that the new regime was being constructed to accommodate and protect the traditional ruling groups, who for decades had felt threatened by the demands of the masses. The loss of a certain degree of freedom seemed to many a fair price to pay for greater security; and anyway, what had that 'freedom' amounted to with the liberal state, but a licence to strike, protest, and subvert the nation? Moreover, the restraints imposed by fascism turned out to be, for the middle classes at least, negligible or just irritating, rather than genuinely oppressive.

The appeal of the fascist regime lay in its attempt to resolve many of the problems that had beset the liberal regime. The power of the state, which had seemed so undermined in the past by the concern with individual rights, was reinforced, above all, with Alfredo Rocco's Public Safety Law of 1926. This rejected 'the dogma of personal liberty as the foundation and goal of society', and made the security of the state (now conceived of as a living organism with rights of its own, in accordance with Nationalist ideas) all important. The police were given greater powers of arrest, and could send a man into 'internal exile' (*confino*) for up to five years for a suspicion simply of *intending* to engage in subversive activities. Citizens lost all possibility of redress against decisions of the executive. Government and state were now one.

In pronouncing its rejection of the 'principles of 1789', fascism was heir to that broad current of idealist thought, stretching back (albeit with certain variations) through Gentile and Croce to De Sanctis and Mazzini, which had emphasized the need to forge a moral community or 'nation' in Italy, and so repair the damage done by centuries of division and servitude in the peninsula. Without an ethic of collective loyalty, deriving from a strong sense of national identity, the individualism and materialism inherent in liberal ideology would, they had argued, operate corrosively and breed selfishness and disorder. Fascism sought to remedy this. It aimed to discipline the workforce using a new structure of trade unions (the so-called 'corporate state') and simultaneously educate them politically through propaganda. If the regime appeared in many regards reactionary, its experiments in the orchestration of consent often struck contemporaries (and not just in Italy) as novel and progressive.

THE FASCIST ECONOMY

Fascism's scorn of materialism and preference for spontaneity over planning deprived it of a coherent economic strategy. Will, not reason, shaped the fascist universe. 'For me', Mussolini told parliament in December 1925, 'life is all about struggle, daring, and determination.' This voluntarist outlook coloured the regime's attitude to the economy. Italy's relative poverty, it was alleged, had been due mainly to the lethargy of the old liberal ruling class: what was needed was a new aggressive spirit to rouse the latent energies of the nation. Hence the belligerent tone of Mussolini's principal initiatives. The 'battle of grain' (1925) was followed by the 'battle of the lira' (1926), and the 'campaign for the national product'; and industry

was called upon to form a 'common front' to resist the threat posed
to Italy by foreign competitors.

The language of battle was intended as a surrogate for the socialist
rhetoric of class and became particularly marked from 1925 as
fascism reinforced its ties with employers. If wages were cut, or
conditions of work harshened – as they tended to be in the later
1920s – this was because the well-being of the nation required such
sacrifices. The enemy was not within, but overseas: all Italians,
whether managers or employees, were engaged in a common struggle
to make the country strong and ward off attempts by the older
industrial states to prevent Italy from becoming a serious economic
competitor. The idea of an international 'plutocratic' conspiracy was
used increasingly by the regime in the 1930s to explain, and justify,
Italy's growing international isolation.

In the first years of his government Mussolini adopted an orthodox financial policy intended chiefly to reassure (and win over) the
economic establishment. Public spending was reduced, and efforts
made to balance the budget; taxes on war profits were reduced or
abolished; and Giolitti's controversial proposal for a register of
shareholders was shelved. Mussolini was fortunate in that his advent
to power coincided with an upturn in the world economy. This, and
the ending of the extraordinary charges for war expenditure which
had weighed so heavily on the exchequer in 1921–2, helped him to
achieve a budget surplus in 1924–5. The success of his economic
programme in 1923–4 was an important factor helping him to
weather the storm brought on by the murder of Matteotti.

The creation of the one-party state after 3 January 1925 obliged
Mussolini to rethink his economic strategy. He still needed the
support of industrialists and landowners for political reasons (and
the PNF was anyway in no position to provide an alternative
managerial class); but he now came under pressure from powerful
sections of the party, above all in the trade unions, who wanted the
fascist revolution to entail the restructuring of the state along syndicalist lines. In the spring of 1925 the fascist unions (or 'corporations'),
led by Edmondo Rossoni, became increasingly militant, staging
several major strikes: that of the Lombard engineering factories in
March involved more than 100,000 workers. The employers grew
alarmed; so did Mussolini, and he now set out to tame the unions.

In April 1926 one of the key items of fascist legislation, the Syndical Law, was passed. It was the work mainly of the Minister of Justice, Alfredo Rocco, a great admirer of the German economy with its cartels and monolithic unions, and whose ambition it was to regulate and discipline the Italian economy in the interests of production. His chief concern was to bring labour under the control of the state. The law offered some sops to the syndicalists: for example, it confirmed the fascist unions in their monopoly of negotiations and set up an independent tribunal to provide compulsory arbitration whenever a dispute was deadlocked; but its substance was highly conservative. It banned strikes and go-slows; and above all, it failed to subject the employers to state or party supervision.

The result was an economic system which left the employers with the whip-hand. While the workers were represented in negotiations by centrally appointed PNF officials (in general middle-class graduates), managers were able to speak for themselves. Mussolini continued to refer to 'corporatism' and the 'corporate state', partly in deference to leading fascists such as Giuseppe Bottai, for whom the Syndical Law was simply a staging post on the road to mixed unions (or 'corporations') of workers and employers and a planned national economy; but in reality the balance of power had tipped firmly against the syndicalist wing of the party. Edmondo Rossoni was sacked in 1928, and the Confederation of Fascist Syndicates, of which he had been head, was split up and, in effect, politically destroyed.

Henceforward, whatever it was to be, the 'corporate state' would not be syndicalist. Nor would it benefit the working classes. Despite such grandiose documents as the 1927 Charter of Labour, with its proclamation of guarantees on a variety of social and labour issues (almost all unfulfilled), it was clear that fascism had little in real terms to offer either industrial workers or peasants. During the late 1920s wages were substantially reduced in many sectors following a major revaluation of the lira, and though the cuts were supposed to be broadly in line with the fall in prices, millions of workers in fact experienced a decline in living standards. The formal creation of the 'corporate state' in 1934, did nothing to alter this: the twenty-two new 'mixed' corporations of employers and employees lacked power, and all the important economic decisions continued to be made as before.

The consequences of pandering so much to the employers were particularly dire in the South – economically as well as socially. Mussolini had announced on the eve of the March on Rome that he intended to solve the southern question; but once in power, he looked to win over the great landowners and refused to take steps that might cost him their support. This was especially galling to the government's principal agricultural expert, Arrigo Serpieri. In 1924 he introduced a radical bill on 'integral land reclamation' (*bonifica integrale*), which was designed to force landowners to contribute to the costs of improving their estates, or else face expropriation. The southern landlords (Serpieri's principal target) were furious and lobbied to have the expropriation clause removed. They succeeded, thereby destroying any real chance that 'integral land reclamation' would have much effect in the South.

The programme of 'integral land reclamation' had rather more impact elsewhere in Italy, though in general its achievements were much less dramatic than fascist propaganda alleged. The novelty of the scheme lay in its provision of a comprehensive ('integral') and interlocking package of measures (such as irrigation works, aqueducts, dams, roads, and houses) to transform designated areas. In some places, for example the Tuscan Maremma and the Roman Campagna, the results were quite impressive. The most striking (and most publicised) success came in the Pontine Marshes to the south of Rome, where thousands of hectares were transformed into small farms and villages. However, in most cases 'integral land reclamation' was applied too unsystematically to have any real effect on agriculture.

Serpieri's failure to force the southern landowners to contribute their share to land reclamation (he tried in 1934 to have expropriation reintroduced, and was sacked) was symptomatic of the government's impotence in the South during the fascist period. The PNF here was largely controlled by the *latifondisti*; and without any independent political representation, the peasantry had no effective means of resistance against wage cuts or breaches of contract. The living standards of southern labourers and smallholders appear to have fallen in the inter-war years, in some cases perhaps dramatically (above all in the 1930s); and the fact that the United States had, after 1921, introduced quotas on the number of immigrants it would accept, shut off the South's most important safety valve.

The full extent of the South's suffering under fascism can only be guessed at, as the regime banned discussion of the 'southern question' (on the grounds it had now been resolved) and forbade damaging references in the press to poverty or crime. Many smallholders undoubtedly went bankrupt in the later 1920s as a result of the revaluation of the lira. They could now no longer meet their mortgage repayments and had to sell out. The world recession after 1929 was probably even more ruinous, as it caused a huge drop in exports of goods such as citrus fruits, on which numerous small southern farmers had depended. The increasing poverty in the South led tens of thousands of peasants to quit the land and move to the big cities (despite official interdictions: beggars were bad for the regime's image) (cf. Table 6). It also, in all likelihood, encouraged a growth in crime.

Given that the South had always suffered from overcrowding, the regime's attempt to increase the Italian population through its much vaunted 'demographic campaign', seems particularly odd. It was an instance, however, of the primacy of politics over economics under fascism. Mussolini launched the campaign in 1927, declaring that the Roman Empire had declined because of its falling birth rate and that one of contemporary Italy's greatest assets was its demographic vitality. His main source for these ideas was Corrado Gini, a demographer who had been heavily influenced by contemporary French and German theories of decadence. However, Mussolini was probably also encouraged by Catholic and clerical groups: he was actively pursuing a resolution of the 'Roman question' at this time, and a campaign to raise Italy's birth rate would certainly have been welcome to the Vatican.

The demographic campaign was a mixture of propaganda and financial incentives. Large families were extolled; prolific mothers were given prizes and received by the Duce (who quickly had two more children himself); family benefits were introduced in the 1930s, together with tax reliefs on children, 'birth grants', and 'marriage loans'; and a special punitive tax was imposed on unmarried men. However, these and other measures seem to have had little impact on the birth rate, which continued its long-term, steady decline – especially in the North, where it fell below replacement level in some areas. The population did rise: from 41 million in 1931 to around

Plate 30 The 'battle of grain'. On the left is a poster advertising a national wheat exhibition, 1927 ('year five' (A(nno)V) of the regime). On the right, an advertisement for a national wheat-growing competition. The head and torso are classical, though perhaps more Greek than Roman.

47 million in 1950; but this was due mainly to declining mortality rates –and was well short of Mussolini's target of 60 million (Table 5).

The high birth rate among the peasantry was one reason why the regime devoted so much propaganda to agriculture and 'rurality'; but fascism did not put its money where its mouth was, especially after the onset of the Great Depression. In the 1930s many of the agricultural initiatives of the liberal period (such as the *cattedre ambulanti*) were scaled down or discontinued. Moreover, prices in industry did markedly better than those in agriculture. The one important exception was wheat, which, thanks to the 'battle of grain' (launched in 1925 to make Italy self-sufficient in cereal after a disastrous harvest) received heavy protection. This encouraged the production of grain, but also shielded inefficient farmers; and in the South the long-term results were particularly deleterious, as wheat displaced other crops (and also pasture) and created a dangerously inflexible (and hence vulnerable) situation of near monoculture.

Industry under fascism continued to progress along the lines laid down during the Giolittian period, with particular growth in the chemical, electrical, and machine sectors. By the mid-1920s Italy was the world's largest exporter of artificial fibre (rayon); and synthetic dyes, pharmaceuticals, and fertilisers all did well too. The railways were electrified; and the telephone and radio industries developed fast. The car industry was hampered by the limited size of the home market, producing just 55,000 vehicles in 1929 (compared with about 250,000 in Britain); but in general, machine manufacturing flourished. Light industry (clothing, leather, wood) made important technological advances and laid the foundations for the post-war success of many smaller concerns, above all in regions such as Tuscany, the Marche, Emilia–Romagna, and the Veneto.

During the 1930s, in response to problems brought on first by the revaluation of the lira in 1926–7 and then by the Great Depression (which in general affected Italy less severely than the more industrialised countries), the regime took several important but largely unplanned initiatives that profoundly influenced the country's future economic development. From the late 1920s a number of banks were in trouble, as companies they had invested in began to collapse. By 1931 the Bank of Italy was itself under threat. The government intervened and set up two agencies: IMI (Istituto Mobiliare Italiano) in 1931, and IRI (Istituto per la Ricostruzione Industriale) in 1933, which rescued the banks and took over their shares. The state soon found itself controlling the equivalent of over a fifth of the capital of Italy's industrial firms – steel, shipping, and electricity in particular. In Europe, only the Soviet Union claimed a larger public sector.

IRI proved particularly successful. It was initially intended as a temporary holding company, to sort out the firms it controlled and then return them to the private sphere; but in 1937 it became a permanent agency. Its companies often straddled the private and public sectors, and it bought and sold shares in a competitive way. Much of its success was due to its independence of the fascist party. It was run by Alberto Beneduce, who had been a minister in Ivanoe Bonomi's government of 1921–2; and under his guidance it became a training ground for a new progressive generation of managers, whose experience and skills were to contribute vitally to the reconstruction of the Italian economy after the war and the 'economic miracle' of the 1950s and 1960s.

Another important development of the 1930s, with major long-term implications for the Italian economy, was the introduction of welfare schemes. To a large extent (as with IMI and IRI), these were reflex responses to problems created by the Depression and did not amount to a coherent economic or social policy. Family allowances were started in 1934, largely to compensate workers for the loss of income resulting from the imposition of a forty-hour week. Insurance against sickness and accidents was incorportated into wage agreements; and in the later 1930s Christmas bonuses and holiday pay were introduced. All this put a great strain on the exchequer; but the regime was always more concerned with ensuring and engineering political support than it was with maintaining financial orthodoxy.

As heir to Italy's long tradition of idealist thought, fascism set out to build a nation on spiritual, not material, foundations. This helps explain the improvisatory quality of many of its economic initiatives. Economic growth was not essential to the regime; forging a collective identity through propaganda and eventually war, was. The liberal state had foundered, so it was argued, through its 'agnosticism' – its failure to recognise that nations did not live by bread alone, and that without ideals (or a 'mission' to use a Mazzinian term) they had no moral defences against the disintegrating tendencies of private or sectional or local self-interest. To a large extent, fascism was an attempt to construct a national community in Italy.

FORGING THE FASCIST NATION

Fascism began as the movement of an elite: young men who believed that their moral strength had rescued Italy from the ignominy of neutrality in 1915 and then carried the nation to victory in 1918. Although many of the movement's initial ideas were soon sacrificed on the altar of political expediency, the regime retained an elitist faith in the creative and purifying powers of the superior will. Mussolini said that fascism's main task was to fashion a new type of Italian, with new values and new ways of behaving. This savoured of eighteenth-century utopianism; but in contrast to the Enlightenment, fascism sought to remodel society by appealing not to reason but to the irrational in man: fascism, according to one *squadrista*, was a revolt against 'intellect' and 'the men of culture' in the name of 'faith, will, and enthusiasm'.

The attempt to forge a new national community struck a chord with those many critics of the liberal state who had long been concerned about the emotional gulf separating the masses from the political institutions. Fascism set out to bridge this gulf. It aimed to replace Italy's flaccid parliamentary system with a more vital regime built around myths and symbols, leadership cults, and the deliberate orchestration of collective hopes, fears, and insecurities. However, this experiment in cultural engineering was somewhat half-baked. Fascism was never a 'totalitarian' system, and in practice was forced to compromise with a variety of value systems, many of them highly conservative. By the 1930s 'fascist man' was no longer a young barbarian. He was a patriotic, hard working, church-going father.

One of the most striking aspects of the regime's attempt to engineer consent was the 'cult of the Duce'. Fascism gloried in the heroic individual: great men, not impersonal material forces, were the motors of history. After 1925 Mussolini was subject to a process of near deification, instigated mainly by his brother Arnaldo, and furthered by a chorus of journalists, place seekers, and genuine admirers. Among the latter, the most remarkable was Mussolini's mistress Margherita Sarfatti, a highly intelligent patron of the arts, whose best-selling 1926 biography, *Dux*, depicted Mussolini as the incarnation of all that was essentially Roman: 'Roman in spirit and in countenance, Benito Mussolini is a resurrection of the Italic archetype, that reappears time and again down the centuries.'

During the 1930s the 'cult of the Duce' reached extraordinary heights. Mussolini's aphoristic injunctions ('believe, obey, fight', 'live dangerously', 'better one day as a lion than a hundred years as a sheep') were painted up everywhere, along with such slogans as 'Mussolini is always right'. Journalists were obliged to report his actions and speeches in eulogistic terms (and the applause he received was always 'interminable', 'ecstatic', or 'thunderous'). Achille Starace, the dull-witted but loyal party secretary for most of the 1930s, took the cult to absurd extremes, stipulating, for instance, that PNF officials stand to attention when talking to the Duce on the telephone. For all its transparency, the 'cult of the Duce' does appear to have generated a good deal of real popular enthusiasm and affection for Mussolini, and helped give the regime a measure of cohesion that would otherwise have been lacking.

Plate 31   The cult of the Duce. Mussolini addressing a crowd
in a stadium at Venice. During the 1930s (partly under the
influence of nazism) fascism made increasing use of choreo-
graphic staging in its bid to mobilise the masses.

In many ways, the 'cult of the Duce' was the regime's official religion; and paying lip-service to the greatness of Mussolini was the main (and often the only) criterion of political loyalty demanded by the regime. The result was a good deal of freedom, in practice, for discussion and even criticism. One reason, presumably, why only eleven of the country's 1,200 university professors refused in 1931 to swear an oath of loyalty to the regime was because they knew it would be no barrier to them continuing to say more or less what they wanted in academic journals or behind the closed doors of lecture halls. If anything, indeed, it might leave them freer than ever, for fascism, like the Catholic Church, was prepared to tolerate much in return for the vestiges of conformity.

The 'cult of the Duce' had another important political purpose. It in effect placed Mussolini above both the government and the fascist party, and helped deflect criticism from him. The country's economic problems and the rampant corruption and inefficiency of the bureaucracy were not his fault, it could be asserted, but the fault of incompetent ministers or venal civil servants, who betrayed the trust of the great man and wilfully left him in the dark as to the real sufferings of the people. One particular butt of popular criticism was the PNF. From the late 1920s it shed any remaining residues of idealism and intellectual vitality and became overwhelmingly a machine for patronage and preferment, with its membership rising to more than 2.5 million by 1939. Most joined, as the joke had it, *Per Necessità Famigliari* – 'for family reasons'.

However, the fascist party was seen by the regime as an important instrument for building consent. Young people were a particular target, partly because the movement had from the beginning made a cult of vitality and rejuvenation (*Giovinezza* – 'Youth' – was the title of its anthem), and partly, too, out of concern for political indoctrination. The youth organisations of the PNF assumed increasing importance from 1926 when they were united into a single institution, the Opera Nazionale Balilla, comprising the Balilla (for boys of eight to fifteen), the Avanguardie (fifteen to eighteen), and the Piccole Italiane (for girls). The emphasis was very heavily on sport, but there was also a strong paramilitary element, with uniforms, parades and rallies, gymnastic displays, and plenty of propaganda to foster loyalty to, and pride in, the nation (and the PNF).

Fascism's most effective experiments in consent building were concerned with leisure. The Opera Nazionale Dopolavoro, set up in 1925, ran a huge network of local clubs and recreational facilities (many of them formerly controlled by the Socialists), with libraries, bars, billiard halls, and sports grounds. The Dopolavoro circles arranged concerts, plays, and film-shows, laid on day-trips to the sea and outings to the countryside, and provided extremely cheap summer holidays for children. In some areas they distributed welfare relief. By the end of the 1930s the Dopolavoro organisation had nearly 4 million members and probably succeeded in penetrating the working classes more than any of the party's other agencies. However, it was more active in the North than in the South; and in many small rural centres its activities were often desultory.

Film and sport were the most popular forms of mass entertainment in Italy in the inter-war years, and the regime exploited their potential as instruments of social control. However, they were used more for diversion than as tools for party propaganda, and were political only in so far as the regime openly encouraged them and helped give them a 'national' edge. The country's film industry was subsidised, and foreign imports restricted; but the majority of Italian productions during the 1930s were escapist comedies or dramas, whose affluent middle-class ethos (symbolised by the 'white telephone') made them little different from their Hollywood counterparts. Of the relatively few commercial films with a clearly 'fascist' theme, one or two only enjoyed any success with the general public – Blasetti's *Vecchia Guardia*, for instance.

Sport was regarded as a good 'fascist' activity: Mussolini's alleged prowess at the steering wheel and on horseback were given much publicity. The regime greatly encouraged motor racing, football (Italy won the World Cup twice in the 1930s), cycling, boxing, and skiing; and in the 1930s party officials were obliged to set a good example by jumping in public through hoops or over vaults. Flying was seen as particularly 'fascist'. Two of Mussolini's sons were pilots, and Italo Balbo, the former *ras* of Ferrara, was fêted as a national hero for his long-distance flights. The regime undoubtedly derived a good deal of political capital from its close identification with sport; and it was largely thanks to fascism that sport became such a 'national' element in Italian culture.

Plate 32 Women mobilised. Mussolini reviewing members of
fascist women's organisations in front of the Arch of Constantine, Rome. The regime assigned women a very traditional role
as child raisers and 'angels of the hearth', but it also involved
them as never before in national political life.

Fascism's desire to be 'totalitarian' (Mussolini first gave the term
currency) should have worked against any understanding with the
Church; and there was certainly friction: in 1928 the Catholic Boy
Scouts (a rival to the fascist youth organisations) were shut down.
Nonetheless, the political advantages of an agreement with the pope
were too great for Mussolini to overlook, and in 1929, amid great
fanfares, the Roman question was finally settled. The Vatican became
a sovereign state and a large sum was handed over to compensate
for the loss of papal territories in 1860 and 1870. However, the most
important provisions came in an accompanying concordat. Religious
teaching was extended to secondary as well as primary schools, and
Catholic Action, the Church's main lay organisation, was guaranteed
autonomy provided it kept out of politics.

The resolution of the Roman question was a great political coup
for Mussolini. It increased his personal prestige, internationally as
well as at home; and more importantly, it allowed fascism to realise
the dream long harboured by the liberal state of using the Church as

an instrument for securing mass political consent. Indeed, no sooner were the Lateran Pacts signed, than the government staged a plebiscite. Voters were asked to accept or reject a single list of 400 candidates for a remodelled (and largely consultative) Chamber of Deputies. The clergy lent active support to prefects and party officials; and the results looked extraordinarily impressive: more than eight and a half million voted YES, only 136,000, NO. The regime had a new degree of moral legitimacy; and Mussolini – 'the man sent by providence', as the pope called him – appeared impregnable.

However, the reconciliation with the Church was bought at a high price. By conceding independence to Catholic Action, with its large network of parish-based organisations, fascism surrendered any serious claim to a monopoly of ideology. The longer-term political risks were considerable, as Catholic Action was explicitly seen by the Vatican as a tool for penetrating civil society and training up a Catholic lay elite. Mussolini knew the dangers. In 1931 he launched an attack on Catholic Action, and charged it with breaking the concordat. The Church made concessions. However, Catholic Action continued to be a powerful force in Italian society, with around a million members in the 1930s. Its student association, FUCI, was particularly influential: many of the post-war Christian Democrat leaders passed through its ranks.

Certain aspects of fascism dovetailed with Catholic ideology: its opposition to socialism and liberalism, its sense of hierarchy and ritual, and its belief in the virtues of rural life (and the evils of urbanisation). However, fascism was essentially pagan in spirit. Its 'new man', moulded by the youth organisations and party propaganda, was to be a warrior – virile, patriotic, disciplined, and austere; its 'new woman', a warrior's wife – loyal and dutiful, a nurturer of children and a guardian of the family home. It was to the Rome of the Caesars, not of the popes, that fascism looked for its spiritual model; and it was ancient Rome that provided the regime with most of its symbolism. 'Fascism, in its entirety', wrote a leading educationalist in 1929, 'is the resurrection of Roman-ness (*romanità*).'

The cult of ancient Rome formed part of fascism's attempt to manufacture a new national identity. Liberalism and parliamentary democracy could be dismissed as foreign imports; fascism, by contrast, was indigenous, a revival of the real genius of Italy and its people going back, via the Renaissance, to the time of the Caesars. 'Roman-ness' permeated all corners of fascist life. The fascist symbol – a bundle of rods with a projecting axe head – was Roman; so too was the fascist salute; Roman history was given prominence in school curricula; the Militia and youth organisations were modelled on the Roman army; 21 April, the traditional date of the founding of Rome, became a public holiday; and the rhetoric of the regime was saturated with Latinate terms and Roman allusions.

Painting, architecture, and sculpture also experienced the imprint of 'Roman-ness', though in general the regime never developed a coherent policy towards the arts. This was partly because Mussolini was not very interested in them; but also and perhaps primarily because the struggle between the progressive and the conservative tendencies within fascism was echoed, virulently, in the sphere of culture, and proved difficult to resolve. However, the *Novecento* group of painters, who gathered around Margherita Sarfatti, attracted a good deal of official patronage in the 1920s, probably because their 'modern' form of classical art seemed to bridge the traditionalist and progressive camps. The same applied to the 'imperial' style of architecture in the 1930s, which used ancient Roman forms (the round-headed arch in particular) in a modern idiom.

The cult of 'Roman-ness' was one aspect of the regime's desire to strengthen feelings of national identity; another was its attempt to purify the Italian language. The campaign against foreign words began in 1926, but it was only from the second half of the 1930s that serious steps were taken to eradicate them and introduce 'Italian' equivalents: 'cocktail' now became *arlecchino*, 'cognac', *ratafià*, and so on. This rather bizarre experiment in nationalism reflected a new degree of cultural interventionism by the regime on the eve of the Second World War, and stemmed largely from the growing influence of nazi Germany. In 1937 a Ministry of Popular Culture was established to provide more systematic control over the press and media, and to intensify political propaganda.

Schools were an obvious instrument of propaganda, and from the late 1920s the regime sought to devise curricula that conformed to the requirements of the new fascist era. The biggest changes occurred at the elementary level, where a uniform state textbook was introduced in which all subjects were taught using Mussolini's life

Plate 33   The 'imperial' style of architecture. Marcello Piacen-
tini's Palace of the Civilisation of Labour, designed in 1940–1
for the Esposizione Universale di Roma (E.U.R.). A modern
reworking of ancient Roman motifs.

or aspects of the PNF as illustrative material. In secondary schools,
the government was forced to be rather less heavy handed, partly
because it could not impose the same degree of discipline on the
teachers as in primary schools (where it was easier to find replacement staff), but also because the middle classes – whose children
packed the *licei* – would have bridled at too much blatant propaganda. Instead, courses were made more nationalist in character,
with greater stress on the *Risorgimento*, Italy's role in the First
World War, and the achievements of Italian intellectuals.

However, the impact of fascist propaganda, whether in the schools
or in other areas of national life, was always bound to be muted.

Without any systematic purge of the bureaucracy, key sections of the state continued in the hands of the old elites; and Mussolini was never in a strong enough position to ensure that they toed the line. His power depended from the start on the negotiated cooperation of big business, the army, the great landowners, and other groups; and their freedom from party control meant that a good deal of their corporate ethos probably remained intact during the inter-war years. The influence of the Church, with the guaranteed independence of Catholic Action and the increased amount of religious instruction in schools, added further to the plurality of values.

One of the biggest obstacles to the attainment of consent by the regime lay in the economic hardships faced by much of the population. If men did not live by bread alone – as fascism eagerly asserted – they could not do without it. Reports from the South, particularly in the late 1930s, spoke of severe poverty. 'Your Excellency must appreciate the reality here in Sicily', the party secretary was told in 1937: '[In Palermo] hordes of people live in the backstreets who cannot find work, and go to bed without even a bowl of soup . . . As one lady said to me, "I do not understand why everyone suffers and yet nobody rebels".' Two years later another report referred to families in the interior of Sicily having only 'roots and herbs' for food. Corruption and organised crime were also rife in the island – though in public nobody dared refer to the mafia, since it was no longer supposed to exist under fascism.

A final problem with fascism's attempt to engineer consent was its intellectual hollowness. The regime was built in effect on the negation of politics: the cult of the Duce, patriotic rhetoric, parades, uniforms, films, football, and trips to the sea, were little compensation for the lack of serious ideas and real debate. By the early 1930s it was clear that fascism had lost ideological momentum; and the still birth of the 'corporate state' in 1934 was for many the final straw. What had the regime left to offer? The fascist party was a corrupt clientelistic machine, run by dull middle-aged placemen; the bureaucracy was inefficient; and everywhere cynicism and indifference seemed rife. Among the young – and especially young graduates, whom the regime had counted on for its new generation of leaders, and whose numbers increased fast in the inter-war years (see Table 10) – frustration began to grow alarmingly.

Table 10 *Students attending university*

	1861	1880	1900	1920	1940	1960	1970	1980	1987
Austria	8043	13264	24140	21967[b]	–	40815	57297	121000	184000
France				49931	76485	210900	651368	864000	985000
Germany (West, from 1960)				119412	49702	212021	411520	818000	1,067000
Spain	7679	15732[a]		23508	33763	62105	168612	424000	646000
United Kingdom				58952[c]	44034	130000	259000	340000	367000
Italy	6504	11871	26033	53239	127058	191790	560605	764000	813000

Notes: [a] 1882. [b] 1921. [c] 1922.

Note the disproportionate growth in student numbers in Italy during the inter-war years.

Source: B. R. Mitchell, *International Historical Statistics, Europe 1750–1988* (N.Y., 1992).

The failure of the regime to win widespread ideological support among intellectuals was a source of considerable weakness – just as it had been for the liberal parliamentary system before it. The stultifying tedium of so much of middle-class life under fascism – well evoked in Alberto Moravia's famous first novel, *Gli Indifferenti* (The Time of Indifference) (1929) – drove the more sensitive and intelligent to gaze longingly abroad for hope and cultural inspiration; at the United States, for instance, or even the Soviet Union. The idealisation of America, indeed, seems to have developed fast among all classes in Italy during the 1930s, helped by imported Hollywood films. Faced with signs of growing disaffection, Mussolini looked for fresh ways to galvanise the regime and generate a sense of political purpose. He found an answer in war.

THE WAR AND THE END OF FASCISM

As a product of the revolt against positivism, fascism placed great stress on will, action, and the creativity of violence. War was the consummate fascist activity; and one fundamental reason why the regime took such pains to forge a powerful sense of collective identity was in order to make Italians ready to fight and die for their country. 'I consider the . . . nation to be in a permanent state of war', Mussolini declared in December 1925. Not surprisingly, therefore, many of fascism's initiatives had an overtly military dimension. The demographic campaign, the promotion of sport and physical fitness, the youth organisations, and the drive for greater economic self-sufficiency (beginning with the 'battle of grain') were all designed, on one level at least, to make Italy ready for war.

However, as with so much else fascism did not pursue a consistent course of action. Like many of those for whom the events of 1915–18 had been a supreme moral and political experience, Mussolini was keen to perpetuate the values and rhetoric of war; but throughout the 1920s fascism fought its battles primarily against domestic and impersonal enemies: the PSI, the Communists, liberals, *Popolari*, foreign grain, and demographic decline. Apart from the bombardment of Corfu in 1923, Mussolini gave little serious thought to aggression or expansion overseas. He regarded fascism as an essentially Italian phenomenon. Only from the end of the 1920s did he endeavour (with the help of the philosopher Giovanni Gentile) to make universal claims for it as an ideology and doctrine.

Once the regime had been consolidated at home, Mussolini began to turn his attention increasingly to foreign policy. Here, as elsewhere, fascism was somewhat eclectic. In 1920–1 the movement had exploited the rhetoric of the 'mutilated victory'; and the idea of trying to revise the Versailles settlement remained popular with many in the party. Quite how this was to be achieved, though, was unclear. Mussolini attempted to destabilise the Balkans from 1926 by backing local terrorist groups; but with only limited success. A particularly important influence on fascist foreign policy was Nationalism: the idea of Italy as a 'proletarian nation' that needed, for demographic reasons, to embark on imperial expansion in the Mediterranean, was one that was taken up by fascism, and expounded insistently from the later 1920s.

Mussolini's main tactic in foreign policy was to try and win concessions through sudden unsettling shifts between belligerence and amenability. From January 1933, however, he had a rival at this game. Initially, he was almost dismissive of Hitler; but the German leader's withdrawal from the League of Nations startled him: Mussolini's monopoly of unpredictability seemed under threat. In 1934 the Austrian chancellor Dollfuss (whom Mussolini had looked upon as a protégé) was assassinated in a nazi coup: his wife had been staying with Mussolini at the time. Mussolini was furious and ordered a mobilisation of his troops on the Brenner. He was fast beginning to feel upstaged, and his thoughts turned increasingly to some dramatic gesture of his own abroad.

Since the late 1920s Mussolini had spoken increasingly of Italy's need for colonial expansion. This, he claimed, was justified due to the country's surplus population. In 1932, following a particularly brutal campaign to suppress rebellious tribesmen in Libya (and which involved the use of gas and concentration camps), preliminary plans were made for the invasion of Ethiopia. In October 1935 these plans were implemented. The conquest of Ethiopia was hugely expensive, not least because of the sanctions imposed by the League of Nations; and married women were even asked to give their wedding rings to boost gold reserves. However, the principal costs were political. Italy lost its credibility with the international community

(Britain and France in particular) and Mussolini was driven irrevocably towards Germany. By the end of 1936 he was referring to a 'Rome–Berlin Axis'.

For all its disastrous results, the conquest of Ethiopia appears to have been genuinely popular in Italy. The painful memories of Adua, in 1896, were effaced: the widow of Crispi's luckless commander, Baratieri, sent Mussolini a telegram thanking him for having avenged her husband. Even Benedetto Croce approved. Mussolini's stock at home was probably never higher, and in May 1936 he announced to ecstatic crowds from the balcony of Palazzo Venezia the foundation of the Italian Empire. A major new thoroughfare, the Via dell'Impero, flanked with maps of the old Roman Empire, was inaugurated in the heart of Rome between the Capitol and the Colosseum, symbolising fascism's inheritance of the mantle of the Caesars.

Ethiopia gave Mussolini a dangerous sense of self-confidence. He became convinced that the western democracies were decadent. He saw the Oxford Union debate of 1933, with its famous anti-war vote, as a sure sign that the British no longer had the resolve to fight. The future, it appeared, lay with fascism. In the second half of 1936 he began sending forces to Spain to help General Franco against the Republicans. There was no real reason to do this, and common sense was against it; but common sense now figured less and less in his calculations. The Civil War continued much longer than he had expected and drew in large numbers of Italian troops and aeroplanes. It also dashed any hope of a reconciliation with France and Britain, pushing Italy more firmly than ever into the arms of Germany.

In the autumn of 1937 Mussolini visited Germany and was treated almost like a demi-god. He pledged himself to support Hitler in 'fascistising' Europe, and announced that the two countries would 'march together right to the end'. The trip culminated in a dramatic open-air rally in Berlin, with Mussolini addressing a vast crowd of several hundred thousand in a thunder storm. Henceforward Mussolini was to all intents and purposes in thrall to Germany; and under the influence of nazism, fascism underwent a final metamorphosis, reverting to its anti-bourgeois radicalism of 1919–20 and attempting, with an air of almost comic absurdity, to manufacture the 'new man' that it had so signally failed to create in the previous decade and a half.

In 1938 the regime introduced its 'reform of customs'. Hand-shaking was suddenly banned as unhygienic: the 'Roman salute' had to be used instead – the right forearm raised vertically. The polite form of address, *Lei*, was regarded as too unmanly, and was also banned. It was replaced with *Voi*. Civil servants were forced to wear uniforms and restrictions were laid on the drinking of coffee, which was now felt to be a decadent habit. That these reforms were introduced mainly to impress Hitler and underline the ideological kinship of nazism and fascism, was clear from the imposition of a new march on the Italian army, the '*passo romano*'. This was simply the German goose-step. Its introduction caused particular offence to the king, who cared more deeply than anything, perhaps, about the dignity of the army.

The most notorious instance of Italy imitating nazi Germany was the passing in November 1938 of racial laws. Italian Jews were banned from marrying 'Aryans', from holding jobs in the public sector, from joining the party, and from owning more than fifty hectares of land. This was extraordinary. Only a few years before Mussolini had explicitly denied the existence of any racial question in Italy; and for a long time he himself had had a Jewish mistress. The Italian Jews were few in number – about 45,000 – but they included many highly respected academics and businessmen. They were also well assimilated. The overwhelming majority of Italians accordingly felt a deep sense of outrage at the new laws; and the Church also condemned them.

If the racial laws and the 'reform of customs' encouraged an erosion of support for the regime, no less politically damaging was Italy's economic situation in 1936–9. The sanctions imposed by the League of Nations after the invasion of Ethiopia forced Italy to shift much of its trade towards Germany (see Table 8); but Italy had little to offer Germany and its trading position was thus weak. Its ability to purchase crucial primary materials was now radically curtailed, and in 1936–8 it was able to import only about half what it could in 1913. Italian industry was in serious trouble. Trading licences, cartels, and price fixing were all introduced; but the cost to the tax-payer of sustaining Italy's manufacturing output was nonetheless enormous. Particularly unpopular was the 'forced loan' of 5 per cent of the value of housing.

With imports restricted, the government embarked upon a policy of economic self-sufficiency or 'autarky'. Certain areas of industry received special encouragement. Aluminium, for instance, expanded rapidly. Most of it was produced at Porto Marghera, a large manufacturing zone near Venice, built up after 1922 and employing 15,000 people by 1939. Oil exploration was pursued with new vigour by the state petroleum company, AGIP: by 1939 it could supply over a quarter of national needs. Efforts were made to find synthetic alternatives for imports: wool was replaced by *lanital* (made from cheese), and cotton by rayon. However, such initiatives had limited success. In 1939 domestic production covered only about one-fifth of all the primary materials that Italy needed. The country was in no position to face a war.

Whether the increasingly radical and anti-bourgeois character of the regime at the end of the 1930s was ideological in inspiration or was a pragmatic attempt to compensate for waning middle-class support by wooing the masses, is unclear. The indications are, though, that Mussolini's sense of reality was fast slipping in the late 1930s, a tendency not helped by an entourage of mediocrities and sycophants, scared to tell him the truth. He was also ill and in near continual pain. He ranted about the need for a war to make Italians tough; they needed to be thrashed constantly, he said: they had no sense of discipline or obedience. His belligerent rhetoric was in part deliberately calculated to frighten the British and French and wring concessions from them; but the signs are also that at times he believed it.

The truth was that Italy's army (like its economy) was ill-prepared to sustain a prolonged modern war: it lacked both equipment and training. Despite all its martial rhetoric, the regime had failed to do any serious strategic planning. The navy had virtually no aircraft carriers (though it did have some excellent battleships and a first-rate submarine fleet); the army had only 1,500 tanks in 1939, almost all of them light (Mussolini thought these were more suited to the Italian character); and the air force lacked long-range bombers and its fighters were too slow. Essential transport vehicles were also in desperately short supply. Little thought had been given, it seems, to the kind of conflict that Italy might be involved in: there were apparently no plans, even, for a war in the Mediterranean.

Most of the problems with Italy's armed forces were due to poor leadership. The officer corps was conservative and elderly and painfully out of date: it still clung to the notion that morale – not technology – was the key to success. Another fatal weakness was the intense rivalry between the army, the navy, and the air force. This resulted in a lack of cooperation and was probably the main reason why there were so few aircraft carriers and why Italy's anti-aircraft defences proved so inadequate. However, it was Mussolini himself who was most to blame. He imagined he had some military skill, and insisted on being minister for war, the navy, and the air force, simultaneously; but his decisions (if he made them) were rarely based upon sound consultation and derived instead from a dangerous faith in his own intuition.

In August 1939 Count Ciano, Mussolini's Foreign Minister and son-in-law, learned of Hitler's intention to invade Poland. He was horrified: Italy was militarily committed to Germany under the 'Pact of Steel' of the previous May, and now risked disaster. Unfortunately, Hitler had probably told Mussolini of his plans during one of their meetings, and Mussolini may have given the impression that he agreed with them: he fancied he spoke German well and no interpreters had been present. An escape route had to be found. Mussolini quickly announced he would fight only if Germany sent 17,000 trains full of munitions, an impossible quantity as he knew; and when war broke out in September he proclaimed, with some satisfaction at his choice of words, that Italy was 'non-belligerent'.

By the following May, however, with Denmark, Norway, Belgium, and Holland invaded and France being overrun, Mussolini found it hard to refrain from joining in. In the spring of 1939 he had annexed Albania (for some years effectively an Italian protectorate) as compensation for Hitler's seizure of Czechoslovakia; he now looked for more substantial pickings, above all in the Mediterranean. On 10 June 1940, amid a public mood marked more by perplexity than enthusiasm, he announced that Italy was entering the war; and a few days later he ordered his army to advance into the French Alps. The poor showing of the Italian troops in this brief campaign underlined Italy's lack of military preparedness and exposed the absence of serious planning. However, Mussolini was sure that the hostilities would soon be over and that Italy would emerge the dominant power in the Mediterranean.

This was his most serious blunder. Italy had been dragged into a war for which he had prepared it with little more than bluster and rhetoric. The next three years witnessed a succession of military fiascos. In the late autumn of 1940 Mussolini suddenly invaded Greece: the Italian forces were routed, and Germany had to step in to salvage the situation. Worse still, the Italian navy was heavily defeated at Cape Matapan and never recovered. In the spring of 1941 the east African empire was lost; and the same year Mussolini insisted on committing over 200,000 men to the ill-fated attack on the Soviet Union. In North Africa, the battle of El Alamein paved the way for the capitulation here of the Axis forces in May 1943 and the loss, after more than thirty years, of Libya. By July 1943 Italy itself faced invasion.

On the home front, morale was eroded by food shortages and allied bombing. Rationing of most basic items was introduced in 1941; and a decline in agricultural output, and the tendency of many peasants to withhold produce from the state (either for their own consumption or for the black market) resulted in growing hardship in the cities. Aerial bombings added to the distress; and defeatism was widespread. In March 1943 Italy experienced its first serious labour unrest for nearly twenty years when over 100,000 workers in Turin went on strike. The protests soon spread to other parts of the North and were clearly political as well as economic in character. They were fanned by Communist organisers operating clandestinely in many factories. Fascist Italy was not only crumbling from without, but also from within.

With defeat looming, the air in Rome became thick with intrigue and plots. The problem was how to get Italy out of the war. The court was the focal point for much of the scheming, as the king still had the constitutional right to dismiss Mussolini and choose a successor. Furthermore, the army had remained loyal to the crown, as had the *carabinieri* and the police. However, the king (who was anyway not very courageous) dared not act too conspicuously for fear of jeopardising his own position. Fortunately for him, a number of leading fascists had themselves come to the conclusion that the only hope of salvaging something from the ruins was to get rid of Mussolini.

On 10 July 1943 Allied forces landed in Sicily and met with very little opposition. The islanders, indeed, welcomed the invaders. Their loyalty to fascism had been eroded by years of neglect, the ravages of war, and by such extraordinarily insensitive gestures as Mussolini's decision in 1941 to transfer all Sicilian-born officials to the mainland – a clear sign of his lack of faith in the islanders. On the evening of 24 July the PNF's main executive body, the Grand Council, assembled. Dino Grandi, a senior party figure, presented a motion calling upon the king to resume his full constitutional powers: it was part of a well-prepared plot. After a long debate, the motion was carried. The following day Mussolini visited the king and was arrested. Fascism had come to an end; and despite having sworn to defend the Duce with their lives, none of the PNF's 4 million members offered the slightest show of resistance or protest.

9

The Republic

The fall of Mussolini was met with enthusiasm and a widespread feeling that the war would soon be over. When Pietro Badoglio, the new prime minister, announced that fighting continued, few, and not least himself, believed it. The government's aim was to humour the Germans until an armistice had been signed quickly change sides, and then, with Allied help, seize Rome. Unfortunately there were delays, and by the time an armistice was signed on 3 September, the Germans had poured reinforcements into the peninsula. Besides, the Italian army had no real stomach for a fight, on whoever's side; and although it had been agreed that Italian troops would aid an American offensive to capture Rome, in the event no support was forthcoming. The Italian forces simply dissolved and the Germans took Rome instead.

This left Italy divided. The king and his government fled Rome to escape the nazis, and set up residence in Brindisi: an act easily construed as cowardice, which sealed the fate of the monarchy in 1946. Meanwhile the Germans had seized Mussolini from his prison on the Gran Sasso mountain, taken him up north, and installed him at the head of a puppet government on the shores of Lake Garda. The Republic of Salò, as this last incarnation of fascism was called, was notable for the brutality of its various police forces (some of them just private criminal gangs) and for attempts to resurrect the syndicalist elements of the early movement: a law of 1944, for instance, declared that half of the management board of large firms should consist of representatives elected by the workers.

However, it was too late to convince the working classes that fascism was on their side. Communist activists were already operating in factories, and in March 1944 they organised a successful general strike in the North. What limited support the Republic of Salò had came from extremists such as Roberto Farinacci, or from middle-class time servers. Mussolini himself was ill and isolated. He had no real power and was pushed around mercilessly by the nazis. His favourite child, Edda, had deserted him: he had ordered the execution of her husband, Count Ciano, for voting against him at the Grand Council meeting of 24 July. It was thus in effect an act of mercy as well as justice when partisans caught and shot him in April 1945, along with his mistress, Claretta Petacci, while he was trying to flee north over the Alps.

The Allied push from the South was a slow and painful affair. The Germans resisted strongly, and the Americans were anyway keen to harness resources for the offensive in France. The slowness of the advance, however, allowed time for the emergence of a resistance movement, something that was very important for Italy's political future. The first partisan groups appeared in the autumn of 1943. Many of them consisted of former soldiers or escaped prisoners of war, who took to the hills to escape the nazis and survived with the support of the local peasantry. They carried out acts of sabotage and commando raids; but they also settled old scores, which meant that at times the resistance movement resembled a civil war as much as a war of liberation.

The partisans were soon drawn into the sphere of organised politics, much as the *squadristi* had been over twenty years before. The Communist Party claimed the largest following, with perhaps 50,000 resistance fighters, more than half of all those actively involved. Next came the Action Party, a radical, liberal, and democratic formation led in the main by high-minded intellectuals eager to wipe out the moral stain of fascism. They and their leader, Ferruccio Parri, were to be the most determined advocates of a political purge of the administration. The next biggest group were the Christian Democrats, whose partisans could count on the active support of many clergy. Finally came the Socialists and the Liberals, the

Plate 34 The end of fascism. The bodies of Mussolini and his mistress Claretta Petacci (fourth and fifth from the left), suspended, along with other executed fascists, in a petrol station in Piazzale Loreto, Milan, 29 April 1945.

former allied to the Communists, the latter small, and monarchist in tendency.

The strength of the Communists lay heavily in their organisational skill. After the fall of fascism 3,000 of their leaders were released from prison and immediately set to work winning support among partisans and factory workers. In the spring of 1944 the party secretary, Palmiro Togliatti, returned from exile in Moscow and declared his willingness to join the government of the king and Pietro Badoglio. This was a decisive moment, known subsequently as the *svolta di Salerno* (Salerno turning-point). The decision to cooperate in a broad anti-fascist alliance was due in part to Stalin's wishes, but it also reflected Togliatti's own musings. Having seen the left crumble in the early 1920s, he had concluded that Italy still had a long way to go before a socialist revolution could succeed. Democracy, he felt, was a prerequisite.

The prospect of the Communists participating in government did not commend itself to the Allies, or at least not to the British; but they were unable to stop it. In June 1944, following the liberation of Rome, the leaders of the main resistance parties forced the resignation of General Badoglio (whom Churchill had supported strongly, largely because he seemed a good royalist: he was eager to shore up the monarchy as a bulwark against a Communist take-over) and established their own coalition under the elderly Ivanoe Bonomi. This was in effect a coup. It revealed the self-confidence of the anti-fascist forces, a self-confidence that was sometimes to make it hard for them to understand why the Allies should view Italy with some misgivings.

In the unliberated North, provisional local governments were set up known as Committees of National Liberation. They varied in composition from region to region, but as in Rome they tended to cover the spectrum of anti-fascist parties. Their activities were coordinated by a supreme body, the CLNAI. With the end of the war in sight, a general insurrection was proclaimed to liberate the main cities ahead of the Allies. The number of partisans suddenly grew from about 80,000 in March 1945 to about a quarter of a million by the end of April; and as intended, the major centres of the North were handed over to the British by anti-fascists. This was of great psychological importance; but it was economically significant, too,

for the partisans were able to prevent the Germans from blowing up
factories and machinery as they withdrew.

The partisans provided an important contribution to the defeat of
fascism; but their contribution to political mythology was much
more significant. The new order in Italy would be built upon the
'values of the Resistance': democracy, freedom, honesty, account-
ability, openness, and modernity. Italy would begin again: it would
wipe away the stains of fascism and liberalism, destroying the old
structures of power and releasing the pure pent up moral energy of
its people. 'Get rid of the prefect!', declared Luigi Einaudi, future
President of Italy, in July 1944: 'Abolish every trace of [the] centralised machine ... The unity of the country does not come from
prefects ... It is made by Italians, who must learn at their own
cost and making mistakes to govern themselves.'

The cleansing 'wind from the North', as it was known, was
combined with a deep sense of national humility and a strong desire
to be accepted back into the international community. This was not
just the result of defeat. It was also part of Italy's long dialectic with
modernity, that had begun in the eighteenth century and then continued during the *Risorgimento*, and which had given rise over the
decades to much political impatience and anger. Fascism had sought
a solution in an indigenous identity; but its failure had only increased
the sense of disquiet: 'Fascism', said the writer Corrado Alvaro in
1944, '... was a window flung on to Europe, through which
modern-day concerns rushed in to assail a country that despised
itself and sought its illusions elsewhere.'

The desire for moral renewal, however, was soon frustrated. To
start with, the 'wind from the North' did not reach the South, which
had been liberated by the Allies and had thus produced no resistance
movement and no new ruling elite. Here, 1945 meant a confirmation
of the old order: the big landowners and their bourgeois (and mafia)
clienteles, who by turns had been liberals and fascists, just as their
grandfathers had been Bourbonists and moderates. In the second
place, renewal broke down in the face of political realities. The men
of the Resistance – like the *squadristi* in 1922 – too often lacked the

skills needed to run a modern government. Moreover, many were Communists or revolutionary Socialists; and that in the era of the Cold War put them beyond the pale.

The years 1945–8 marked the triumph of continuity. The symbols, the rhetoric, and even the constitution changed; but most of the old personnel and many of the former institutions remained untouched. For those who had believed in a new moral order, the sense of disappointment was great; and their frustration was to prove a major source of instability in the years to come, encouraging anti-system parties, protest movements, and terrorism, and feeding a stream of literature and journalism that denounced the Republic and its rulers. In the South, the discrediting of the state helped to provide a moral alibi for those who perpetrated or colluded with organised crime. The gap between 'real' and 'political' Italy seemed wider than ever.

In May 1945, the war over and the partisans poised to assume control of the government in Rome, Italy had three fundamental domestic problems to resolve. First was the question of a purge: how far should fascists or fascist sympathisers be punished or removed from public posts? Second was the institutional question: what type of constitution and government should post-war Italy adopt? Third was the question of the economy: how to deal with the immediate issues of runaway inflation, unemployment, and reconstruction, and also longer-term structural issues, particularly the North–South gap. All these problems were on top of the major diplomatic questions of the peace treaty and Italy's place in the new international order.

The problem of the purge proved especially difficult. Many of the most notorious fascists, among them Farinacci and Starace, had already been arrested and shot by partisans; and throughout the spring and summer of 1945 the reprisals and vendettas continued in a largely indiscriminate manner: perhaps 15,000 people were killed in April, May, and June alone. The question, though, was who, or perhaps more realistically, who was not, a fascist? Millions of Italians had joined the PNF; millions had enrolled in the unions; and hundreds of thousands of industrialists, landowners, state employees, and intellectuals had benefited from the regime and colluded with it – or at least done nothing to oppose it. Had they all been 'fascists'?

Not surprisingly, perhaps, there was confusion and resentment when the Committees of National Liberation set up 'purge commissions' and began proceeding against fascist supporters. The situation grew even more fraught when Ferruccio Parri, the leader of the Action Party and prime minister from June 1945, decreed that 'collaborators' with the nazis or with the Republic of Salò were liable to criminal sanctions. Many courts balked at this and refused to convict, for judges and juries often knew that they were as culpable as the accused. In the end, pragmatism or a sense of collective sin won out, and attempts to conduct a systematic purge were dropped. Ferruccio Parri resigned in disgust, and in 1946 a general amnesty was issued, drawn up by the Communist leader, Togliatti.

The consequences of all this were far-reaching. The bureaucracy remained staffed with people who had been taken on and promoted for political or clientelistic reasons, and who had worked for a regime in which the state was regarded as being prior to the individual and in which citizens had no rights: the idea of public service and hence of efficiency (in practice at least) had been alien to fascism. The failure after 1945 to give a democratic ethos to the administration seriously weakened the credibility of the new Republic in the eyes of many ordinary Italians. It also frustrated well-meaning politicians. Time and again, important pieces of legislation did not get converted from law into practice: they simply ground to a halt in a mass of unprocessed papers in Rome or on the desks of local government officials.

The failure to purge the bureaucracy had other important political results. It meant that many policemen, judges, and prefects remained in their posts despite having fascist sympathies. One consequence was that for a decade at least the law was often interpreted in a highly illiberal way. Former partisans were convicted of 'crimes' committed in 1943–5, while supporters of the Republic of Salò were frequently acquitted. In 1953 the writer and publisher of a screenplay about Mussolini's attack on Greece were referred to a military court as 'soldiers on leave' (a category that applied to all men under sixty-five), and sent to gaol, for 'defaming the Armed Forces in combat'. A particularly open-ended crime (and one with major implications for press freedom) was 'defamation of the state institutions'. In 1957 550 charges were brought under this head.

Plate 35   Italy in 1945, an awkward and unholy alliance. Catholic books, rosaries, and devotional images share a notice board with Socialist and Communist Party writings. Tucked discreetly in the bottom left is some fascist party material.

One reason why the political will to conduct a purge was not greater lay in the importance that was attached to the institutional question. It was widely assumed (and the assumption reflected a legalistic tendency among Italian politicians, many of whom were lawyers) that the best safeguard against a repeat of 1922 was a well-drafted constitution. This was politically convenient given the psychological need in 1945 to be done with the past, but it was also rather myopic. It meant that great care was taken to reverse the worst formal aspects of fascism, but only at the cost of reproducing some of the main weaknesses of the old liberal system. Moreover, while outward appearances changed, the substance (as with the bureaucracy or the 1931 fascist penal code) was often retained.

The first issue to be decided was that of the monarchy. Victor Emmanuel was deeply compromised by fascism, and his flight from Rome in September 1943 had further weakened his position. In a bid to save the dynasty, he abdicated in May 1946 in favour of his son, Umberto. A month later, on 2 June, the same day as elections for the Constituent Assembly, a referendum was held, and by a majority of just 2 million (12.7 to 10.7 million) a republic was voted in. Particularly striking was the political cleavage between North and South: Rome and the South voted for the monarchy (79 per cent in Naples), the North rejected it (77 per cent in Emilia and 85 per cent in Trentino). The Republic, like its predecessor in 1860, was thus born of disagreement.

Nowhere was backing for the new republic more qualified than in Sicily. The island had always had an autonomist tradition, and had reacted to unification in 1860 by opposing, often violently, attempts to impose centralised control. Fascism had not altered this: it had conducted a harsh campaign against the mafia during the later 1920s, but had then abandoned the island to its own devices. Towards the end of the war a number of landowners worried by the prospect of a return to democracy (and the strength of the left in particular), spearheaded a movement to make Sicily independent. For a time it had considerable popular support. It even had its own army, which carried out guerrilla operations against the police and military. Among its commanders was the bandit, Salvatore Giuliano.

The unrest in Sicily provided a backdrop to discussions in the Constituent Assembly. In the elections of 2 June the Christian Democrats had gained 207 of the 556 delegates, the Communists 104, and the Socialists 115. The Action Party secured only seven seats, and was dissolved in 1947. The delegates' main concern was to fashion a political system that guaranteed the maximum possible freedom. Parliament was to consist of two chambers, both elected with universal suffrage, male and female. The President was to have very limited powers; there was to be proportional representation; the judiciary was to form an independent branch of government; and, above all, there was to be regional government, with a number of areas, among them Sicily, having autonomy and their own special statutes and elected parliaments.

This concession to regionalism was partly designed to weaken the power of central government and to promote local democracy; but it also reflected fears about separatism, not only in Sicily but in other peripheral areas too: Sardinia, the French-speaking Valle d'Aosta, and the German-speaking South Tyrol. The hurried granting of autonomy to these 'special' regions effectively killed off separatism as a political issue by 1948. However, the delegates to the Constituent Assembly had displayed an Achilles' heel. Their eagerness to prevent a possible dissolution or diminution of the national territory showed the extent to which they were still caught up in the emotional dilemma presented by the *Risorgimento*: how to combine freedom with unity.

This dilemma operated like an under-tow that qualified or ham-strung many of the provisions in the Constitution. Regional govern-ment, for instance, was not in fact implemented – apart from in the 'special' regions – until 1970. The Constitutional Court remained a phantom until the late 1950s. A number of important rights were seriously hedged about. Article 40 said that the right to strike should be exercised 'within the framework of the laws regulating it'. No such laws were introduced, and the only relevant legislation on the statute books was that passed under fascism, which was not repealed. Even the powers given to the autonomous regions were often dis-regarded. In Sicily, the police were supposed to be under the control of the island's president: in practice this could never be permitted.

The Constitution (which came into force on 1 January 1948) contained many inconsistencies. These were the result not only of human fallibility and the pressure of events, but also of attempts to accommodate the wishes of groups as diverse as the Christian Democrats and the Communists. Hence a frequent recourse to blanket rhetoric and ambiguity. Equally important, though, was the question of political insecurity. A new order was being built on the ashes of two failed regimes; the risks involved were great. To hand out freedom was all very well in theory: but what if, in practice, that meant the freedom to subvert liberalism itself? This was the dilemma of 1860. It was no mere oversight that the Republic retained the public security law and the 1931 penal code, and with them the tools of coercion.

On the face of it, it was perhaps surprising that the Communists proved as cooperative as they did in the Constituent Assembly. Even when it came to the issue of Church–state relations, they supported the Christian Democrats and far right, and ensured that the 1929 Lateran Pacts were incorporated wholesale into the Constitution. Togliatti, however, was determined to appear moderate and conciliatory: he refused to exploit the social unrest that swept much of the industrial North after the war, and disregarded the insurrectionary promptings of the party hardliners. He also (and this is less easy to understand) declined to use the unrest simply to improve his bargaining position. It was as if he had been traumatised by the fate of the left in the 1920s and 1930s, and was determined to appease the bourgeoisie at all costs.

This was a very dangerous strategy. It left the initiative entirely with the conservative parties and above all with the Christian Democrats, who were able to ensure that the essence of the old liberal and fascist order passed into the new Republic. Togliatti had no doubt calculated, rightly, that post-war Italy would form part of a western capitalist alliance, and that this would make revolutionary action almost impossible. However, he ended up with the worst of both worlds: used, and then in 1947 brushed aside, by the centre and right, who could always claim that his support for parliamentary democracy was merely a smoke-screen; and also mistrusted, if not abandoned, by those Communists (presumably the vast majority) who had hoped that the party would be a force for radical change at the very least.

Togliatti was influenced in his political strategy by the writings of his friend Antonio Gramsci. Gramsci had spent the last ten years of his life in prison reflecting on the course of Italian history and in particular the problem of why Italy's bourgeoisie had always failed to win moral ascendancy ('hegemony') over the working classes. Gramsci's meditations – contained in a set of notebooks smuggled out of prison after his death in 1937 – were a mixture of Crocean idealism and Marxism. He argued that a successful revolution had to be preceded by a war of ideas, to win people over mentally to socialism. The campaign would be led by intellectuals, and would involve the gradual indoctrination of society through various cultural channels. It is no coincidence that Gramsci greatly admired the Catholic Church, which he saw as in many respects a model revolutionary force.

In the struggle for ideological supremacy, the Church was to be the main rival to the PCI after 1946. Togliatti's efforts to integrate his party into the democratic framework of the Republic were prompted by a desire to secure the Communists a sound base within civil society from which to launch a war of ideas and undermine the cultural hold of the Church. Up to a point he succeeded. During the late 1940s and 1950s the PCI attracted to its cause a huge array of major writers, film-makers, and artists, whose works undoubtedly influenced many Italians, especially among the younger generation. However, the Church had the advantage of history on its side; and its roots ran deep, above all in rural areas.

Moreover, the Church now had the Christian Democrats (DC) to champion its cause. The DC was not strictly a confessional party: indeed its secretary, Alcide De Gasperi, remembered well what had happened to Don Sturzo and the PPI in 1923, and was determined to free the party as much as possible from any dependence on the Vatican; but it did espouse Catholic values and relied heavily on the Church's moral and organisational support for success in elections. From the 1950s the DC set out, like the fascist party before it, to colonise civil society through a plethora of para-state organisations; and while the Communists were urging their followers to read Steinbeck or Dos Passos, the DC was waging its campaign for hegemony with a rather more lethal weapon – money.

However, it was not just access to public funds, and the creation of large clienteles, that gave the Christian Democrats the edge over the Communists; nor was it the less high-brow approach to culture. Far more important was something that neither party could really control: the rise of consumerism. From 1945 Italy was locked economically as well as politically into the world of the advanced industrial economies, with all that this implied for expectations and values. Whilst the PCI struggled to promote the image of the Soviet

Union, and with it an austere morality of self-sacrifice in the interests of the collectivity, cinema, television, glossy weekly magazines, and a variety of other new media poured out a much more seductive message of private consumption. The dreams of most ordinary Italians in the 1950s were made in Hollywood, not Moscow.

Of course, the extent to which Italy became part of the industrialised west also depended on strategic decisions made by post-war governments. Fascism had been identified in the 1930s with state intervention and the attempt to create a national self-sufficient economy. It was partly in reaction to this that free trade became a dogma of the early years of the Republic; though the fact that many of the levers of economic power were controlled by doctrinaire old-school liberals such as Luigi Einaudi (Governor of the Bank of Italy from 1945 to 1948, Budget Minister in 1947–8, and President of Italy from 1948 to 1955), also encouraged this choice of direction. The result was that of all the post-war western economies, Italy's probably had the least state planning and intervention.

The principal beneficiaries of this were the major export industries. They could take advantage of the fact that they had suffered less damage than many of their competitors in northern Europe, and also that their main sources of power, the hydro-electric plants, were still intact. The government helped them with lenient foreign exchange controls, which provided wonderful opportunities for currency speculation. The result was that in the first years after the war sectors such as textiles experienced an extraordinary boom. The downside, though, was the effective abandonment of planning: with foreign currency in the hands of the exporters, it was very difficult for the government to control what types of goods were imported, and therefore which areas of the economy got what, and when.

In a sense this was a reassertion (though it had never really disappeared under fascism, even in the 1930s) of the traditional balance of economic power in Italy: those sectors that were already strong, and had political influence, could make their wishes prevail. This was certainly evident with American aid, a key element in the post-war recovery. From 1943 to 1948 Italy received over 2 billion dollars' worth of assistance from the United States, with a further 1.5 billion under the Marshall Plan over the next four years. Textiles again appear to have benefited disproportionately; and big public and private companies, such as Finsider (the steel giant) and Fiat, also did very well, buying the new plant which finally allowed them to 'catch up' with the leading industrial nations.

In the area of labour relations, the period of reconstruction also saw the industrialists asserting themselves to good effect. American aid, in the form of food and fuel, took the edge off working-class unrest; but the employers still needed to ensure the compliance of the unions. CGIL, the national confederation, had been reconstituted in 1944. In 1946 it bowed to pressure from the main employer's organisation, Confindustria, and accepted mass lay-offs. At the same time nation-wide wage settlements were reached which had, as a condition, that individual plants should in future not seek special agreements. This spelled an end to the influence of local shop floor representatives, and left the employers in undisputed control of factories. CGIL also failed to win acceptance for its cherished scheme of planning commit-tees to be composed of managers and workers.

Though the balance of power remained firmly with employers, the workers did succeed in securing some important gains. The pay settlements of 1945–6 guaranteed minimum national wages in indus-try, and concessions were also granted on holidays and an annual Christmas bonus. The principal gain, however, was the introduction of the *scala mobile*. This was a mechanism for pegging workers' salaries automatically to inflation and preventing the kind of erosion in living standards that had occurred under fascism. It was conceded with remarkably little fuss by the industrialists, and remained in place until 1985, when it was modified with a referendum. However, despite these safeguards, Italian workers remained among the lowest paid in Europe during the 1950s.

One crucial factor in the employers' favour was the abundance in Italy of manpower. Forty-four per cent of the workforce was still engaged in agriculture at the end of the war, and in the South especially levels of unemployment were severe. Without a reservoir of plentiful (and hence cheap) labour, many Italian factories would have struggled to survive: most were tiny (90 per cent employing five people or fewer), and among the larger firms, work practices and management techniques were often archaic. This situation changed little in the 1950s, as the majority of industrialists showed little desire to explore new ideas or methods. Instead (and as in the past), they looked to the government to ensure them an inexpensive and compliant workforce; and until the 1960s this is what they got.

Any fears they had that the left might trouble their sleep unduly, by influencing the government, were alleviated in 1947. In January the Socialist Party (which, under the leadership of a one-time friend of Mussolini, Pietro Nenni, was more pro-Soviet than the Communist Party) split down the middle, and a new centrist party was formed. The Church, meanwhile, had grown impatient at the Communists' presence in government; and with the onset of the Cold War, so, too, had the Americans (who were after all giving aid partly to allay the threat from the left). The southern middle classes were also perturbed. In these circumstances, the Christian Democrat prime minister, Alcide De Gasperi, felt constrained to eject the Communists and Socialists from his coalition in May 1947.

A year later, on 18 April 1948, the first post-war parliamentary elections in Italy were held. The campaign was bitterly fought. The Church threw its weight unashamedly behind the Christian Democrats. Cardinals, bishops, and priests fulminated from pulpits about the consequences of not backing the 'party of God'. Catholic Action became a huge electoral machine: special 'civic committees' were set up across the country to mobilise support. Women now had the vote: as better church-goers than men, they were a natural constituency of the Christian Democrats; but they had to be made to turn out. The Americans also did their best to ensure that the Communists were debarred from power: they conspicuously stepped up the aid programme in the first months of 1948. They also considered plans for military intervention in the event of a victory by the left.

The Communists had little with which to retaliate. The cult of Stalin or *Baffone* ('big moustache') was certainly strong – and remained so among Italian workers and intellectuals until Khrushchev destroyed the Stalinist myth overnight in 1956; but the international situation, as well as American money and the bitter opposition of the Church, told against them. The Communist *coup d'état* in Prague in February 1948 dented the party's image badly and played into the hands of those who claimed that the far left could never be trusted to abide by the rules of democracy; while a promise, almost on the eve of polling, by Britain, France, and the United States, to restore Trieste to Italy (its loss had been perhaps the most galling feature of the 1947 Peace Treaty), provided further assistance to the Christian Democrats.

The outcome of the 1948 elections was an overwhelming victory for the Christian Democrats. They won 48.5 per cent of the votes and 305 of the 574 seats in the Chamber of Deputies – the only time in the history of the Republic when a single party has secured an absolute majority. The Communists and the Socialists together gained 31 per cent of the votes, nearly 8 per cent less than in 1946. However, while the number of PCI deputies went up from 106 to 140, that of the Socialists dropped from 115 to only 41, a consequence largely of the PSI's disastrous split the previous year. The pattern of Italian politics for the next forty years was now set: the system was polarised between two major parties, the Christian Democrats and the Communists, with the latter effectively consigned to permanent opposition. Italy, to all intents and purposes, was again a one-party state.

ITALY IN THE 1950S

After the 1948 elections the Christian Democrats set out to consolidate their power. Like Mussolini in 1925, De Gasperi needed to broaden his power base: in his case, away from the Vatican and the organisation of the Church, towards the elites of industry and finance, and downwards towards the masses. The fascists had found it hard to secure working-class support; the liberals before them, impossible. Mussolini had tried to acquire it through rhetoric and propaganda, and in the 1930s, a measure of welfare. This had not been particularly successful, but in a sense it had not needed to be: there were no serious elections to worry about and the regime could use censorship and coercion to keep discontent out of sight. The Christian Democrats, however, had a more difficult task.

The Church had been their indispensable ally on the road to power, but it did not require much political acumen to see the dangers inherent in this partnership. Popes came and went with alarming frequency; and policy changed with them. Furthermore, though the moral authority of the Church was still quite strong in Italy, especially in the rural areas of the North and in parts of the South, it was unclear how long this would endure against the rising tide of secularism. The Christian Democrats needed a firmer basis for their power. Their solution was to build on the foundations already laid down by fascism and create a party structure closely intertwined with that of the state and primed with public money.

Their first task, however, was to deal with the South. This was urgent, not just because of the appalling neglect by fascism, but also because the peasants now had the vote and were politically important in a way they had never been before. The end of the war presented a familiar picture: hundreds of thousands of labourers marching to occupy estates that were either uncultivated or which they deemed public property by virtue of their having once been common land. However, there was an important new aspect to the agitation: the presence of the Communists, who, under the influence of Gramsci, had discarded the Italian left's old repugnance for the South and decided that southern peasants were as vital to the revolutionary process as northern industrial workers.

Between 1944 and 1946 the Minister of Agriculture was a Communist from Calabria, Fausto Gullo, who attempted to alter the pattern of landholding in the South with a series of elaborate decrees. His aim, however, was not just to satisfy the material needs of the peasants. He wanted also to mobilise them and strengthen their tenuous sense of class by, for instance, encouraging the formation of cooperatives. The landowners fought back, often with violence: in Sicily, dozens of left-wing leaders were murdered in these years, and on 1 May 1947 the bandit Salvatore Giuliano trained his machine guns (at the behest of local right-wing mafia elements) on a peasant May Day rally near Palermo. Eleven people were killed.

The Christian Democrats were alarmed by these developments. They had no wish to see peasant individualism replaced by collectivism; and they did not want to alienate the large landowners and mafia bosses, who in the South were electorally often of greater significance than the Church. Accordingly, in the summer of 1946 they took control of the Ministry of Agriculture, and set out to unpick the work of Gullo and allay the fears of the owners of the great estates and their middle-class allies. The southern 'notables' responded by abandoning the far right-wing parties, such as the Monarchists, the Liberals, or in the case of Sicily, the Separatists, and moving their support to the Christian Democrats.

The electoral benefits of this were seen in 1948, when the Christian Democrats increased their share of the poll in the South compared to 1946. However, the problem of the southern peasantry still remained. Had the Christian Democrats been a homogeneous party of an orthodox conservative kind, the issue might have been politically quite simple: they could have continued to back the landowners, and employed the old formula of police and public works to contain the peasantry. But the Christian Democrats were a mixture of currents, some of them deeply progressive, particularly on social issues. Moreover, the party as a whole was imbued with Catholic inter-class ideology, and this was overlaid with a commitment (in public, at least) to 'social justice'.

It was therefore not easy to abandon the southern peasants. After all, Don Sturzo, whom the Christian Democrats regarded as a founding father (and who only died in 1959), had begun his career in eastern Sicily setting up peasant cooperatives. However, ideology was not the sole consideration. Practical politics came into it also: could the great landowners be expected to exert the same degree of local influence in the world of the 1950s, and beyond, as their fathers and grandfathers had done? And what of the Communists? If, after the fig leaf of American aid had been removed, the Christian Democrats were seen as perpetuating the old order and with it the ills of unemployment and poverty, the peasants would desert them and go over to the left.

Accordingly, in 1950 the Christian Democrats passed three laws to break up the great estates in much of southern Italy, and parts of the Centre and North, too. Special state 'reform agencies' were created, with the power to expropriate land above a particular acreage or value that was either unfarmed or else 'unimproved'; and this was then distributed to local peasant families on the basis primarily of need. The agencies provided cheap long-term credit, technical assistance for new farmers, and conducted improvement works. In all, about 700,000 hectares were divided up during the 1950s, and an estimated 120,000 peasant families benefited. However, this was only about five per cent of the rural population, and a great majority of peasants remained either landless, or else had plots that were too small or of too poor quality to be economically viable.

In part, it was the sheer scale of the problem that was to blame.

Plate 36   North and South in the 1950s. Above, assembly line
at the Fiat Mirafiore factory, Turin, in 1955, with six- and four-
seater '600's. The Fiat '600' was Italy's first mass-produced car.
Below, a Sicilian cartmaker at work beside a shrine to
St Joseph, the patron saint of carpenters.

Italy was not a rich country in the 1950s, and the state could never realistically have provided the funds needed (even if heavy taxation had been a viable option) to transform the South into a land of prosperous small farmers. However, other less venial factors also account for the limited impact of the reforms. For instance, some landowners avoided expropriation by dividing up their estates ahead of the laws among members of their own family; others claimed exemption by pointing to a small shed, a cattle stall, or some equally modest investment, as evidence that the land had been 'improved'. Still others made use of the old methods of influence and string-pulling.

However, the rather half-hearted character of the agricultural reforms was perhaps also an expression of the northern industrial bias of the republic. Fascism had never seriously identified itself with modernisation, and in its propaganda and policies had done much to uphold traditional values and practices, above all in the countryside. It was partly in reaction to this that the new regime placed economic growth high on its agenda; and growth was equated almost instinctively by both left and right with industrialisation. The Communists saw the formation of a modern factory culture as vital to 'progress', while the Christian Democrats realised that political consent and economic success were inseparable in a mass democracy: and the easiest path to economic success, it seemed, lay through industry.

This had been Giolitti's view half a century before; but the price then, as in the 1950s, was the economic subordination of the South, and its exploitation as a reservoir of easy government votes. Just as Giolitti had played on the vulnerability of the *latifondisti* to build a majority in parliament, so the Christian Democrats set out from the early 1950s to buttress their power by creating huge clienteles in the impoverished southern towns and cities. The North was politically unreliable: the industrial cities were bastions of the left, and civil society relatively mature and articulate, but also volatile. The South, by contrast, was easier to control, at least politically: votes and money usually went hand in hand. All that was needed was to have access to the till.

As the dominant party of government from 1948, the Christian Democrats could use their position to make sure that public funds served their electoral needs. State bodies, such as the Cassa per il

Mezzogiorno (set up in 1950 to foster development in the South, with billions of lire at its disposal), were run by party men and became machines for the distribution of patronage. The process was simple: supporters of the Christian Democrats received preference with subsidies, contracts, or jobs, in exchange for votes. There was no absolute guarantee that the *quid pro quo* would be delivered on polling day; but it suited a client to have his patron returned to power, for therein lay his own best interest.

This system of 'state clientelism' was remarkably efficient. Given the levels of unemployment and poverty in the South, the mere promise of a job or a loan was enough to create a patron–client bond. This promise did not always have to be fulfilled: the important thing was to ensure that the supplicant was kept in hope. Another advantage of the system was that it dovetailed with the traditional feudal ethos of the South. The allocation of favours to kinsmen or friends had long been regarded not just as an economic necessity, but also as a symbol of power and even as a virtue in its own right. As an American researcher found in Basilicata in the mid-1950s, it was not in the interest of local politicians to act impartially, for it was always expected as a matter of course that they would give preference to clients.

The moral foundations of 'state clientelism' were further buttressed by the Christian Democrats' stress on the sanctity of the family. During the 1950s the Christian family was constantly held up as the nucleus of society, whose rights had to be defended against the claims of the state. As a well-known Catholic author put it in 1958: 'Family duties, founded on faith, love, and unity, are of a superior order . . . to social duties.' At one level, this was an ideological weapon with which to counter the collectivist teachings of the left; and its effectiveness was helped by the fact that it harmonised with the views of the Church. But it also had a more insidious dimension: if the family and family values were sacred, where did this leave the state? In specific terms, did public officials have as their first duty friends and relatives, or the law?

One of the consequences of this uncertainty as to the claims of public over private was the growth from the 1950s of 'corruption'. Welfare agencies, state companies, and local government were all transformed into enclaves of party power catering more to the needs of individual bosses (for whom 'preference votes' were vital at elections) than to the interests of the collectivity. Pay-rolls grew inflated, as staff were taken on to expand clienteles: their suitability for the post was often immaterial. In Naples by 1968 there were over 15,000 municipal employees, a rise of nearly 400 per cent in fifteen years. The result of all this, not surprisingly, was a mounting sense of frustration in many quarters, as services ground down and the bureaucracy became prey to sclerosis.

In the short term, however, the Christian Democrats' colonisation of the state paid off. It consolidated their hold on power, and helped to free them from dependence on the Church. It was a process that affected the whole country, but the most flagrant abuses occurred in the South, the area that the party secretary Amintore Fanfani singled out from 1954 as the principal target for expansion. The overcrowded southern cities saw enormous increases in party membership during these years (by 1961 Cosenza in Calabria had almost as many card-holders as Turin, Milan, and Genoa combined); and most of them became the virtual baronies of individual Christian Democrats: Giovanni Gioia (and after him Salvatore Lima) in Palermo; Silvio Gava in Naples; Antonino Drago in Catania.

The growth of the Christian Democrats in the 1950s mirrored the similar expansion of the fascist party in the 1930s. In both cases the need for a job or job security was more important than ideology. In the South, the process of expansion was helped by the failure of the land reforms. After 1950 hundreds of thousands of peasants left the countryside and moved into the southern cities looking for work. Here they joined the armies of the unemployed and destitute, who were all too willing to offer their support to the Christian Democrats in return for the prospect, however faint, of a job. The lucky ones found a post in local government; some drifted into crime, a growing industry in the South; the majority soon packed their bags again and headed north, where they furnished the cheap labour on which so much of Italy's 'economic miracle' was built.

FROM 'ECONOMIC MIRACLE' TO SOCIAL PROTEST: ITALY IN THE 1960s

In the mid-1950s Italy was still in many regards an underdeveloped country. Some sectors of its economy – for example, cars, steel, and chemicals – were comparatively advanced; but these oases of modernity were restricted almost entirely to the north-west. Manufacturing in general was labour intensive and artisanal in character. Agriculture was still the largest single category of employment, with over 40 per cent of the work force; and here too backwardness prevailed. Apart from the prosperous Po valley, farming was marked by low growth rates and an increasing fragmentation of holdings, particularly in the Centre and South. Between 1947 and 1955 the amount of land cultivated in units of less than ten hectares rose by 10 per cent to almost 9 million hectares.

The standard of living of most Italians was low. A government enquiry of 1951–2 revealed that close on a million families, nearly all in the South, never ate meat or sugar; and more than 2,700,000 families were classified as 'poor' or 'needy', equivalent to a quarter of the total population. Most desperate, perhaps, were the southern day labourers, whose wages were often less than half those of their counterparts in the North. Much of the country's accommodation lacked amenities: only 7 per cent of households had electricity, drinking water, and an inside toilet. Illiteracy was still widespread, and in some southern towns the only printed matter available was missionary newsletters or political leaflets.

By the mid-1960s Italy was no longer a backward country. Industry had boomed, with investments in manufacturing rising by an average of 14 per cent a year between 1958 and 1963. Firms such as Zanussi, Ignis, and Candy had become international household names; the scooter industry had appeared from almost nowhere. Fiat had leapt ahead, making cheap compact family models, of which the '600' was the best known. By 1967 it was selling more cars in the Common Market than any other firm, Volkswagen included. Living standards had improved greatly. Per capita income rose by 134 per cent between 1952 and 1970. In Britain, in the same period, it went up just 32 per cent. Most Italians could now afford to eat meat regularly. They could also afford to store it: in 1958 13 per cent of families owned a refrigerator; in 1965 55 per cent (cf. Table 1).

This extraordinary transformation – almost certainly the most dramatic in the country's history – was the result of a number of factors. One of particular importance was Italy's involvement from the outset in the Common Market. De Gasperi had been a strong supporter of European integration, which he saw as a safeguard of international peace and a guarantee (if indirectly) of political stability. He also saw it as a tool for correcting the main structural imbalances in Italy's economy, and especially (through the free movement of labour) its huge problem of unemployment. It was largely due to De Gasperi's vision and energy that in 1957, three years after his death, Italy became a founder member of the European Economic Community (EEC).

The benefits of the EEC to Italy were enormous. Despite the fears of many industrialists, the most advanced sectors of the economy were sufficiently strong by the late 1950s to confront the challenge of free trade. Italy was thus well placed to profit from a new surge in world demand. Between 1958 and 1963 Italian exports increased on average by 14.4 per cent per annum, with the percentage going to EEC countries nearly doubling. Industrial output grew by over 8 per cent per annum, a faster rate than any other country except Japan and perhaps West Germany. In 1951 Italy made 18,500 refrigerators; by 1967 the figure was over 3 million. Plastics production went up fifteen-fold in a decade, while Olivetti (arguably the most progressive firm in Europe) quadrupled its production of typewriters between 1957 and 1961.

This extraordinary achievement – which turned Italy almost overnight from a land of peasants into a modern industrialised nation – was the result not only of high investment and increased demand, but also, and perhaps crucially, of new sources of cheap energy. In the past Italy had been handicapped by its lack of coal; in the age of oil, this mattered less. Large deposits of natural gas were found in the Po valley in 1944 and some (admittedly poor quality) oil was struck off Sicily. The state-owned petroleum company, ENI (run by an exceptional entrepreneur, Enrico Mattei), made beneficial deals with other oil-producers, and Italian industry had the cheapest energy in western Europe. At the same time a modern and efficient steel industry had been developed, largely through government investment.

The fact that the mixed economy, built up in the 1930s, was retained after the war, was another important ingredient in the 'economic miracle'. IRI continued in being, and was responsible among other things for the telephone network and the construction of motorways. IRI firms (such as Alitalia and Alfa Romeo) were in general well managed and competitive in this period, and provided important fillips to the rest of the economy. The state did not in any real sense 'plan' the miracle; but it did a great deal to facilitate it through its support for these companies, and by helping develop the country's infrastructures. It also kept interest rates low and ensured that taxation favoured industrial investment.

However, the 'miracle' was not achieved without severe costs. To begin with, it was geographically limited. It was concentrated in the north-west and parts of the north-east and Centre: the South was left almost untouched. The gap between the two halves of the peninsula accordingly widened, and in 1971 per capita income in the North was double that of the rest of the peninsula. Secondly, the boom in the consumer industries was not matched by a similar development in public services. The state of schools, hospitals, public transport, and housing was often in stark contrast to the glamorous and stylish world of sports cars, high-fashion, and aperitifs depicted in films such as Fellini's *La Dolce Vita* (1959).

Thirdly, the miracle relied heavily on cheap labour. Hundreds of thousands of peasants, many of them from the South, poured into the northern cities, and the conditions in which they lived and worked were often appalling. The population of Milan rose by over 400,000 between 1951 and 1967; that of Turin by the same amount (becoming, in the process, the third largest 'southern' town in Italy after Naples and Palermo) (see Table 6). The immigrants would sleep rough or in squalid *pensioni*, four or five to a room. They were rarely employed for less than ten or twelve hours a day; they had short contracts of three to six months; and the conditions of safety, especially in smaller factories or on building sites, were poor: eight construction workers were killed in accidents in just one month in Turin in July 1961.

The 'economic miracle' gave many peasants their first taste of a regular income; but it also caused profound dislocation, real and psychological. During the 1950s and 1960s over 9 million Italians migrated to a new region of the country. Men and women, often illiterate, whose families had rarely stirred beyond their rural communities for centuries, and who spoke dialect only, suddenly found themselves amid the neon lights, the hoardings, and the traffic of a huge bustling city: 'I felt alone, like in a forest without a single living soul', recalled Antonio Antonuzzo, a Sicilian peasant who came to Milan in 1962 after his small family farm had failed. Uprootedness, as much as a sense of social injustice, drove many (including Antonuzzo) into collective politics and sowed the seeds of 1968.

The fears of those who had always felt that economic modernisation would, like Pandora's box, unloose a plague of evils, seemed in danger of being realised. In the 1950s the authorities tried to minimise the political threat through repression. Battles with the police were common; and the prosecution of left-wing activists at times suggested that little had in fact changed since the fascist period. In the province of Bologna alone between 1948 and 1954, two workers were killed and nearly eight hundred injured in clashes with the police. Some 14,000 charges were brought for public order offences, and these included crimes of incitement, such as selling the PCI newspaper *L'Unità* in the street or putting up political posters.

The Church did its best to help the government, through its propaganda war against the left and its denunciations of modern culture. Supporters of communist, materialist, or anti-Christian doctrines were excommunicated, while Catholic Action, under the energetic leadership of Luigi Gedda, sought to mobilise the faithful against the 'Red Threat' using almost every conceivable device, from films to pilgrimages and rallies. Father Riccardo Lombardi, the so-called 'microphone of God', became famous for his radio sermons defending Christian values and attacking socialism. Night-clubs, jazz, and other aspects of modern life were condemned by the Church as licentious; and a renewed emphasis on the cult of the Virgin Mary helped publicise Catholic teachings on the family and sexuality. In 1949 the pope proclaimed Our Lady patron saint of the *carabinieri*.

Fortunately for the Christian Democrats, the threat of economic and social change causing a build-up of revolutionary pressure on the left was much reduced by the events of 1956. In that year Nikita Khrushchev made his dramatic revelations about the Stalinist purges in the 1930s. Overnight the myth of Stalin ('the man who has done most for the liberation of the human race', according to an obituary headline in *L'Unità* in 1953) was fatally damaged. A further blow to the PCI came with the suppression of the Hungarian revolution, which made the idea of the Soviet Union as the land of true democracy hard to sustain. Togliatti tried to put a brave face on things; but by 1957 perhaps 400,000 had left the PCI in disgust. Henceforward, the party was compelled to distance itself from Moscow and stress more than ever its commitment to an 'Italian road to Socialism'.

The effect of 1956 on the Italian Socialist Party was even more profound. Until then the PSI had probably been closer to the Soviet Union than the PCI. However, Pietro Nenni, the party leader, condemned the invasion of Hungary strongly. He also criticised Togliatti's Jesuitical attempts to defend it; and henceforth the Socialists gave up shadowing the PCI and began moving towards the centre ground of social democracy. This was a godsend for the Christian Democrats. They now had a chance to transform the PSI (Italy's third largest party, with just under 13 per cent of the vote in the 1953 elections) into a coalition partner and thus isolate the PCI; and with the new social tensions being produced by the economic miracle, a shift in the government axis leftwards looked increasingly necessary.

Providence lent a hand in another way, too. In 1958 the cautious and deeply conservative Pius XII died, and was succeeded by John XXIII. His brief pontificate (he died in 1963) was a watershed: it marked the start of a profound reappraisal of the Church's character and role in society, a move prompted by an awareness that many orthodoxies had come to seem outdated and were being widely challenged by laymen and clergy alike. The Vatican looked to distance itself from party politics (especially in Italy) and concentrate more fully on its universal spiritual and pastoral mission. It also, with the opening of the Second Vatican Council in 1962, introduced a new liberal approach to many social and doctrinal issues. These developments gave the Christian Democrats an ideal backdrop against which to conduct negotiations with the Socialists.

In December 1963 the Socialists entered government, beginning a series of centre-left coalitions which, it was widely hoped, would bring about major reforms in areas such as housing and education, and reduce the gap between North and South. However, much less was achieved than expected. In the first place, the PSI failed to maintain a united front. In 1964 its left wing split off to form a new party, so reducing the influence of the PSI within the coalition. This made it easier for the Christian Democrats to dictate terms and prevaricate over legislation they found awkward (for example the introduction of regional government). Secondly, most industrialists, especially in those small firms that had done little to modernise in the 1950s, were unenthusiastic about socio-economic reforms that would have increased their labour costs.

A third reason for the inability of the centre-left governments of the 1960s to achieve more in the way of reforms was the insecurity, bordering at times on paranoia, of both the PSI and the Communists. Memories of how the working-class movement in Italy had been shattered in 1920–1 by the fascists acting in collusion with the police, the army, and parts of the political establishment made many on the left nervous about a possible right-wing coup. One result of this insecurity was a reluctance on the part of the Socialists to stand up to the Christian Democrats. Another was the refusal of the Communists to intervene strongly at the grassroots level, and agitate energetically for reform. Both parties feared that if the centre-left formula broke down, the country would be thrown into the arms of reactionaries.

Their fears were not without foundation. The absence of a political purge in 1945 had left some branches of the bureaucracy (the secret services and military in particular) with enclaves of fascists, ready to plot against the Republic. In 1964 the head of the *carabinieri*, Giovanni De Lorenzo, drew up plans for what may well have been a coup; and it is just possible that the President of Italy, the right-wing Christian Democrat Antonio Segni, was implicated. Six years later Prince Valerio Borghese, a war hero of the Republic of Salò, seized the Ministry of the Interior briefly with a handful of followers; and during the 1970s there were plenty of indications (many of them in due course substantiated) that elements of the security forces were colluding with neo-fascist terrorists to undermine the state.

The threat to the Republic from such plots was perhaps never as great as was sometimes believed. The Italian army had no tradition of political interventionism, and it is hard to imagine (particularly as many of the 200,000 or so annual conscripts had left-wing sympathies) that it could have provided serious support for a coup. However, the important point about this subterranean manoeuvring was that it helped to discredit the authority of the state. An odour of corruption hovered about Rome, an odour that seemed to have been dispelled during the late 1940s and early 1950s by the 'wind from the North'. Moral outrage, a traditional rallying ground for Italian intellectuals, was now added to the growing social and economic disquiet of workers; and the results were politically explosive.

The failure of the centre-left governments to respond adequately to the social tensions created by the 'economic miracle' was made worse by the increasing paralysis of the public sector. The Christian Democrats' strategy of using state-owned companies and the bureaucracy to build up mass party clienteles accelerated after the 1950s; and like the sorcerer's apprentice, the system developed a life of its own and began to slip out of their control. Civil servants, managers of IRI firms, and local and regional politicians, saw that one of the best ways of increasing their power and protecting themselves against the changing fortunes of patrons in Rome, was to set up their own personal clienteles, insinuating friends and supporters into posts. As a result, the state bureaucracy came to resemble a medieval kingdom: a patchwork of feudal lordships, each semi-autonomous, and quite ready if the occasion suited to rebel against the centre.

In this situation, economic efficiency, consistency, and logic all suffered, and state-controlled enterprises, which had generally done well in the 1950s, saw their profits begin to decline. IRI started doing badly from 1963, and even ENI went into the red after 1969. Some of the most glaring instances of mismanagement occurred in the South, where, in an attempt to bridge the growing gap between the two halves of the peninsula, the government decided to switch funding from agriculture and infrastructure (the main targets in the 1950s) to industry. However, politics again got the better of planning. A number of large factories were built, but they tended to be capital-, not labour-intensive, and so did little to relieve local unemployment. Moreover, their siting was often determined by clientelistic rather than economic considerations, which meant that huge plants (soon to be dubbed 'cathedrals in the desert') sprang up in unlikely and sometimes remote spots, cut off from necessary back-up facilities.

It was not the fault of the centre-left governments alone that the

South benefited so little from these attempts at industrialisation. Part of the problem lay in the corrupt character of much of southern society. Local entrepreneurs often submitted tenders that were fraudulent or ill-thought out, and were awarded contracts on the basis of political preference, rather than merit. However, there was perhaps a more fundamental problem with trying to industrialise the South. How fair was it to expect that an area with little history of industry, and a workforce that was more attuned to agriculture than manufacturing, might be readily kick-started into becoming a successful factory-based society, particularly given the growing competitiveness of companies in the North?

However, the main obstacle to economic and social progress in the South lay in the values and structures of the Christian Democrat state. In the 1860s the Piedmontese had tried – for a time at least, and often brutally – to introduce a sense that the law stood above private interests and ought to be respected and obeyed for the sake of the 'nation' or the 'national good'. Unfortunately, this 'nation' had turned out to be made up of a very narrow elite, and seemed to cater primarily to the needs of the North. This severely limited the moral authority of the state in the South. After 1945 the Christian Democrats had done nothing to alter this situation; if anything, they had made it worse. In their concern to keep the Communists at bay and entrench themselves in power, they had turned clientelism into a self-sustaining method of government and thereby reinforced many of the most corrupting and debilitating features of southern society.

THE REVOLTS OF 1968–1973

In the late 1960s and early 1970s Italian society was convulsed by a series of protest movements. At one level, these were the judgement of a generation on the Republic and specifically on the failure of the politicians to meet the needs and expectations of a society that had undergone such rapid changes in the preceding decade. The causes of the unrest were many, and the fact that similar upheavals took place in other countries, makes it impossible to see Italy's experience in isolation. The fashion for Marxism, the rejection of authority, the disparagement of consumerism, the dislike of the family, anger over the Vietnam war, enthusiasm for Mao's China – these were common to the protesters of Paris and Washington, as well as Turin and Rome. However, Italy was unique in the breadth and also the duration of its culture of protest: in one form or another, and with varying shades of intensity, militant opposition to the state continued for many years after it had abated elsewhere.

The first explosion of unrest occurred in 1967–8 amongst university students. Their anger was in part directed at the educational system, which since the early 1960s had expanded rapidly without having the necessary resources to cope. In 1962 compulsory secondary education had been introduced up to the age of fourteen, and in a few years the school population had nearly doubled. At the same time entrance to university had been made easier, and student numbers here too had almost doubled (see Table 10). The results were severe overcrowding – the university of Rome had been designed for 5,000 students: by 1968 it had 60,000 – inadequate teaching, and administrative chaos. What is more, there were almost no state grants, and this contributed to a very high drop-out rate, especially among undergraduates of working-class background who could not rely on their parents for financial support.

However, the disruption of university lectures, the sit-ins, and the clashes with the police that punctuated the winter and spring of 1967–8, were not merely a demand for a better system of education. They were also an expression of more fundamental grievances; and these, under the influence of what can be broadly categorised as Marxist thought, were converted into a general critique of the whole of Italian society and its values. Italy had for a long time tended to produce more graduates than its economy could absorb, but the rapid expansion of the educated middle classes after the 1950s had made the problem unusually acute. The prospect of unemployment, or having to compete with thousands of others for a humble bureaucratic post in a system where it was often contacts rather than qualifications that really counted, blighted the expectations of the young and turned many of them into rebels with a cause readily to hand.

To begin with the student movement was essentially spontaneous, and lacked any structured programme. Those involved seemed more concerned to preach (and where possible practise) a new ethical system based on opposition to authority, libertarianism, and collectivist values, than to organise themselves for any specific political goals. However, in the second half of 1968 this changed. A feeling grew that Italy, and indeed much of Europe, was living through a period of potential revolution, and this led to the formation of numerous Leninist and Stalinist groups, many of which were prepared to countenance using violence to attain their goals. Among these groups were Potere Operaio, Lotta Continua, and *Il Manifesto*, all of which became household names in the course of the next few years.

Together these groups constituted Italy's 'new left', and they exceeded in both size and vitality any comparable movements elsewhere in Europe in this period. However, they found it almost impossible to cooperate, and spent much of their time justifying or defending complex theoretical positions, which had usually been derived from a very narrow and schematic analysis of society. They turned out a constant stream of journals, pamphlets, and newspapers; and although these were intended to raise revolutionary consciousness, they were usually so opaque and abstract as to be unintelligible to most people. Their chances of winning a mass following were accordingly slight; and in desperation, during the 1970s, some of their members turned to terrorism in the hope of securing with violence what they had failed to achieve by means of the printed word.

The support offered to these revolutionary groups by students and intellectuals reflected a widespread disillusionment among the young with the Italian Communist Party. Up until 1956 the PCI had provided the most obvious rallying point for anyone seeking an alternative to the current system; but the events of 1956, and the entry of the Socialists into government, had left the PCI tactically and ideologically bewildered. During the 1960s it seemed paralysed by indecision: frightened of alienating its middle-class voters by resorting to direct action, and yet unclear as to what peaceful and democratic route to power was now open to it with the left so severely split. The 'new left' was born, as the PCI itself had been nearly half a century earlier, of a sense of frustration among the young at the timidity of the old guard.

Naturally, the desire for revolutionary action would never have been so strong had the conditions for it seemed less favourable. In 1968–9 the workforce of northern Italy erupted into militancy after years of inaction, and a huge wave of strikes, factory occupations, and demonstrations swept through the country, culminating in the 'Hot Autumn' of 1969. The causes of this unrest were both economic and social. Unemployment had declined during the boom years and yet industrial wages were still the lowest in western Europe; and the quality of housing, transport, education, and health care was for many Italians abysmal. Furthermore, expectations had risen, fuelled by the glittering images of consumerism dangled before growing audiences in television advertisements and game-shows, in films, and in the glossy weekly magazines that had become so popular in the 1960s.

There was certainly a strong political dimension as well to the labour unrest, in that the workers were voicing dissatisfaction not just with their material conditions, but also with the parties and trade unions of the centre and left, which, they understandably felt, had failed them; and this was why revolutionary groups such as Potere Operaio and Avanguardia Operaia thought they now had a chance of gaining mass support, and why they started to set up cells in the factories of Milan, Turin, Genoa and elsewhere. However, they miscalculated. While the student supporters of Lotta Continua or *Il Manifesto* (many of whom were from well-off middle-class families) claimed to despise the materialism of capitalist society, those they wanted to lead into the new collectivist dawn had yet to enjoy the fruits of affluence. The rank and file and the self-proclaimed generals were marching in opposite directions.

It was not surprising, therefore, that the workers were appeased largely through economic concessions. Industrial wages nearly doubled between 1969 and 1973; a new pension law was passed; changes in the tax system benefited the less well-off (in theory at least); and a law of 1971 offered the prospect (for the most part unrealised) of an increase in the quantity of public housing. On many of these reforms, the trade unions acted as mediators, and as a result they were able to improve their standing dramatically with the workers: membership of the two principal confederations rose by more than 60 per cent between 1968 and 1975. The upshot of all this was that industrial unrest was steered into constitutional channels, making the possibility of a revolution more remote than ever. By 1974 it was clear that the impetus for collective agitation was fast declining.

Plate 37 The campaign for the introduction of divorce. A demonstration in Rome in 1970. Women were active in the protest movements of the late 1960s and during the 1970s, and the Italian feminist movement became a major political force in these years.

Tension was further defused by several other reforms which, in certain respects, profoundly altered the character of the Italian state. In 1970 regional government was finally introduced, more than twenty years after being enshrined in the Republic's constitution. Each region (there were fifteen excluding the five special autonomous regions that had already received their own governments) had an elected council and the power to legislate in areas such as housing, health, and agriculture. This was a major development. It resulted, as the Christian Democrats had always feared, in the emergence of left-wing administrations in the 'red zone' of Tuscany, Umbria, and Emilia–Romagna. It also (and this may have been of greater long-term significance) gave the wealthy regions of the North and Centre a taste for decentralisation.

The year 1970 also saw the introduction of a law allowing for the holding of national referenda, a 'Workers' Statute' (guaranteeing such important rights as that of appeal to the courts against unfair dismissal), and, perhaps most dramatic of all, a law on divorce. This was the culmination of a four-year campaign led by the League for the Institution of Divorce (LID), a pressure group of a kind rarely seen before in Italy, that mobilised progressive middle-class opinion and whose success encouraged other similar extra-parliamentary initiatives in the next few years. The Christian Democrats were opposed to the new law and responded by promoting a national referendum to have it repealed. They failed: the 1974 referendum provided a clear victory for lay opinion, with nearly 60 per cent of voters choosing to retain the divorce law. For some this was a sign that the era of Christian Democrat hegemony might be coming to an end.

RECESSION, TERRORISM, AND THE 'HISTORIC COMPROMISE'
1973–1982

The reforms that followed the revolts of 1968–9 alleviated tensions but did not resolve them; and they did little to foster confidence in central government. The spread of urbanisation, higher living standards, greater access to education, and fresh opportunities for leisure helped to raise expectations and made the shortcomings of the state seem worse than ever. In 1970, according to a European survey, 72 per cent of Italians were 'highly' or 'completely' dissatisfied with the way their democracy operated. In 1976 the figure was more than 80 per cent, compared with around 46 per cent dissatisfaction in Britain and under 20 per cent in Germany, and an average for the European Community as a whole of 45 per cent. Terrorism in the North, and in the South a growth in organised crime, were among the causes and effects of this lack of confidence in the institutions.

On one level, consumerism had undoubtedly worked to integrate the nation. It had given Italians a new set of unifying symbols, that had helped break down divisions which education, military service, propaganda, religion, and even war had failed to destroy. People travelled more. In 1948, when De Sica made his film *Ladri di Biciclette* (Bicycle Thieves), Italians rode bicycles; by 1970 they used cars – over 10 million of them, a five-fold increase in the space of a decade (see Table 11). Television, arguably the most potent of all instruments of standardisation, had entered nearly every home: in 1965 less than 50 per cent of families had a set; by 1975 the figure

Table 11 *Private cars in use (in thousands) 1914–1987*

	1914	1920	1930	1940	1950	1960	1970	1980	1987
France	108	157	1109	1800	1700[a]	5546	12900	19130	21970
Germany (West									
Germany from 1950)	55.3	60.6	489	1416[b]	516	4489	13941	23192	27908
United Kingdom	132	187	1056	1423	2258	5526	11515	14772	17421
Italy	22	31.5	183	270	342	1995	10181	17686	24307

Notes: [a] 1951. [b] 1939.

The triumph of consumerism in post-war Italy.

Source: B. R. Mitchell, *International Historical Statistics, Europe 1750–1988* (N.Y., 1992).

was 92 per cent. Language had become more uniform – though in the mid-1970s nearly 30 per cent of the population still used dialect only.

However, these enormous changes were accompanied by others that served to weaken collective ties and to dilute, and even destroy, older symbols of identity. Regular church attendance declined swiftly: from almost 70 per cent of adults in 1956 to 35 per cent in 1972. Catholic Action, which in 1966 still had over two and half million members, all but withered away in the course of the 1970s, with most of the defections occurring among the young. Family units grew smaller and family ties perhaps weaker – although kinship and patronage remained crucial for finding jobs, especially in the South, and perhaps even gained in importance during the recession of the 1970s. Old patterns of community life were fatally eroded by migration to the cities.

Materialism, as many nineteenth-century conservative observers had feared, could dissolve as well as integrate; and Italy's politicians added hugely to the problem by failing to link consumerism to any collective national ideals. In the post-war years, and during the 1950s, the need to make up for fascism, and the ideological struggle between the D C and the P C I, had injected a strong moral note into public life; but by the 1970s all this had gone. The instruments of party politics – clientelism in particular – had become ends in themselves, means of preserving power and distributing favours rather than achieving a social vision; and significantly, ethical terms such as *patria* and 'nation' had now almost disappeared from public life.

The moral failure of Italy's ruling class was highlighted by a succession of scandals. Early in 1974 it was found that certain politicians, mostly Christian Democrats, had been receiving money from petroleum companies in exchange for political favours. The same year a neo-fascist organisation called the Rosa dei Venti was discovered to have been carrying out acts of terrorism in preparation for a *co.·p d'état*: among those implicated were a number of senior figures in the secret services and the armed forces. In 1976 two government ministers were prosecuted for taking bribes from the American company, Lockheed: one, the Social Democrat, Mario Tanassi, went to prison.

The declining moral credibility of the parties – above all, the

Christian Democrats – was made worse by economic recession. Since the 1950s Italy had become heavily dependent on cheap oil, and by 1973 three-quarters of its total energy requirements came from this one source. Accordingly, the decision of OPEC to raise its oil prices in 1973 by 70 per cent, had devastating effects. Prices soared; and the industrialists could no longer offset higher costs with lower wages: the unions were now too strong. So the government was obliged to devalue the lira. This helped exports, but it pushed up domestic prices, and throughout the 1970s Italy was trapped in a vicious spiral of inflation that it seemed wholly unable to control.

Another aspect of Italy's economic crisis in the 1970s – and one that was to prove particularly intractable – was the huge public debt. The rising costs of education and health, the enormous expenditure on the South, the growing demands on the state insurance fund (Cassa Integrazione Guadagni), which from 1975 guaranteed 80 per cent of pay, for a year, to anyone laid off), new training and welfare measures to help the unemployed, and the massive losses sustained after 1974 by the state-owned IRI firms, resulted in a deficit of over 30,000 billion lire in 1979. By 1982 public expenditure as a percentage of GDP was higher in Italy, at 55 per cent, than in any other west European country. In 1970 the figure had been 38 per cent and in 1973, 43.5 per cent.

The government was forced to borrow heavily from abroad, raise taxes, and put up interest rates. Recession set in and unemployment rose. However, the situation in the 1970s was not entirely negative for the economy. In the Centre and North, and especially in the north-east (which had a strong tradition of family-based production), small firms sprang up, often illegally, which undercut large-scale manufacturers by employing non-unionised labour and skimping on social security payments (and usually taxes, too). They were frequently advanced, technologically, and were able to mass-produce items such as shoes and clothes for the export market. The size of this 'black' economy is hard to gauge, but one estimate suggests that it accounted for between 15 per cent and 20 per cent of the workforce in 1979.

One reason why Italy's governments found it almost impossible to restrain public spending was because support for the coalition parties had become so tightly linked to clientelism. Any attempt to

Table 12 *Per capita GDP (at parity of purchasing power) 1870–1988*
(USA = 100)

	1870	1913	1950	1973	1988
France	67	54	44	66	70
Germany	63	53	38	69	73
Great Britain	120	78	61	66	68
Italy	61	36	28	55	68
North-west		49	44		88
North-east/Centre		36	27		73
South		27	18		46
Japan	27	22	15	60	73
USA	100	100	100	100	100

Note the persistent gap between North and South.
Source: V. Zamagni, *Dalla periferia al centro* (Bologna, 1990).

instigate cuts produced vehement protests from the party, or current within a party, that thought its voters would be most disadvantaged. Here was a serious, and possibly fatal, flaw in the system built up by the Christian Democrats. By making politics a matter of retaining power at almost any cost, with just a thin (and increasingly transparent) ideological veneer of holding communism at bay, the Republic's rulers had trapped themselves in a vicious spiral: as their moral hold on the electorate evaporated, their survival depended on buying votes; but the strain on the economy threatened in the longer run to be ruinous.

The dangers were particularly great given the disastrous situation in the South after 1973. The failure of the government's attempts to trigger an industrial take-off here in the 1960s left the South dependent on public money. Furthermore, the world recession closed off emigration, which had done more than anything since the war to keep tensions in the South under control. By the mid-1970s unemployment was three times the level in the North; and although average per capita income had trebled in the space of a generation (thanks largely to remittances), it was still just half that of the rest of the country (cf. Table 12). It was against this background of increasing frustration and resentment that organised crime began to escalate in both scale and violence.

Mafia gangs and networks had long been a feature of southern society, and had flourished in the vacuum created by the absence or ineffectiveness of the state authorities. Until the 1950s they had been most conspicuous in the rural areas of western Sicily and in parts of Calabria and Campania; but the enormous influx of public money into the South opened up new and far more lucrative possibilities of gain than such traditional activities as controlling the land market or monopolising local water supplies. The focus of mafia activity moved to the cities: it was here that state funds and public contracts were allocated; and here, too, that a new generation of politicians was based, eager to build up their clienteles and willing, all too often, to trade patronage and protection for preference votes.

The tightened links between the mafia and politicians made the problem of organised crime more insidious than ever. In 1962, after several years of vicious gang warfare in Sicily, a parliamentary commission of enquiry was set up to investigate the mafia. It collected a wealth of information on almost every aspect of the phenomenon, and showed, in particular, how far the mafia had penetrated regional and local government in a bid to ensure control of building contracts, public works, and credit. Its findings led to a major new anti-mafia law in 1965; and during the next few years tens of thousands of suspects were imprisoned or sent into a form of 'internal exile' outside Sicily. This might have helped to contain organised crime, but did not solve it.

The strength of the mafia lay not just in political protection. Arguably of greater importance, was the fact that it could draw on a set of values and ideas which enjoyed a measure of popular legitimacy and which could be used to justify criminal violence. Silence before the law (*omertà*), vendetta, hostility to the state, honour, physical courage, and the reciprocation of favours formed a powerful ideological cocktail that was as serviceable and alluring to the unemployed of the Palermo (or Naples) slums in the 1970s, as to their peasant forebears. The economic recession from 1973, and the closing off of legal paths to enrichment, gave the values of the mafia or the Naples *camorra* renewed validity, especially with international drug trafficking beginning to offer such spectacular and dramatic occasions for profit.

The success of Sicilian mafia families in displacing the Marseilles clans as the main suppliers of heroin to the United States (by the late

1970s Palermo was estimated to be producing four or five tons annually – 30 per cent of total US consumption) gave them access to massive sums of capital, which, recycled, could be invested in a broad range of business activities, from transport to tourism. Elsewhere in the South, too, especially in Campania and Calabria, drug trafficking led to a growth in the power and influence of criminal gangs, helped, it seems, by new levels of organisation: in Naples, Raffaele Cutolo controlled the so-called Nuova Camorra Organizzata, while in Sicily, the various mafia factions were federated in a structure known as Cosa Nostra.

As organised crime increased, so did violence; and by the early 1980s the state was in danger of losing control entirely in some areas of the South. One particularly disturbing development was the growing number of murders of public officials and politicians, which gave the unrest the appearance at times of a civil war. In Sicily, the victims of Cosa Nostra included leading magistrates, such as Pietro Scaglione (1971) and Cesare Terranova (1979), the President of the Region, Piersanti Mattarella (1980), and the highly respected local Communist, Pio La Torre (1982). La Torre's murder precipitated the appointment to Palermo of Italy's best known *carabiniere* general, Carlo Alberto Dalla Chiesa. His mandate was to fight the mafia; but he made little progress: on 3 September 1982 he too was assassinated.

The threat to the state from organised crime in the South was matched in the North by the challenge of terrorism. This came from both neo-fascist and left-wing groups. The workers' and student revolts of 1968–9 led to a revival in the fortunes of the extreme right, and its vote increased in the 1972 elections to 8.7 per cent. At the same time, various neo-fascist terror groups were founded, and these were almost certainly responsible for many of the earliest and most vicious bomb attacks, including that in Piazza Fontana, Milan, in 1969, in which sixteen people were killed. The right-wing terrorists operated according to a 'strategy of tension'. Their aim was to spread chaos and frustration and so trigger a military crack-down and an end to democracy.

Neo-fascist violence was never very well organised; and though it enjoyed support in powerful places, it was unable to sustain itself on a serious level beyond the mid-1970s. Its last major act, after a lull of a few years, was a bomb on Bologna station in August 1980, which killed eighty-five people. However, just as the challenge from the extreme right seemed to be declining, that from the far left began to increase. This might not have been entirely fortuitous, for whatever the intentions of the Red Brigades or Prima Linea, the real beneficiaries of left-wing terrorism were likely always to be the far right. The neo-fascists in a sense no longer needed their own 'strategy of tension': the revolutionaries could provide it for them.

Left-wing terrorism, like its right-wing counterpart, was born out of the ferment of the late 1960s. The Red Brigades were founded in Milan in 1970 by a group of young idealists who thought a revolution was imminent, and who believed that a more voluntaristic approach was needed than that espoused by the 'new left' – Lotta Continua and Potere Operaio in particular. These first terrorists included disenchanted middle-class intellectuals, such as Renato Curcio, and militants from working-class families, such as Alberto Franceschini. A large number came from the 'red zone' of Emilia–Romagna; many had fathers or uncles who had been in the Resistance; and a curiously high percentage had grown up in a fervent Catholic environment.

The Red Brigades were inspired by foreign models of terrorism, especially the Tupamaros of Uruguay. They also saw their struggle as a continuation of the Resistance. To begin with, however, their actions were restricted mainly to propaganda and assaults on property, and it was only from 1974 that the level of violence escalated to the point where the first murders took place. This qualitative change coincided with an influx of recruits to terrorism from the 'new left', which underwent a crisis in 1975 after a disastrous showing in the June elections. Supporters of groups such as Lotta Continua were now forced to accept that a revolution via the ballot box was not practicable: for many, the armed struggle seemed the only way forward.

By 1976 well over a hundred separate left-wing terrorist organisations were active in Italy. Many of them found a theoretical justification for their killings in the writings of 'new left' Marxist intellectuals, among them Toni Negri, a sociology professor at Padua university and apologist of revolutionary violence. The main victims of the terrorist groups were so-called 'servants of the state': judges,

Plate 38   The body of the president of the Christian Democrats, Aldo Moro, shot by the Red Brigades, found in a car boot in via Caetani, Rome, 9 May 1978. Via Caetani was half-way between the Christian Democrat and Communist Party headquarters – a symbolic choice of location by the terrorists.

policemen, industrialists, and also journalists; and the declared aim, at least of the Red Brigades, was to use indiscriminate murder to paralyse Italy's ruling classes with fear, and thereby immobilise the state and clear the way, in a period of world economic crisis, for the unfettered development of the revolutionary class struggle.

Above all, the Red Brigades aimed at a 'disarticulation' of the political system through a strike at the 'heart of the state'; and it was this idea that led to their most notorious action: the kidnapping, imprisonment, and murder in the spring of 1978 of Aldo Moro, the president of the Christian Democrats and dominant political figure of the period. For nearly two months Moro was held in a hideout in Rome. His captors issued various communiqués to the press, while Moro himself wrote a series of letters to his colleagues and family, begging them to procure his release. However, despite 13,000 men being drafted to the case, nearly 40,000 house searches, and 72,000 road-blocks, Moro's 'prison' was never found, and on 9 May his corpse was left dumped in the centre of Rome, a stone's throw from the headquarters of the DC.

Despite the Christian Democrats' refusal on moral grounds to enter into negotiations with the terrorists, the government could take little credit from the episode. Some commentators, most famously the Sicilian novelist Leonardo Sciascia, denounced the Christian Democrats for their hypocrisy: what 'moral' resolve had they ever shown during the previous thirty years in tackling corruption, inefficiency, or the mafia? The episode was also highly mysterious. How could the police and intelligence services, after nearly a decade of fighting terrorism, have proved so ill-informed? Some suspected a conspiracy: Moro had after all been working hard to bring the Communists into government, something many on the right would undoubtedly have loved to stop.

Moro's assassination was the high-water mark of Italian terrorism. The sense of moral outrage engendered by the murder forced the government to act with new vigour; and the results were evident in the sweeping arrests of 1979–81. The violence, however, continued. If anything it was worse in 1978–9 than before; but this was a sign of disintegration rather than of a strengthened offensive. Disputes among the terrorists about tactics grew, leading many to break away and set up rival organisations. At the same time the violence became increasingly gratuitous, and this alienated a large number of those who had earlier shown some sympathy for the armed struggle. By 1982 the state had gained the upper hand; and terrorism in Italy was almost dead.

The political backdrop to the years of terrorism was provided by the so-called 'historic compromise' of the PCI. By the early 1970s the centre-left formula that had dominated the 1960s had run its course. The Socialists had failed to convert their alliance with the DC into more votes, and after the elections of 1972 they passed into opposition. Meanwhile, the PCI had a new leader, Enrico Berlinguer, a wealthy Sardinian with a strongly Catholic family, who believed that Italy's best hope of moral and social progress, and of extricating itself from the immobility of the previous years, lay in an alliance with the DC. He also feared a right-wing coup in Italy were the left to try and come to power on its own: the

overthrow of the socialist government of Salvador Allende in Chile
haunted him.

In October 1973 Berlinguer proposed an 'historic compromise'
between the three main parties, the PCI, the PSI, and the DC. The
Communists, he said, would be willing to help restore Italy's
economy, uphold law and order, and respect the Church; in return
they wanted reforms and a share in overall policy. For the Christian
Democrats, the proposal had much to recommend it. They had lost
the Socialists as a coalition partner, and their authority was being
undermined by corruption and the growing inefficiency of the state.
They also badly needed support in tackling the recession and fighting
terrorism. Accordingly, some of the more moderate Christian Democrats, in particular Giulio Andreotti and Aldo Moro, responded
favourably to Berlinguer's overtures; and the DC and PCI began to
converge.

Initially, the gains for the PCI were considerable. In the regional
elections of June 1975 the Communist vote went up by more than
6 per cent compared to 1970: and across northern and central Italy,
a string of left-wing local administrations were formed. The PCI
was just 2 per cent behind the DC; and the national elections of
the following year were held in an atmosphere of intense excitement,
not least because the situation in much of Europe appeared highly
propitious to the left. Berlinguer looked to reassure international
opinion, announcing on the eve of polling his support of NATO;
but despite a further advance, the PCI failed to overtake the DC.
Nonetheless, Berlinguer's strategy seemed to be working, and the
PCI agreed to back the new government to the extent of abstaining
on votes of confidence.

The 'historic compromise', however, had its price. It won the PCI
new support among the middle classes, but perplexed many of the
party's traditional voters, who were less sure than ever about what
the 'Italian road to socialism' really meant. It also required results, in
the shape of workable reforms, to justify itself; but as the Socialists
had found during the 1960s, this was not easy to achieve. Some
important items of legislation were certainly passed in 1976–9: regional government was strengthened, the health service restructured,
lunatic asylums closed, abortion made legal, and broadcasting dereg-
lated; but many of these innovations were vitiated by the corrupting

effects of party clientelism on the bureaucracy, to which the PCI, eager for its own share of the spoils, now began to contribute. In March 1978 the PCI became part of the government majority, though it still had no cabinet ministers. Thereafter, however, relations between the two main parties deteriorated. The murder of Moro, the election of a new, conservative pope, John Paul II, and the Soviet invasion of Afghanistan, helped to rekindle old feelings of mutual mistrust; and the fact that many workers had grown intolerant of the PCI's calls for austerity (to help solve the country's economic problems) and were starting to leave the party, showed how difficult (and politically dangerous) it was to try and subordinate sectional economic interests to those of 'the nation'. Early in 1979 the Communists went into opposition; and in June the electorate passed judgement on the preceding three years: the PCI's share of the vote dropped by 4 per cent.

The 'historic compromise' had not been altogether negative. It had helped the country to ride out the storms of terrorism and recession; and for a while, at least, it had fostered hopes that the system might still be redeemed. However, the timidity of the PCI, its fear that if it pressed too hard it might trigger the collapse of democracy, meant it failed to take sufficient advantage of the various movements of protest and reform (including a fresh wave of student unrest in 1977) that had sprung up, particularly among the young, since the late 1960s. The feminists, the new left groups, the tiny but highly vocal Radical Party, and various other organisations in both North and South, agitated, often militantly, on a broad spectrum of issues including unemployment, housing, sexual equality, police powers, prisons, and family law. Their cries were too often unheeded; and by the late 1970s disillusionment had set in.

The moral failure of the PCI was compounded by its short-sighted insensitivity towards the PSI. During the 'historic compromise' Berlinguer lavished most of his attention on the Christian Democrats, and treated the Socialists very much as if they were a junior, indeed almost insignificant, partner. This was galling to the young and ambitious new PSI secretary, Bettino Craxi. He never forgave the Communists their high-handedness and concluded that he had nothing in future to gain from any alliance with them. He looked, instead, to rebuild the centre-left formula of the 1960s, but this time with the PSI behaving less passively. From 1979 the Communists were thus isolated; and any chance of the Republic having a government that did not include the DC had seemingly vanished.

POSTSCRIPT: TOWARDS A NEW IDENTITY?

The air of crisis that hovered around the political institutions at the end of the 1970s and beginning of the 1980s gave way after 1983 to an interlude of optimism and at times even of national pride. This new atmosphere was created largely by economic factors. The recession finally came to an end in 1984, and was followed by a period of such rapid growth that by 1986 some commentators were talking of a 'second economic miracle'. Inflation, which in 1980 had stood at 21 per cent, dropped in 1987 to 4.6 per cent; while GDP, which had grown on average by just 0.8 per cent per annum in 1978–82, grew by an average of 2.5 per cent per annum in 1983–7. In 1987 the Italian government announced that Italy had for the first time overtaken Great Britain economically to become the world's fifth industrial power, behind the United States, Japan, Germany, and France. This claim was robustly contested by the British government; but it may well have been correct (cf. Table 12).

The boom was part of a world-wide economic upturn; but the competitiveness of Italian firms in the 1980s was also due to a dramatic reduction in levels of manning. Fiat led the way in September 1980 when it laid off 24,000 workers, among them nearly all the leading militants of recent years; and despite huge strikes, the trade unions proved unable to block the move. Other companies followed suit; and the result was that unit labour costs in Italian industry were reduced to levels similar to those of the 1960s. Among the sectors that benefited most were engineering and fashion (the clothing firm Benetton was one of the success stories of these years). The small and medium-size firms of the Centre and north-east were especially dynamic: by the late 1980s some provinces of the Veneto, Tuscany and the Marche had one small business for every twenty-five inhabitants. Public confidence in Italian industry soared, and the value of shares on the Milan stock exchange more than quadrupled between 1982 and 1987.

The fruits of the 1980s boom were far from being uniformly distributed, however. An official enquiry in the mid-1980s found that nearly 7 per cent of the population in the Centre and North of Italy lived below the poverty line, while in the South the figure was more than 18 per cent. One of the most impoverished categories was that of the young urban unemployed; and again it was the South that was most seriously affected. In 1988, some 45 per cent of southern males between the ages of fourteen and twenty-nine were looking for a job; and among young women the percentage was higher still. The implications of this for crime, not least organised crime, were enormous. Part of the problem was demographic: the birth rate in Italy fell steadily in the 1970s and 1980s (as in other western countries), but the rate of decline was less marked in the South than in the more prosperous North (which by the early 1990s had the lowest birth rate of any west European country).

The economic boom of the 1980s was helped by – and contributed to – a fresh spirit of political optimism. This came partly from the state's success in defeating terrorism; but it also stemmed from a new climate of moral regeneration, which for a time seemed to dispel the cynicism and corruption that had characterised Italian politics in the 1960s and 1970s. Between 1978 and 1985 the President of the Republic was an elderly Socialist and ex-partisan, Sandro Pertini, whose blunt populist manner, and frequent upbraiding of the government, parliament, and the parties, made him almost certainly the best-loved politician in Italy since Mussolini, and injected a badly needed note of moral authority into the institutions. At the same time, the Christian Democrats under the leadership of Ciriaco De Mita embarked upon a programme of 'renewal' designed to restore their credibility.

The climate of political optimism in the 1980s was encouraged by a loosening of the Christian Democrats' hold on government. In June 1981 Giovanni Spadolini, a historian and the leader of the small but highly respected Republican Party, became the first non-Christian Democrat prime minister since 1945, at the head of a five-party coalition of Christian Democrats, Socialists, Social Democrats, Liberals, and Republicans. He was followed between 1983 and 1987 by the PSI secretary, Bettino Craxi, whose government was not only the longest since the war, but also in some respects one of the most

Plate 39   Lawyers, judges, and film crew take a break during
the first 'maxi-trial' of members of Cosa Nostra, 1986. The
'bunker' courtroom in Palermo was built specially for the trial,
and for security reasons was linked directly with the prison.

successful. Italy, it seemed, had broken out of the strait-jacket of
forty years of DC dominance; and the prospect now emerged of the
Socialists replacing the Communists as the second biggest party, and
giving post-war Italy, for the first time ever, a viable opposition.

The hope also grew that organised crime might finally be brought
under control. The assassination of Carlo Alberto Dalla Chiesa in
Palermo in September 1982 stung the authorities into action; and
over the next few years, spurred on by a vigorous and unremitting
press campaign, the police rounded up thousands of *mafiosi*. Among
them were several prominent political figures. A major breakthrough
occurred when the judge Giovanni Falcone persuaded the mafia
boss Tommaso Buscetta to talk. Buscetta's testimony revealed the
existence of the well-structured Cosa Nostra, with its initiation
ceremonies and an apparently rigid hierarchy; and it was largely
thanks to his testimony that in February 1986 456 mafia suspects
went on trial in Palermo. Various other 'penitents' (*pentiti*) were also
induced to come forward, and commentators began to speak optimis-
tically of the collapse of *omertà* and the impending demise of the
mafia.

All this optimism was painfully short-lived. At the end of the 1980s the boom came to an end. In September 1990 Fiat, which in the previous few years had confirmed its position as Europe's leading car manufacturer, announced it was shedding jobs and cutting production by 10 per cent. Other companies followed suit. Much more alarming, however, than the onset of recession was the realisation that the years of prosperity had done nothing to change the basic structural weaknesses in the economy, and above all had failed to resolve the problem of the huge public sector deficit. Since the early 1970s spending on social services and state industries had soared, and by 1983 had reached 58 per cent of GDP. The Craxi government had taken some steps to reduce the budget deficit, cutting public expenditure and trying to curb tax evasion; but it had not been very successful. In 1985 the public debt stood at 85 per cent of GDP; by 1992 it had risen to 120 per cent.

The crisis in public finances brought the spotlight increasingly to bear on the country's political institutions; for it was becoming clear that the only real hope of sorting out the economic chaos was if Italy's parliamentary and party system were first reformed so as to promote governmental stability and strengthen the hand of the executive. In 1983 the Craxi government had set up a commission of enquiry to explore the possible options: but its findings had failed to command general support. Some politicians (notably, for a time, Craxi himself) argued that Italy should adopt a presidential form of government along French lines; but such suggestions had to contend with the legacy of fascism, which had given many a deep mistrust of any proposal to curtail the powers of the Chamber. The fact that Craxi was often portrayed in political cartoons as a reincarnation of Mussolini was indicative of the problems facing the idea of strong government.

The need for institutional reform was made more pressing still by the growing fragmentation of parties after the collapse of Communism in eastern Europe in 1989–91; for the end of the Soviet Union ironically removed a key stabilising element in the Italian political system. Fear of the PCI coming to power had been one important reason why the Christian Democrat vote had held up so well since the Second World War; with the bogey of Communism removed, the Christian Democrats lost a good deal of their *raison d'être*. In the elections of 1987 they had raised their share of the national vote slightly to 34.3 per cent – a result in part of De Mita's attempts to clean up the party's image; but in the 1992 elections they fell to 29.7 per cent, the first time in the history of the Republic that they had dropped below 30 per cent. Their support was now concentrated more than ever in the South, where ideology traditionally counted much less than public money in elections.

The events in eastern Europe and the Soviet Union had an even more devastating effect on the PCI. In 1990, after protracted and agonised debates, a majority of PCI delegates voted to dissolve their party and reconstitute it as a social democratic force. In January 1991, exactly seventy years after its foundation, the Italian Communist Party came to an end and was replaced by the Democratic Party of the Left (PDS). However, a minority of hardliners broke away to form their own party, thereby weakening the PDS and adding to Italy's accelerating political fragmentation. In the 1987 elections the PCI had gained 26.6 per cent of the vote; in 1992 the Democratic Party of the Left won just 16.1 per cent, the hardliners (PRC) 5.6 per cent. The PDS was still Italy's second largest party, but only just; and Italy now had fourteen different parties in the Chamber, probably a record for post-war Europe.

The decline of the Christian Democrats and the disappearance of the PCI did not work to the benefit of the Socialists. The PSI gained some ground in the mid-1980s, increasing its share of the vote from 11.4 per cent to 14.3 per cent between 1983 and 1987; but this was far from being the breakthrough it had hoped for. A good deal of the problem lay with the party's image. Many people disliked Craxi's aggressive style and mistrusted his ill-disguised thirst for power (evident after 1987, when the DC resumed the premiership, in his repeated attempts to bring down the government); but more important, perhaps, were the growing signs that the PSI had become as deeply corrupt as ever the Christian Democrats had been. In the April 1992 elections the PSI vote fell back to 13.6 per cent. Simultaneously, a major scandal broke involving kick-backs in the Milan city council – one of the bastions of the PSI; and in the course of the next year dozens of leading Socialists were imprisoned. Early in 1993 Craxi himself was implicated and forced to resign as PSI secretary.

The Milan scandal proved to be the tip of an iceberg. Evidence of fraud and corruption on a colossal scale surfaced in dozens of cities, thanks largely to the zealous investigations of a Milanese magistrate, Antonio Di Pietro. By the spring of 1993 the scandal of *tangentopoli* ('bribetown') threatened to discredit, if not destroy, the entire political and business establishment in Italy: a thousand businessmen and politicians (mostly Christian Democrats and Socialists) were in gaol, and well over a thousand others were subject to enquiry. The principal charge was of having taken kick-backs and bribes in return for the awarding of public contracts – a practice apparently almost routine in many municipalities. Much of the money obtained in this fashion had ended up in central party coffers.

The crisis of moral authority sweeping through the Italian political system in the early 1990s did not spare even the highest office of state. In 1985 Sandro Pertini had been replaced as President of the Republic by Francesco Cossiga, a respected Christian Democrat, who had been Minister of the Interior at the time of Aldo Moro's kidnapping and murder. In 1990 it was revealed that Cossiga had been involved back in the 1950s in setting up a secret counter-revolutionary strike force known as 'Gladio'; and evidence emerged that this organisation may later have been involved in right-wing terrorism. Cossiga found himself under investigation; and the pressure he faced might have been a factor behind an extraordinary series of intemperate, and often ill-judged, attacks that he launched on a string of targets, including his own party, the judiciary, and the Northern League, a rapidly growing northern protest party.

Adding to the crisis facing Italy's political system in the early 1990s was a resurgence of mafia activity in the South. By 1990 levels of violence were back to where they had been a decade earlier; and in some regions, above all Campania and Calabria, they were probably greater than at any time since the 1860s. Nor, despite the fearless work of judges such as Giovanni Falcone, and the revelations of Tommaso Buscetta and other *pentiti*, had the situation in Sicily been improved. Many of those who had been arrested in the mid-1980s were free after a few years: either there was not enough evidence to convict them, or else the courts failed to reach a verdict within the statutory period of time. The authorities were clearly back on the defensive. In May 1992 Falcone, his wife, and his body-guards were blown up by a massive bomb. A few weeks later Italy's second most important anti-mafia judge was also assassinated.

The atmosphere of moral and economic confusion inclined many in Italy to turn to the European Community for salvation. Italy had always been among the most strongly pro-European of the EC member states – a sentiment rooted historically in the desire, dating back to the eighteenth century, to avoid being relegated to the position of a second-rate power on the periphery of the continent. However, by the beginning of the 1990s integration with Europe no longer appeared to be the political and economic panacea it had once seemed. The inability of successive Italian governments to match their pro-Community rhetoric with deeds, and ensure that EC legislation was properly implemented, meant the country was increasingly out of line with the other member states; and this, together with the problems of the uncontrolled public debt and the budget deficit, threatened to put Italian firms at a huge disadvantage within the single market.

The feeling that Italy might now be left behind economically was especially galling to the middle classes of the North. They had done well in the 1970s and 1980s, largely owing to the success of the small-business sector; and they now risked a serious drop in living standards, thanks (in their view) to the incompetence and corruption of central government. Above all, they resented the fact that the taxes they paid to Rome were used to prop up the parasitic South and to fund what seemed to be an increasingly hopeless battle against organised crime; and in a bid to tackle the country's economic crisis, the government was now looking to increase taxes and curb fiscal evasion. In the elections of 1992 nearly 9 per cent of the electorate – 17 per cent in the North – voted for the Northern League, a recently formed party, whose platform combined a vehement hostility to central government, the South, and immigrants, with a call for Italy to be turned from a unitary republic into a federation.

The Northern League was composed principally of two regionalist parties, the Venetian League and the Lombard League, neither of which had enjoyed serious political success before the end of the 1980s. It was led by a charismatic senator, Umberto Bossi, and offered a curious mixture of the new and the old. It strongly supported high-technology small firms, but politically it looked to

AVVISO AGLI UTENTI

* Siamo momentaneamente assenti. Chi volesse lasciare un messaggio può parlare dopo il segnale acustico.

Plate 40   The political and moral crisis of the early 1990s. The caption to this cartoon from the national newspaper, *La Republica*, October 1992, reads: 'Advice to users: we are momentarily out. If you wish to leave a message, please speak after the tone'.

the past for inspiration, and glorified in particular the communes of the Middle Ages: its symbol was the medieval knight, Alberto da Giussano, one of the leaders of the Lombard League which had defeated the Emperor Frederick Barbarossa at the Battle of Legnano in 1176. Much of the Northern League's rhetoric focused on the strength of regional traditions and the damage done to Italy by centralisation. Among its ideologues was the nineteenth-century federalist, Carlo Cattaneo.

The hybrid character of the Northern League – simultaneously unconventional and conservative – reflected an atmosphere of curious ambivalence surrounding what was now generally referred to as the collapse of the First Republic. That many people were avid for change was certain: but quite how much change, and along what lines, was far less clear. As in 1922 and in 1945, the desire to remove the trappings of the old regime, and in particular to sweep away the leadership of the 'guilty men', was perhaps stronger than the desire to alter the substance of the former system or ask awkward questions about the responsibility of ordinary Italians for what had gone wrong. In part the difficulty was historical: Italy's past offered few obvious solutions to the current crisis. Bossi put his faith in regionalism, and talked of creating a northern republic of Padania; but such a proposal lacked the emotional sanction of history.

Another major problem with regionalism, and certainly with federalism, was that it risked condemning the poorer areas of Italy to financial ruin. These areas, the South in particular, had for decades been dependent on massive state subsidies for their survival. They had also looked to the state to mitigate, if not solve, the scourge of organised crime, which, despite the setbacks of the early 1990s, still remained a powerful threat. The fears of these poorer areas contributed to a surge in support for the neo-fascist far right, for decades little more than a marginal force in Italian politics, but which, from 1991, under the leadership of the young and suavely plausible Gianfranco Fini, became a significant beneficiary of the vacuum created by the collapse of the Christian Democrats. Fini marketed the MSI as a democratic 'post-fascist' force, committed to the defence of 'national and Catholic values', and this helped it (or rather the Alleanza Nazionale as it now styled itself) to win 13.4% of votes in the general elections held in March 1994. In the South the Alleanza Nazionale averaged over 20% of the vote.

The most remarkable success story of the 1994 elections, however, was that of Forza Italia, a party founded just two months beforehand by the media tycoon and owner of AC Milan football club, Silvio Berlusconi. Like the Northern League, it was a curious mixture of the old and the new. It was strongly patriotic, and displayed the tricolour prominently in its party symbol; but its patriotism, and indeed the whole ethos of the party, drew heavily on the language and imagery of football – arguably the most powerful vehicle for national sentiment in Italy in the 1990s. It espoused dogmatic free market principles, and talked of creating a second economic miracle by freeing Italy's entrepreneurs from the shackles of the state bureaucracy. Yet Berlusconi himself, who made much of the fact that he was a 'new' man in politics, had been one of the most conspicuous beneficiaries of the old and corrupt clientelistic system. A good deal of his success as a businessman had been due to his close ties in the 1980s with Craxi and other discredited figures of the First Republic. What is more, he was in danger of being sucked into *tangentopoli*: his brother and business partner, Paolo, was arrested in February 1994; and many people speculated that Berlusconi's principal motive for entering the political arena might be to secure his own immunity from prosecution and save his endangered business empire.

Forza Italia secured 21% of the vote in the elections, and Berlusconi became prime minister at the head of a right-wing coalition comprising his own party, the Alleanza Nazionale and the Northern League. It was a somewhat unlikely coalition, and Berlusconi and Bossi were soon locked in a power struggle: the players might have changed but the old political tactics continued. Berlusconi's promises of an economic miracle were exposed as hollow rhetoric: far from encouraging competition he seemed more concerned with protecting his own business interests and damaging those of his rivals. He even made an ill-judged attack on the independence of the Bank of Italy. His electoral talk of reducing taxes and generating a million new jobs proved (not surprisingly) illusory. The underlying structural problems of the economy persisted, and the budget deficit continued to grow, making Italy's chances of rejoining the European monetary system – from which it had been forced out in September 1992 – increasingly remote.

Berlusconi had spoken of his commitment to the fight against corruption. In power, however, he seemed determined to undermine Antonio Di Pietro and his fellow magistrates by claiming that their work was politically inspired. Perhaps he sensed – as was probably the case – that the public appetite for the judicial investigations was beginning to wane. Perhaps, too, as the owner of an agency that controlled most of advertising on television, he had an exaggerated belief in the malleability of public opinion. Whatever the reason, his gauche attempts to derail the anti-corruption campaign contributed to a fast-growing mood of disenchantment with his government. In the autumn of 1995 he faced massive protest demonstrations against his proposals to cut spending on pensions and health. The Milan magistrates then announced he was under investigation for false accounting in his business dealings, and in December his coalition partner, Bossi, withdrew his support, and Berlusconi was forced to resign.

As on a number of occasions since 1860, Italians had put their faith in a man who appeared to offer salvation, only to discover that this faith was largely misplaced. For several years Italy had been living through an almost surreal drama: political parties had dissolved, metamorphosed, or emerged from nowhere; the old names and faces, symbols of a political order that had seemed doomed to permanent immobility, had vanished from the scene, discredited: even Andreotti, a minister in thirty different governments and prime minister seven times, had been caught up in the tide, and was facing trial for alleged links with the mafia. Amidst all this flux the desire for heroes to offset the growing cast of villains was as understandable as it was strong. But the climate was fickle and unpredictable: Di Pietro, who had been treated almost as a demigod at the beginning of the anti-corruption campaign, was himself charged with acting illegally, and spent much of 1996 and 1997 fighting to save his reputation.

A mood of more sober realism began to spread through Italy in 1995. Europe clearly offered the best long-term hope of stability; but that meant coming to grips quickly with the country's economic problems. In particular, it meant reducing the still largely uncontrolled levels of public spending that threatened to exclude Italy from entry into the single European currency. The prime minister from January 1995 was a highly regarded former general manager of the Bank of Italy, Lamberto Dini, who, along with his cabinet of 'non-political technicians', succeeded in pushing through some unpopular but much needed financial decisions, most notably one to bring down the spiralling cost of state pensions. He also pressed ahead with the fight against organised crime in the South; and he made clear his unequivocal commitment to the campaign against corruption. After the somewhat unfortunate experience of Berlusconi, the Dini administration did a good deal to restore Italy's credibility in the eyes of the international community.

In April 1996 elections were held and victory went to a left-of-centre coalition, known as the Ulivo. This comprised several parties, the largest of which was the Democratic Party of the Left, headed by an able politician, the ex-communist, Massimo D'Alema. It won over 20% of the vote. The principal architect of the coalition was a widely respected economist and university professor called Romano Prodi, who now took over at the head of the Republic's fifty-fifth government. In his cabinet were a number of former communists: this was quite remarkable. Even more so, perhaps, was the fact that almost for the first time in its history Italy faced the prospect of having an alternation in government between a left-wing and a right-wing grouping: the Ulivo and the so-called Freedom Alliance headed by Berlusconi and Fini.

Prodi's government pushed ahead with meeting the criteria laid down for entry into the single currency. Taxes were increased and spending on welfare was reduced. However, the public debt remained obstinately high; and many observers felt that a degree of 'creative accounting' was being resorted to in order to help the country qualify for the launch of the Euro in 1999. Luckily, though, a number of other member states faced problems similar to those of Italy, and this, combined with the overwhelming political commitment of many of Europe's leaders to greater integration, helped ensure that in May 1998 Italy was formally accepted for entry into the single currency. This was an extraordinary achievement. Not all Italians were convinced that the sacrifices involved were worth it: in the autumn of 1997 Prodi's government faced a crisis when one of his coalition partners, the Rifondazione Comunista, refused to support a further package of cuts. But the government was quickly reconstituted: if Italy missed out on Europe, where would it stand politically as well as economically?

As the millennium neared its end, Italy certainly had a great deal to be proud of. But the spirit of optimism that in many quarters had greeted the collapse of the First Republic during the early 1990s had given way to a mood of increasing introspection and uncertainty. The hopes that Italy had turned a corner and put behind it former habits and practices seemed a long way still from being realised. Old doubts about Italy's identity and character began to resurface. The push for ever greater integration into Europe, the persistent devolutionist

rhetoric of the Northern League, the continuing fracturing and
transformation of parties, factional quarrels, the fragility of
coalitions, and recurrent governmental instability – Prodi was
replaced by D'Alema in October 1998, and D'Alema by the former
socialist Giuliano Amato in April 2000 – fuelled debates in the press
and elsewhere about whether or to what extent Italy was in any
meaningful sense a nation.

Many of these debates centred, as they had often done at critical
junctures since the Enlightenment, on Italy's history. The sins or
otherwise of the Christian Democrats, the Communists, the
Resistance, fascism, the liberal state and the Risorgimento began to
be argued over with renewed intensity by intellectuals, journalists and
politicians eager to identify the defining threads in a past that was
threatening to unravel following the collapse of the ideological and
political fixities of the First Republic. The success of Berlusconi and
his right-wing coalition partners, including Gianfranco Fini, in the
general elections held in May 2001 intensified the debates.
Berlusconi's presidential-style campaign and his at times shameless
use of his media empire to further his cause and promote his image
raised some uncomfortable memories, and for many commentators
seemed to pose awkward questions about the character not just of
Italy but of Italians themselves.

At one level all this was rather surprising. Italians arguably had
more in common now than any other time in their history. The spread
of communications, the growth of the mass media, enormous
economic advances, and internal migration had all helped to integrate
the population to an unprecedented degree. Language, education,
newspapers, food, sport and leisure, to name but a few categories,
were 'national' as never before. But nations rest heavily on their
collective memories; and in Italy the collective memory is peculiarly
fraught and contested. Furthermore, and somewhat ironically, the
long-standing desire to define or redefine Italy and Italians, which has
been one of the main themes in the country's history in the past two
hundred years, may itself have been a source of division rather than
unity. Italy has much to look forward to in the twenty-first century,
but the signs were that its past will continue to haunt and trouble it
for a long time to come.

A SELECT BIBLIOGRAPHY OF RECENT BOOKS IN ENGLISH (MOSTLY SINCE 1970)

GEOGRAPHY

Bethemont, J. and J. Pelletier, *Italy: a Geographical Introduction* (trans. E. Kofman), London: Longman 1983

Walker, D.S., *A Geography of Italy*, 2nd edn, London: Methuen 1967

LANGUAGE AND LITERATURE

Migliorini, B. and T.G. Griffith, *The Italian Language*, revised edn, London: Faber 1984

Whitfield, J.H., *A Short History of Italian Literature*, new edn, Manchester: Manchester University Press 1980

NATIONAL CHARACTER

Barzini, L., *The Italians*, Harmondsworth: Penguin 1991

MEDIEVAL ITALY (to *c*. 1300)

Abulafia, D., *Frederick II: a Medieval Emperor*, London: Allen Lane 1988

Bowsky, W.M., *A Medieval Italian Commune: Siena under the Nine, 1287–1355*, Berkeley, London: University of California Press 1981

Bullough, D.A., *The Age of Charlemagne*, London: Elek Books 1965

Epstein, S., *An Island for Itself. Economic Development and Social Change in Late Medieval Sicily*, Cambridge: Cambridge University Press 1992

Finley, M.I., *Ancient Sicily. To the Arab Conquest*, London: Chatto and Windus 1968

Halphen, L., *Charlemagne and the Carolingian Empire* (trans. G. de Nie), Amsterdam, Oxford: North Holland Publishing Co. 1977

Herlihy, D., R.S. Lopez and V. Slessarev (eds.), *Economy, Society and Government in Medieval Italy*, Kent, Ohio: Kent State University Press 1969

Hyde, J.K., *Society and Politics in Medieval Italy. The Evolution of the Civil Life 1000–1350*, London: Macmillan 1973

Jones, A.H.M., *The Decline of the Ancient World*, London: Longman 1966

Jones, A.H.M., *The Later Roman Empire 284–602. A Social, Economic and Administrative Survey*, 3 vols., Oxford: Blackwell 1964

Larner, J., *Italy in the Age of Dante and Petrarch, 1216–1380*, London: Longman 1980

Luzzatto, G., *An Economic History of Italy. From the Fall of the Roman Empire to the Beginning of the Sixteenth Century* (trans. P. Jones), London: Routledge and Kegan Paul 1961

Mack Smith, D., *Medieval Sicily 800–1713*, London: Chatto and Windus 1968

Matthew, D., *The Norman Kingdom of Sicily*, Cambridge: Cambridge University Press 1992

Matthews, J., *Western Aristocracies and the Imperial Court AD 364–425*, Oxford: Clarendon Press 1975

Moorhead, J., *Theoderic in Italy*, Oxford: Oxford University Press 1993

Norwich, J.J., *Venice. The Rise to Empire*, London: Allen Lane 1977

Osheim, D.J., *An Italian Lordship: the Bishopric of Lucca in the Late Middle Ages*, Berkeley, London: University of California Press 1977

Richards, J., *The Popes and the Papacy in the Early Middle Ages, 476–752*, London: Routledge and Kegan Paul 1979

Tabacco, G., *The Struggle for Power in Medieval Italy. Structures of Political Power* (trans. R.B. Jensen), Cambridge: Cambridge University Press 1989

Waley, D., *The Italian City-republics*, 3rd edn, London: Longman 1988

Wickham, C., *Early Medieval Italy: Central Power and Local Society, 400–1000*, London: Macmillan 1981

RENAISSANCE ITALY

General overviews

Burckhardt, J., *The Civilization of the Renaissance in Italy* (trans. S.G.C. Middlemore), Harmondsworth: Penguin 1990

Hay, D. and J. Law, *Italy in the Age of the Renaissance, 1380–1530*, London: Longman 1989

Pullan, B., *A History of Early Renaissance Italy. From the mid-Thirteenth to the mid-Fifteenth century*, London: Allen Lane 1973

Baron, H., *The Crisis of the Early Italian Renaissance. Civic Humanism and Republican Liberty in an Age of Classicism and Tyranny*, Princeton: Princeton University Press 1966

Baron, H., *In Search of Florentine Civic Humanism. Essays on the Transition from Medieval to Modern Thought*, Princeton: Princeton University Press 1988

Baxandall, M., *Painting and Experience in Fifteenth-Century Italy. A Primer in the Social History of Pictorial Style*, Oxford: Clarendon Press 1972

Bentley, J., *Politics and Culture in Renaissance Naples*, Princeton: Princeton University Press 1987

Brucker, G., *The Civic World of Early Renaissance Florence*, Princeton: Princeton University Press 1977

Burke, P., *Culture and Society in Renaissance Italy, 1420–1540*, London: Batsford 1972

Dean, T., *Land and Power in Late Medieval Ferrara: the Rule of the Este, 1350–1450*, Cambridge: Cambridge University Press 1987

Dean, T. and C. Wickham (eds.), *City and Countryside in Late Medieval and Renaissance Italy*, London: Hambledon 1990

Denley, P. and C. Elam (eds.), *Florence and Italy: Renaissance Studies in Honour of Nicolai Rubinstein*, London: Westfield College 1988

Gombrich, E. H., *Symbolic Images. Studies in the Art of the Renaissance*, 3rd edn, Oxford: Phaidon 1985

Grendler, P.F., *Schooling in Renaissance Italy: Literacy and Learning, 1300–1600*, Princeton: Princeton University Press 1988

Hale, J.R., *Florence and the Medici: the Pattern of Control*, London: Thames and Hudson 1977

Hale, J.R. (ed.), *Renaissance Venice*, London: Faber 1973

Hartt, F., *A History of Italian Renaissance Art. Painting, Sculpture, Architecture*, London: Thames and Hudson 1970

Hay, D., *The Church in Italy in the Fifteenth Century*, Cambridge: Cambridge University Press 1977

Herlihy, D. and C. Klapisch-Zuber, *Tuscans and their Families*, New Haven, London: Yale University Press 1985

Holmes, G., *The Florentine Enlightenment 1400–50*, London: Weidenfeld and Nicolson 1969

Holmes, G., *Florence, Rome and the Origins of the Renaissance*, Oxford: Clarendon Press 1986

Jones, P.J., *The Malatesta of Rimini and the Papal State. A Political History*, London: Cambridge University Press 1974

Kent, F.W. and P. Simons (eds.), *Patronage, Art and Society in Renaissance Italy*, Oxford: Clarendon Press 1987

Larner, J., *Culture and Society in Italy, 1290–1420*, London: Batsford 1971

Laven, P., *Renaissance Italy 1464–1534*, London: Batsford 1966

Mallett, M.E., *The Borgias. The Rise and Fall of a Renaissance Dynasty*, London: Bodley Head 1969

Martines, L., *Power and Imagination: City-States in Renaissance Italy*, London: Allen Lane 1980

Meek, C., *Lucca, 1369–1400. Politics and Society in an Early Renaissance City-State*, Oxford: Oxford University Press 1978

Norwich, J.J, *Venice. The Greatness and the Fall*, London: Allen Lane 1981

Origo, I., *The Merchant of Prato. Francesco di Marco Datini*, London: Jonathan Cape 1957

Partner, P., *Renaissance Rome, 1500–1559*, Berkeley, London: University of California Press 1976

Rubinstein, N., *The Government of Florence under the Medici, 1434 to 1494*, Oxford: Clarendon Press 1966

Rubinstein, N. (ed.), *Florentine Studies. Politics and Society in Renaissance Florence*, London: Faber 1968

Ryder, A., *Alfonso the Magnanimous, King of Aragon, Naples and Sicily, 1396–1458*, Oxford: Clarendon Press 1990

Skinner, Q., *Machiavelli*, Oxford: Oxford University Press 1981

Stephens, J., *The Italian Renaissance: The Origins of Intellectual and Artistic Change before the Reformation*, London: Longman 1990

EARLY MODERN ITALY *c.1550–c.1800*

General overviews

Carpanetto, D. and G. Ricuperati, *Italy in the Age of Reason 1685–1789*, London: Longman 1987

Cochrane, E. (ed. J. Kirshner), *Italy 1530–1630*, London: Longman 1988

Woolf, S., *A History of Italy, 1700–1860: the Social Constraints of Political Change*, London: Methuen 1979

Acton, H., *The Bourbons of Naples (1734–1825)*, London: Methuen 1956

Berlin, I., *Vico and Herder: Two Studies in the History of Ideas*, London: Hogarth Press 1976

Braudel, F., *The Mediterranean and the Mediterranean World in the Age of Philip II* (trans. Siân Reynolds), 2 vols., revised edn, London: Fontana 1975

Cochrane, E., *Florence in the Forgotten Centuries, 1527–1800*, Chicago, London: University of Chicago Press 1974

Cochrane, E. (ed.), *The Late Italian Renaissance, 1525–1630*, London: Macmillan 1970

Evans, R.J.W., *The Making of the Habsburg Monarchy, 1550–1700: an Interpretation*, Oxford: Clarendon Press 1979

Ginzburg, C., *The Cheese and the Worms: the Cosmos of a Sixteenth Century Miller* (trans. J. and A. Tedeschi), new edn, London: Penguin 1992

Levi, G., *Inheriting Power: the Story of an Exorcist*, Chicago, London: University of Chicago Press 1988

Mack Smith, D., *Modern Sicily after 1713*, London: Chatto and Windus 1968

McArdle, F., *Altopascio: a Study in Tuscan Rural Society 1587–1784*, Cambridge: Cambridge University Press 1978

Rosselli, J., *The Opera Industry in Italy from Cimarosa to Verdi: the Role of the Impresario*, Cambridge: Cambridge Univeristy Press 1984

Sella, D., *Crisis and Continuity. The Economy of Spanish Lombardy in the Seventeenth Century*, Cambridge, Mass., London: Harvard University Press 1979

Symcox, G., *Victor Amadeus II: Absolutism in the Savoyard State, 1675–1730*, London: Thames and Hudson 1983

Venturi, F., *Italy and the Enlightenment: Studies in a Cosmopolitan Century* (trans. S. Corsi), London: Longman 1972

Woolf, S., *The Poor in Western Europe in the 18th and 19th Centuries*, London: Methuen 1986

MODERN ITALY [SINCE *c*.1800]

General overviews

Coppa F.J. (ed.), *Dictionary of Modern Italian History*, Westport, London: Greenwood 1985

Livi-Bacci, M., *A History of Italian Fertility during the Last Two Centuries*, Princeton: Princeton University Press 1977

ITALY IN THE AGE OF THE RISORGIMENTO 1800–1870

General overviews

Hearder, H., *Italy in the Age of the Risorgimento, 1790–1870*, London: Longman 1983

Mack Smith, D., *The Making of Italy 1796–1866*, 2nd edn, London: Macmillan 1988

Woolf, S., *A History of Italy, 1700–1860: the Social Constraints of Political Change*, London: Methuen 1979

Acton, H., *The Last Bourbons of Naples (1825–1861)*, London: Methuen 1961

Beales, D., *The Risorgimento and the Unification of Italy*, new edn, London: Longman 1981

Davis, J.A., *Merchants, Monopolists and Contractors. A Study of Economic Activity in Bourbon Naples 1815–1860*, New York: Arno Press 1981

Davis, J.A., *Conflict and Control: Law and Order in Nineteenth-Century Italy*, Basingstoke: Macmillan 1988

Davis, J.A. and P. Ginsborg (eds.), *Society and Politics in the Age of the Risorgimento*: Essays in Honour of Denis Mack Smith, Cambridge: Cambridge University Press 1991

Ginsborg, P., *Daniele Manin and the Venetian Revolution of 1848–49*, Cambridge: Cambridge University Press 1979

Greenfield, K.R., *Economics and Liberalism in the Risorgimento. A Study of Nationalism in Lombardy, 1814–1848*, revised edn, Baltimore: Johns Hopkins Press 1965

Lovett, C.M., *Carlo Cattaneo and the Politics of the Risorgimento, 1820–1860*, The Hague: Martinus Nijhoff 1972

Lovett, C.M., *Giuseppe Ferrari and the Italian Revolution*, Chapel Hill: University of North Carolina Press 1979

Lovett, C.M., *The Democratic Movement in Italy, 1830–1876*, Cambridge, Mass., London: Harvard University Press 1982

Mack Smith, D., *Victor Emanuel, Cavour and the Risorgimento*, Oxford: Oxford University Press 1971

Mack Smith, D., *Garibaldi*, 2nd edn, London: Hutchinson 1982

Mack Smith, D., *Cavour*, London: Weidenfeld and Nicolson 1985

Mack Smith, D., *Cavour and Garibaldi, 1860: a Study in Political Conflict*, 2nd edn, Cambridge: Cambridge University Press 1985

Ridley, J., *Garibaldi*, London: Constable 1974

ITALY 1870–1918

General overviews

Clark, M., *Modern Italy, 1871–1982*, London: Longman 1984

Mack Smith, D., *Italy: a Modern History*, 2nd edn, Ann Arbor: University of Michigan Press 1969

Seton-Watson, C., *Italy from Liberalism to Fascism 1870–1925*, London: Methuen 1967

Barbagli, M., *Educating for Unemployment: Politics, Labor Markets and the School System, Italy 1859–1973* (trans. R. Ross), New York: Columbia University Press 1982

Bell, D.H., *Sesto San Giovanni: Workers, Culture and Politics in an Italian Town, 1880–1922*, New Brunswick, London: Rutgers University Press 1986

Bellamy, R., *Modern Italian Social Theory: Ideology and Politics from Pareto to the Present*, Cambridge: Polity 1987

Blok, A., *The Mafia of a Sicilian Village, 1860–1960. A Study of Violent Peasant Entrepreneurs*, Oxford: Blackwell 1974

Bosworth, R.J.B., *Italy, the Least of the Great Powers: Italian Foreign Policy before the First World War*, London: Cambridge University Press 1979

Bosworth, R.J.B., *Italy and the Approach of the First World War*, London: Macmillan 1983

Coppa, F.J., *Pope Pius IX: Crusader in a Secular Age*, Boston: Twayne Publishers 1979

Coppa, F.J. (ed.), *Studies in Modern Italian History. From the Risorgimento to the Republic*, New York: Lang 1986

De Grand, A.J., *The Italian Nationalist Association and the Rise of Fascism in Italy*, Lincoln, London: University of Nebraska Press 1978

Di Scala, S., *Dilemmas of Italian Socialism: the Politics of Filippo Turati*, Amherst: University of Massachusetts Press 1980

Gibson, M., *Prostitution and the State in Italy, 1860–1915*, New Brunswick, London: Rutgers University Press 1986

Gooch, J., *Army, State and Society in Italy, 1870–1915*, Basingstoke: Macmillan 1989

Hess, H., *Mafia and Mafiosi. The Structure of Power* (trans. E. Osers), Farnborough: D.C. Heath 1973

Jemolo, A.C., *Church and State in Italy 1850–1950* (trans. D. Moore), Oxford: Blackwell 1960

Kertzer, D.I., *Family Life in Central Italy, 1880–1910: Sharecropping, Wage Labor, and Coresidence*, New Brunswick: Rutgers University Press 1984

Ledeen, M. A., *The First Duce: D'Annunzio at Fiume*, Baltimore, London: Johns Hopkins University Press 1977

Lowe, C.J., and F. Marzari, *Italian Foreign Policy 1870–1940*, London: Routledge and Kegan Paul 1975

Renzi, W.A., *In the Shadow of the Sword: Italy's Neutrality and Entrance into the Great War, 1914–1915*, New York: Lang 1987

Snowden, F.M., *Violence and Great Estates in the South of Italy: Apulia, 1900–1922*, Cambridge: Cambridge University Press 1986

Tannenbaum, E.R. and E.P. Noether (eds.), *Modern Italy: a Topical History since 1861*, New York: New York University Press 1974

Toniolo, G., *An Economic History of Liberal Italy, 1850–1918*, London: Routledge 1990

Webster, R.A., *Industrial Imperialism in Italy, 1908–1915*, Berkeley, London: University of California Press 1975

Whittam, J., *The Politics of the Italian Army, 1861–1918*, London: Croom Helm 1976

ITALY 1918–1945

General overview

De Grand, A.J., *Italian Fascism: its Origins and Development*, Lincoln, London: University of Nebraska Press 1982

Cardoza, A.L., *Agrarian Elites and Italian Fascism: the Province of Bologna, 1901–1926*, Princeton: Princeton University Press 1983

Cassels, A., *Mussolini's Early Diplomacy*, Princeton: Princeton University Press 1970

Clark, M., *Antonio Gramsci and the Revolution that Failed*, New Haven, London: Yale University Press 1977

Corner, P., *Fascism in Ferrara, 1915–1925*, London: Oxford University Press 1975

Deakin, F.W., *The Brutal Friendship: Mussolini, Hitler and the Fall of Italian Fascism*, London: Weidenfeld and Nicolson 1962

De Felice, R., *Fascism: an Informal Introduction to its Theory and Practice*, New Brunswick: Transaction 1976

De Felice, R., *Interpretations of Fascism* (trans. B.H. Everett), Cambridge, Mass., London: Harvard University Press 1977

De Grand, A.J., *In Stalin's Shadow: Angelo Tasca and the Crisis of the Left in Italy and France, 1910–1945*, DeKalb: Northern Illinois University Press 1986

De Grazia, V., *The Culture of Consent: Mass Organization of Leisure in Fascist Italy*, Cambridge: Cambridge University Press 1981

De Grazia, V., *How Fascism Ruled Women. Italy, 1922–1945*, Berkeley, London: University of California Press 1992

Duggan, C., *Fascism and the Mafia*, New Haven, London: Yale University Press 1989

Ellwood, D., *Italy, 1943–1945*, Leicester: Leicester University Press 1985

Forgacs, D. (ed.), *Rethinking Italian Fascism: Capitalism, Populism, and Culture*, London: Lawrence and Wishart 1986

Gregor, A.J., *Young Mussolini and the Intellectual Origins of Fascism*, Berkeley, London: University of California Press 1979

Gregor, A.J., *Italian Fascism and Developmental Dictatorship*, Princeton: Princeton University Press 1979

Kelikian, A., *Town and Country under Fascism: the Transformation of Brescia, 1915–1926*, Oxford: Clarendon Press 1986

Kent, P., *The Pope and the Duce: the International Impact of the Lateran Agreements*, London: Macmillan 1981

Knox, M., *Mussolini Unleashed 1939–1941. Politics and Strategy in Fascist Italy's Last War*, Cambridge: Cambridge University Press 1982

Koon, T., *Believe, Obey, Fight: Political Socialization of Youth in Fascist Italy, 1922–1943*, Chapel Hill: University of North Carolina Press 1985

Lyttelton, A., *The Seizure of Power: Fascism in Italy, 1919–1929*, London: Weidenfeld and Nicolson 1973

Mack Smith, D., *Mussolini's Roman Empire*, London: Longman 1976

Mack Smith, D., *Mussolini*, London: Weidenfeld and Nicolson 1981

Michaelis, M., *Mussolini and the Jews: German–Italian Relations and the Jewish Question in Italy, 1922–1945*, Oxford: Clarendon Press 1978

Mockler, A., *Haile Selassie's War*, Oxford: Oxford University Press 1984

Passerini, L., *Fascism in Popular Memory: the Cultural Experience of the Turin Working Class* (trans. R. Lumley and J. Bloomfield), Cambridge: Cambridge University Press 1987

Pollard, J.F., *The Vatican and Italian Fascism, 1929–1932: a Study in Conflict*, Cambridge: Cambridge University Press 1985

Roberts, D.D., *The Syndicalist Tradition and Italian Fascism*, Manchester: Manchester University Press 1979

Robertson, E.M., *Mussolini as Empire-builder: Europe and Africa, 1932–36*, London: Macmillan 1977

Sarti, R., *Fascism and the Industrial Leadership in Italy 1919–1940: a Study in the Expansion of Private Power under Fascism*, Berkeley, London: University of California Press 1971

Sarti, R. (ed.), *The Ax Within: Italian Fascism in Action*, New York: New Viewpoints 1974

Segrè C.G., *Fourth Shore: the Italian Colonization of Libya*, Chicago, London: University of Chicago Press 1974

Segrè C.G., *Italo Balbo: a Fascist Life*, Berkeley, London: University of California Press, 1987

Snowden, F.M., *The Fascist Revolution in Tuscany 1919–1922*, Cambridge: Cambridge University Press 1989

Steinberg, J., *All or Nothing: the Axis and the Holocaust 1941–43*, London: Routledge 1990

Tannenbaum, E.R., *Fascism in Italy. Society and Culture, 1922–1945*, London: Allen Lane 1973

Zuccotti, S., *The Italians and the Holocaust: Persecution, Rescue and Survival*, London: Halban 1987

1945 TO PRESENT

General overviews

Allum, P. A., *Italy: Republic without Government?*, London: Weidenfeld and Nicolson 1973

Clark, M., *Modern Italy, 1871–1982*, London: Longman 1984

Ginsborg, P., *A History of Contemporary Italy: Society and Politics, 1943–1988*, London: Penguin 1990

Hine, D., *Governing Italy: the Politics of Bargained Pluralism*, Oxford: Clarendon Press 1993

Kogan, N., *A Political History of Italy: the Postwar Years*, New York: Praeger 1983

LaPalombara, J., *Democracy: Italian Style*, New Haven, London: Yale University Press 1987

Sassoon, D., *Contemporary Italy. Politics, Economy and Society since 1945*, London: Longman 1986

Spotts, F. and T. Wieser, *Italy: a Difficult Democracy. A Survey of Italian Politics*, Cambridge: Cambridge University Press 1986

Adler Hellman, J., *Journeys among Women. Feminism in Five Italian Cities*, Oxford: Oxford University Press 1987

Allum, P.A., *Politics and Society in Post-war Naples*, London: Cambridge University Press 1973

Amyot, G., *The Italian Communist Party. The Crisis of the Popular Front Strategy*, London: Croom Helm 1981

Arlacchi, P., *Mafia Business: the Mafia Ethic and the Spirit of Capitalism* (trans. M. Ryle), Oxford: Oxford University Press 1988

Baranski, Z.G. and R. Lumley (eds.), *Culture and Conflict in Postwar Italy: Essays on Mass and Popular Culture*, Basingstoke: Macmillan 1990

Barkan, J., *Visions of Emancipation: the Italian Workers' Movement since 1945*, New York: Praeger 1984

Barnes, S.H., *Representation in Italy: Institutionalized and Electoral Choice*, Chicago, London: University of Chicago Press 1977

Blackmer, D.L.M. and S. Tarrow (eds.), *Communism in Italy and France*, Princeton: Princeton University Press 1975

Bondanella, P., *Italian Cinema. From Neorealism to the Present*, new edn, New York: Ungar 1990

Caesar, M. and P. Hainsworth (eds.), *Writers and Society in Contemporary Italy: a Collection of Essays*, Leamington Spa: Berg 1984

Certoma, G.L., *The Italian Legal System*, London: Butterworths 1985

Chandler, B.J., *King of the Mountain: the Life and Death of Giuliano the Bandit*, DeKalb: Northern Illinois University Press 1988

Chubb, J., *Patronage, Power, and Poverty in Southern Italy. A Tale of Two Cities*, Cambridge: Cambridge University Press 1982

De Grand, A.J., *The Italian Left in the Twentieth Century: a History of the Socialist and Communist Parties*, Bloomington: University of Indiana Press 1989

Di Palma, G., *Surviving without Governing: the Italian Parties in Parliament*, Berkeley, London: University of California Press 1977

Di Scala, S.M., *Renewing Italian Socialism: Nenni to Craxi*, New York: Oxford University Press 1988

Farneti, P., *The Italian Party System (1945–1980)*, London: Pinter 1985

Forgacs, D., *Italian Culture in the Industrial Era 1880–1980*, Manchester: Manchester University Press 1990

Harper, J.L., *America and the Reconstruction of Italy, 1945–1948*, Cambridge: Cambridge University Press 1986

Hellman, S., *Italian Communism in Transition: the Rise and Fall of the Historic Compromise in Turin 1975–80*, Oxford: Oxford University Press 1988

Lange, P. and S. Tarrow, *Italy in Transition. Conflict and Consensus*, London: Cass 1980

Leonardi, R. and D.A. Wertman, *Italian Christian Democracy: the Politics of Dominance*, Basingstoke: Macmillan 1989

Lumley, R., *States of Emergency: Cultures of Revolt in Italy 1968–78*, London: Verso 1990

Miller, J.E., *The United States and Italy: the Politics of Diplomacy and Stabilization*, Chapel Hill, London: University of North Carolina Press 1986

Moss, D., *The Politics of Left-Wing Violence in Italy, 1969–85*, Basingstoke: Macmillan 1989

Onida, V. and G. Viesti (eds.), *The Italian Multinationals*, London: Croom Helm 1988

Pitkin, D.S., *The House that Giacomo Built. History of an Italian Family, 1898–1978*, Cambridge: Cambridge University Press 1985

Podbielski, G., *Italy: Development and Crisis in the Post-War Economy*, Oxford: Clarendon Press 1974

Pridham, G., *Political Parties and Coalition Behaviour in Italy*, London: Routledge 1988

Ruscoe, J., *The Italian Communist Party 1976–81: on the Threshold of Government*, London: Macmillan 1982

Sassoon, D., *The Strategy of the Italian Communist Party: from the Resistance to the Historic Compromise*, London: Pinter 1981

Tarrow, S., *Peasant Communism in Southern Italy*, New Haven, London: Yale University Press 1967

Tarrow, S., *Between Center and Periphery: Grassroots Politicians in Italy and France*, New Haven, London: Yale University Press 1977

Urban, J.B., *Moscow and the Italian Communist Party. From Togliatti to Berlinguer*, London: Tauris 1986

Walston, J., *The Mafia and Clientelism. Roads to Rome in Post-War Calabria*, London: Routledge 1988

Woolf, S. (ed.), *The Rebirth of Italy 1943–50*, London: Longman 1972

INDEX